Fifth Edition

Planning Your Success

Kendall Hunt
publishing company

Customized version of *Thriving in the Community College and Beyond*
Joseph B. Cuseo, Aaron Thompson, Julie A. McLaughlin and Steady H. Moono

Designed specifically for Des Moines Area Community College
Edited by Sharon Bittner, Hollie Coon, and Melinda Graham-Hinners

Cover images © DMACC

Welcome Photo of R. Denson contributed by Dan Ivis. © Kendall Hunt Publishing Company

*From THRIVING IN THE COMMUNITY COLLEGE & BEYOND: STRATEGIES FOR ACADEMIC SUCCESS AND PERSONAL DEVELOPMENT, 2ND EDITION by JOSEPH CUSEO, AARON THOMPSON, JULIE MCLAUGHLIN, AND STEADY MOONO. Copyright © 2013 by Kendall Hunt Publishing Company.

**From THRIVING IN THE COMMUNITY COLLEGE & BEYOND: STRATEGIES FOR ACADEMIC SUCCESS AND PERSONAL DEVELOPMENT, 3RD EDITION by JOSEPH CUSEO, AARON THOMPSON, AND JULIE MCLAUGHLIN. Copyright © 2016 by Kendall Hunt Publishing Company.

***Authors original works.

www.kendallhunt.com
Send all inquiries to:
4050 Westmark Drive
Dubuque, IA 52004-1840

Revised Printing: 2015

ISBN 978-1-5249-8107-5

Published in the United States of America

Contents

Acknowledgments

Thank you to the counselors, advisors, faculty, and staff who contributed to this book, teach *The College Experience*, and work every day to support DMACC students. Thank you to Sheila Aukes, Dale Chell, Rita Davenport, Dr. Melinda Graham-Hinners, Mary McClure, Pamela Parker, Landi Smith, Thomas Tweedy, Michelle Vaccaro, and Jennifer Wollesen.

Thank you to Sheila Aukes, Rita Davenport, Amanda Rodenborn, Dan Nelson, Dr. Graham-Hinners, Drea Iseminger, Dr. Jenny Foster, and Michelle Vaccaro for their help with editing.

Thank you for the leadership and support from DMACC President Rob Denson, Dr. Joe DeHart, Dr. Kari Hensen, and Dr. Wade Robinson.

Welcome

Welcome to Des Moines Area Community College! We're glad you're here.

On behalf of the Board of Trustees and all of us at DMACC, I'd like to welcome you to one of the **finest educational institutions in America.** In 2016, we were picked #10 of 1,717 two-year institutions in the United States based on value. The more you learn about DMACC, the more you will experience our truly unique approach to education, student support, and engagement.

Whether you're interested in starting a four-year education through DMACC's Transfer Programs, pursuing a rewarding career in STEM (Science, Technology, Engineering and Mathematics) or you want one of our many in-demand career and technical degrees, DMACC offers you over 200 programs and short-term certificates that will help you qualify for the many job opportunities in Central Iowa and throughout the United States. Maybe that's another reason that DMACC was voted by CityView readers as the "Best Place to Continue Your Education" several years in a row.

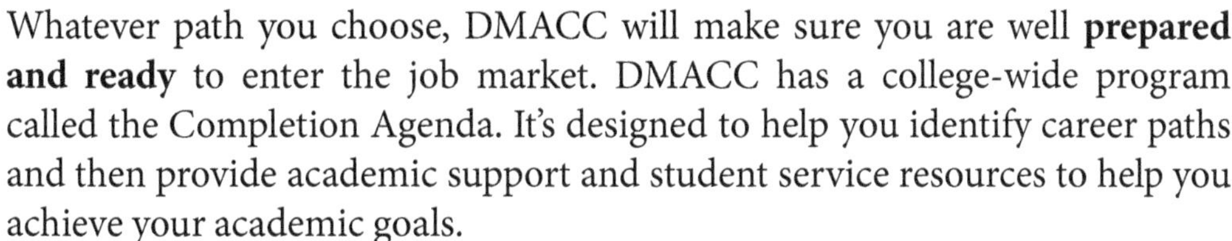

Whatever path you choose, DMACC will make sure you are well **prepared and ready** to enter the job market. DMACC has a college-wide program called the Completion Agenda. It's designed to help you identify career paths and then provide academic support and student service resources to help you achieve your academic goals.

DMACC is dedicated to your personal and professional success through our small class sizes, free tutoring in our academic achievement centers, and the flexibility of our growing list of new Signature Series(™) online classes. Maybe the best part: DMACC offers this outstanding education for **thousands of dollars less** than you will find anywhere else. It's good to know that a great higher education experience is still affordable.

Again, welcome to DMACC. We want you to work hard and enjoy your experience here and be prepared for the opportunities that await you. If you see me around, be sure to stop and say hello.

Sincerely,
Robert J. Denson
President
Des Moines Area Community College

Finish your degree, diploma, or certificate at DMACC before you transfer or make a career move. Why?...

- Increased transferability of coursework
- Opportunity for transfer student scholarships
- Credential to include for employment/promotional applications
- Credential to include for internship applications

Find out more at www.dmacc.edu
or call 800-362-2127.

ANKENY • BOONE • CARROLL • NEWTON • URBAN/DES MOINES • WEST DES MOINES

CAPITOL MEDICAL OFFICE BUILDING | DMACC CENTER FOR CAREER & PROFESSIONAL DEVELOPMENT AT SOUTHRIDGE DMACC TRANSPORTATION INSTITUTE | DMACC CAREER ACADEMY, HUNZIKER CENTER, AMES EVELYN K. DAVIS CENTER FOR WORKING FAMILIES | DMACC AT PERRY VANKIRK CAREER ACADEMY

The Game Plan

Online and In-Class Behavior

1

THOUGHT STARTER | Journal Entry 1.1

LEARNING GOAL

To equip you with a set of fundamental skills that all college students need to get off to a fast and good start in college and that will ease your adjustment to college.

**1. In what three major ways do you think college will differ from high school? If you have been out of high school for a while and are just now returning to school, what are the biggest changes you see?

____

____

____

2. What three personal characteristics, qualities, or strategies do you think will be most important for college success?

____

____

____

____ **

Think About It — Journal Entry 1.2

*Look at the list of differences between high school and college in Snapshot Summary 1.1. Which differences were you most unaware of or most surprised to see?

____

____

____

____

____

____

(continued)

Why?

Snapshot Summary

1.1 Birds of a Different Feather: High School vs. College

High School	College
Your classes are mostly arranged for you.	You arrange your own schedule in consultation with your advisor. Schedules tend to look lighter than they really are.
Your time is structured by others.	You manage your own time.
You go from one class directly to another, spending six hours per day—30 hours per week—in class.	You have free time between classes; class times vary throughout the day and evening; and you spend 12–16 hours each week in class if you are a full-time student.
The school year is 36 weeks long; some classes extend over both semesters, and some do not.	The academic year may be divided into separate semesters or quarters.
Teachers monitor class attendance.	Professors may not formally monitor class attendance; you're expected to have the self-discipline to show up and get down information that's presented in class.
Teachers often write information on the board for you to put in your notes.	Professors may lecture nonstop, expecting you to identify and write down important information in your notes. Notes that professors write on the board are used to supplement or complement the lecture, not to summarize or substitute for the lecture.
Teachers provide you with information you missed when you were absent.	Professors expect you to get information you missed from classmates.
You are given short reading assignments that are then discussed, and often reviewed, in class.	You're assigned substantial amounts of reading and writing that may not be directly addressed in class.
You seldom need to read anything more than once, and sometimes listening in class is enough.	You need to review class notes and read material regularly.
Teachers present material to help you understand the textbook.	Professors may not follow the textbook, but you may be expected to relate class sessions to textbook readings.

You may have studied outside of class for zero to two hours per week.	You need to study for at least two to three hours outside of class for each hour spent in class.
Teachers remind you of assignments and due dates.	Professors expect you to consult the course syllabus for assignments and deadlines.*

Source: Southern Methodist University (2006).

Student *Perspective*

"College teachers don't tell you what you're supposed to do. They just expect you to do it. High school teachers tell you about five times what you supposed to do."

—College sophomore (Appleby, 2008)

Think About It — *Journal Entry* 1.3

*** 1. Considering the information in the Snapshot Summary, how do you currently plan for your classes and study times?

____

____

____

____

____

2. Do you have a note taking strategy?

____

____

____

____

____

3. What strategies do you plan to use to read and learn the material in your textbooks?

____

____

____

____

______________________________ ***

Time Spent in Class

*Since the total amount of time you spend on learning is associated with how much you learn and how successfully you learn, this association leads to a straightforward recommendation: Attend all class sessions in all your courses. It may be tempting to skip or cut classes because college professors are less likely to monitor your attendance or take roll than your teachers were in high school. However, don't let this new freedom fool you into thinking that missing classes will have no effect on your grades. Over the past 75 years, numerous studies have shown a direct relationship between class attendance and course grades—as one goes up or down, so does the other (Credé, Roch, Kieszczynka, 2010; Launius, 1997; Shimoff & Catania, 2001; Tagliacollo, Volpato, & Pereira, 2010). Figure 1.1 represents the results of a study conducted at the City Colleges of Chicago, which shows the relationship between students' class attendance during the first five weeks of the term and their final course grades.

Student *Perspective*

"My biggest recommendation: GO TO CLASS. I learned this the hard way my first semester. You'll be surprised what you pick up just by being there. I wish someone would have informed me of this before I started school."

—Advice to new students from a college sophomore (Walsh, 2005)

FIGURE 1.1

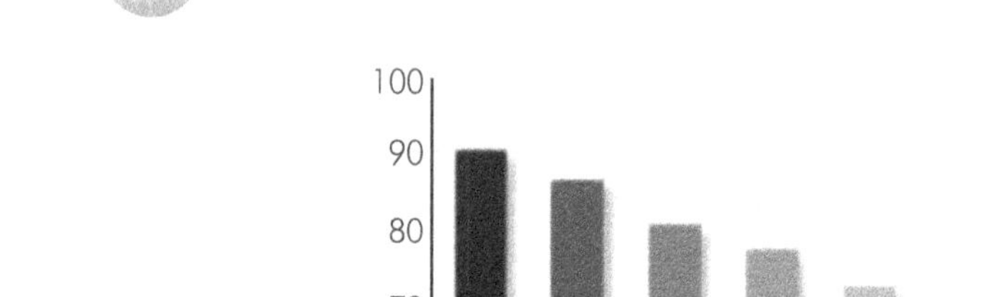

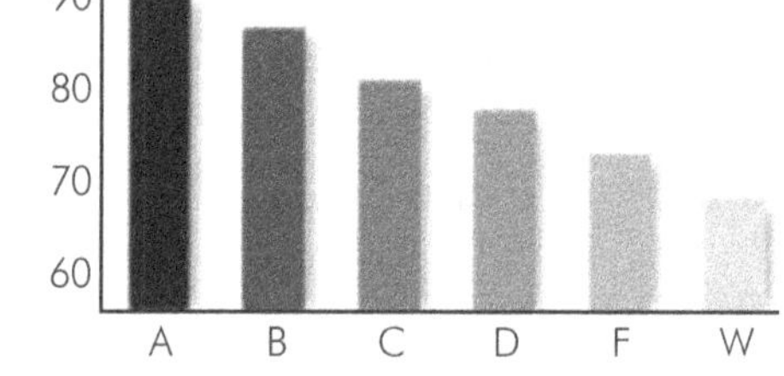

Percentage of Classes Attended and Final Course Grades

Time Spent on Coursework outside the Classroom

You will spend fewer hours per week sitting in class in college than you did in high school. However, you will be expected to spend more time on your own on academic work. Studies clearly show that when college students spend more time on academic work outside of class, the result is better learning and higher grades. For example, one study of more than 25,000 college students found that the percentage of students receiving mostly A grades was almost three times higher for students who spent 40 or more hours per week on academic work than it was for students who spent between 20 and 40 hours. Among students who spent 20 or fewer hours per week on academic work, the percentage receiving grades that were mostly Cs or below was almost twice as high as it was for students who spent 40 or more hours on academic work (Pace, 1990, 1995).

"If you are going to achieve excellence in big things, you develop the habit in little matters. Excellence is not an exception, it is a prevailing attitude."

—Colin Powell, Retired General and former U.S. Secretary of State

Unfortunately, less than 40 percent of beginning college students report having studied for six or more hours per week during their final year in high school (Pryor et al., 2012), only one-third expect to spend more than 20 hours per week preparing for class in college (National Survey of Student Engagement, 2009), and less than 10% say they will study at least two hours out of class for every hour spent in class—which is what most college faculty believe is necessary to do well in college (Kuh, 2005). This trend has to change if new college students are to earn good grades. Just as successful athletes need to put in time and work hard to improve their physical performance, successful students need to do the same to improve their academic performance.

Think About It — Journal Entry 1.4

How are you going to make sure you have the time needed to study in college?

If you need further motivation to achieve good grades, keep in mind that higher grades during college result in higher chances of career success after college. Research on college graduates indicates that the higher their college grades, the higher:

- The status (prestige) of their first job;
- Their job mobility (ability to change jobs or move into different positions); and
- Their total earnings (salary).

The more you learn, the more you'll earn. This relationship between college grades and career success exists for students at all types of colleges and universities regardless of the reputation or prestige of the institution that the students are attending (Pascarella & Terenzini, 1991, 2005). In other words, how well you do academically in college matters more to your career success than where you go to college and what institutional name appears on your degree.

Student *Perspective*

"In high school, you were a dork if you got good grades and cared about what was going on in your class. In college, you're a dork if you don't."

—College sophomore (Appleby, 2008)

Think About It — Journal Entry 1.5

In high school, how many hours per week did you spend on schoolwork outside of class during your senior year? What do you think you will need to do differently in college?

Author's Experience

When I went to college, I had to work to assist my family and to assist in paying for college. Although I was an 18-year-old, I came from a very poor family and it was part of my obligation to assist them financially, while it was more important for me to go to school and graduate so I could have a higher standard of living in comparison to my mother and father. Juggling my work life and school life quickly became a reality to which I had to adjust. Thus, I made sure I made the time to study and attend class as my first priority and worked with my employer to adjust my work hours around my classes. By placing my future above my immediate present, I was able to get my college degree and increase my earnings substantially beyond the earnings I had in college and way beyond my parents' earnings.*

Aaron Thompson

Classroom Basics

*Within College, as within many environments, there will be expectations for behavior. Depending on what kind of course (traditional face-to-face, online, web-enhanced, or web-blended) you are taking, there will be different expectations for which you are held responsible. Other than a few exceptions (i.e., you can wear pajamas in your house to do an online course), most of the following expectations apply to all.

Snapshot Summary

1.2 Types of Classrooms

Traditional (face-to-face) instruction classrooms offer students and instructors an opportunity to see each other and have interaction. This kind of classroom setting and experience enhances the opportunity for collaborative and social learning.

Web-enhanced courses use traditional (face-to-face) instruction but also use some Web-based learning tool (i.e., Blackboard) to enhance the course. You are expected to attend all class sessions and also to check the course Web site regularly. You may even be required to do some of your assignments through the course Web site.

Online courses are designed to bring campus-based classes to students' computers. The instructor provides information posted on a course Web site that guides the student through course content, prompts discussions, and helps students keep pace with assignments. Online courses offer flexibility for many working adults; they can offer an accelerated opportunity for a certificate and/or degree. However, they provide less face-to-face social interaction and fewer degree options in comparison to traditional face-to-face classrooms. You will need to pay special attention to when assignments are due and where to turn them in for the instructor's review. In addition, you may have to go to a central location to take proctored exams or do other assessments (e.g., placement tests). Online courses require discipline. These courses are not as easy as many commercials make them out to be. Sometimes an online class can be more difficult than a traditional course.

Web-blended courses blend on-campus instruction with Web-based instruction. Students meet on campus according to the published schedule of classes with approximately half of the course instruction and/or activities occurring online. The web-blended classroom incorporates characteristics from both the traditional and the online classroom: web-blended classrooms have access to the Internet in order to enhance the learning process. Students have the benefit of having face-to-face interactions along with having assignments available to them online at any time. Web-blended courses create flexible learning options while allowing students to meet face-to-face with instructors and other students.

https://www.csmd.edu/programs-courses/credit/flexible-learning-options/online-learning/

No matter how you take your classes, the first day of class is often the most important and is full of hustle and bustle. There are students of all ages, ethnicities, races, and genders walking with backpacks and energy drinks, looking for their classrooms, or sitting down in front of the computer. Most of these students will be like you, full of newfound curiosities and apprehensions. Questions are being asked of new faces and soon new friends. When you find your classroom (in person or virtually), hopefully the first person you sit next to will become a new friend or study partner. Here you go on your college trip, so enjoy the ride!

Classroom Top Strategies

1. **Adopt a seating location that maximizes your focus of attention and minimizes sources of distraction.** Many years of research show that students who sit in the front and center of class tend to earn higher exam scores and course grades (Benedict & Hoag, 2004; Rennels & Chaudhair, 1988; Tagliacollo, Volpato, & Pereira, 2010). These results are found even when students are assigned seats by their instructor, so it's not just a matter of more motivated and studious students tending to sit in the front of the room: instead, the better academic performance achieved by students sitting in the front and center of the room likely results from a learning advantage provided by this seating location. Front-and-center seating benefits students' academic performance by improving their vision of

material written on the board or screen and their ability to hear the instructor's lectures. In addition, this seating position allows for better eye contact with the instructor, which can increase students' level of attention, reduce their feeling of anonymity, and heighten their sense of involvement in the classroom. Sitting in the front of class can also reduce your level of anxiety about speaking up in class because, when you speak, you will not have numerous classmates sitting in front of you turning around to look at you while you speak.

2. **Sit by people who will support your ability to learn.** Intentionally sit near classmates who will not distract you or interfere with the quality of your note taking. Attention comes in degrees or amounts; you can give all of your attention or part of it to whatever task you're performing. Trying to grasp complex information in class is a task that demands your undivided attention.
3. **Adopt a seating posture that screams attention.** Sitting upright and leaning forward increases your attention because these bodily signals will reach your brain and increase mental alertness. If your body is in an alert and ready position, your mind tends to pick up these physical cues and follow your body's lead by also becoming alert and ready (to learn). Just as baseball players assume a ready position in the field before a pitch is delivered to put their bodies in position to catch batted balls, learners who assume a ready position in the classroom put themselves in a better position to catch ideas batted around in the classroom. Studies show that when humans are mentally alert and ready to learn, greater amounts of the brain chemical C-kinase are released at the connection points between brain cells, which increases the likelihood that a learning connection will form between them (Howard, 2014).

There's another advantage to being attentive in class: you send a clear message to your instructor that you're a conscientious and courteous student. This can influence your instructor's perception and evaluation of your academic performance, which can earn you the benefit of the doubt at the end of the term if you're on the border between a lower and higher course grade.

"For success, attitude is equally as important as ability."

—Walter Scott

Expectations: Classroom Behavior

Research indicates that one key characteristic of successful learners is that they monitor or watch themselves and maintain self-awareness of the following:

- Whether they are using effective learning strategies. For example, they're aware of their level of attention or concentration in class.
- Whether they comprehend what they are attempting to learn. For example, they're aware of whether they're understanding it at a deep level or merely memorizing it at a surface level.
- How to self-regulate or self-adjust their learning strategies to meet the different demands of different tasks or subjects. For example, when reading technical material in a science textbook, they read more slowly and stop to test their understanding more frequently than when they're reading a novel (Pintrich & Schunk, 2002).

"Successful students know a lot about themselves."

—Claire Weinstein and Debra Meyer, professors of educational psychology, University of Texas

For instance, studies show that students who self-monitor their thought processes when solving math and science problems are more effective problem solvers than those who just go through the motions (Resnick, 1986). Effective problem solvers ask themselves such questions as "How did I go about solving this problem correctly?" and "What were the key steps I took to arrive at the correct solution?"

Snapshot Summary

1.3 Reading and Understanding a Syllabus

What's in a syllabus? A course syllabus is a document created by instructors that will probably be given to you on the first day of class. Please pay careful attention to all parts of the syllabus and make a copy to keep with you at all times. You are responsible for adhering to the syllabus. However, your instructor can change the syllabus as he/she deems necessary. A syllabus usually contains the following components (not necessarily in this order):

1. Course department, prefix, number, title, credit hours, semester and year, and course reference number.
2. Meeting times and location, instructor information (name, office location, office hours, contact information).
3. Catalog course description, including prerequisites and/or corequisites (courses students need to have taken before this one or at the same time); prerequisite skill sets (e.g., programming languages, familiarity with software).
4. Text(s) with dates, supplemental text(s), other required readings, and references readings (books, reserve readings, course readers, software, and supplies with information about where they can be obtained). You are expected to have these on the first day or soon after the first day.
5. Student learning outcomes and/or course objectives (this is what the instructor is telling you that he or she will work the lectures around, and you will have learning opportunities around them throughout the course). The tests, quizzes, papers, etc., are based on these objectives.
6. Skills and knowledge students will gain. These are the new items you will have learned after the course is completed. You may hear these referred to as competencies.
7. Course organization. This tells you step-by-step how this course will be taught.
8. Explanation of the topical organization of the course. This will give you an idea of the specific topics that will be covered in class.
9. Course requirements (what students will have to do in the course: assignments, exams, projects, performances, attendance, participation, etc.). Usually the nature and format of assignments and the expected length of written work, as well as due dates for assignments and dates for exams, will be explained.
10. Evaluation and grading policy: what grades are based on, especially your final grade. Always keep up on what grade you have in class and discuss how to improve it with the instructor on a regular basis.
11. Course policies and expectations: may include policies on attendance, participation, tardiness, academic integrity, missing homework, missed exams, recording classroom activities, food in class, laptop use, cell phone use, etc.
12. Other expectations such as student behavior (e.g., respectful consideration of one another's perspectives, open-mindedness, creative risk-taking).
13. Course calendar/schedule (sometimes the instructor will put "tentative" before these words, letting you know it is subject to change). However, this is a class-to-class breakdown of topics and assignments (readings, homework, project due dates).

As a college student, you are responsible for knowing the contents of the course syllabus. It is not the instructor's responsibility to go over it with you. Be sure you read and understand your syllabi for all your courses. If you have any questions, be sure to ask your instructor right away.

You can begin to establish good self-monitoring habits now by getting into a routine of periodically pausing to reflect on how you're going about learning and how you're "doing" in college. For instance, consider these questions:

- Are you listening attentively to what your instructor is saying in class?
- Do you comprehend what you are reading outside of class?
- Are you effectively using campus resources that are designed to support your success?

- Are you interacting with campus professionals who can contribute to your current success and future development?
- Are you interacting and collaborating with peers who can contribute to your learning and increase your level of involvement in the college experience?
- Are you effectively implementing the key success strategies identified in this book?

Classroom Behaviors to Avoid

The following behaviors create confusion in the classroom and disturb the education process. More specifically, they cut down on your opportunity to learn all that you could.

"Behavior is a mirror in which everyone displays his own image."

—Johann Wolfgang von Goethe

- Coming in class late and/or leaving early
- Walking in and out of the classroom during class
- Talking with classmates while the instructor is lecturing
- Disregarding the deadlines set by your instructor or study partners
- Interrupting class with electronic devices or other distractions
- Disrespecting your classmates and/or instructor
- Acting uninterested or sleeping during class
- Working on homework during class
- Cheating on tests, quizzes, papers, or other homework

Student Perspectives

"I wasn't sure what this class was about. Now I understand this class and I really like it. I learned a lot about myself."

"In the start of the semester I thought this class would be a waste of time and busy work. But I realized it is an important way of learning who and what you are . . . I underestimated this class."

—Comments made by first-year students when evaluating their first-year experience course

Technology Is for Learning

Guidelines for Civil and Responsible Use of Personal Technology in the College Classroom

Technology as a Partner

- Turn your cell phone completely off or leave it out of the classroom. In the rare case of an emergency when you think you need to leave it on, inform your instructor.
- Don't check your cell phone during the class period by turning it off and on.
- Don't text message during class.
- Don't surf the Web during class.
- Don't touch your cell phone during any exam, because this may be viewed by the instructor as a form of cheating.

Insensitive Use of Personal Technology in the Classroom: A Violation of Civility

Behavior that interferes with the rights of others to learn or teach in the college classroom is a violation of civility. Listed below are behaviors illustrating classroom incivility that involve student use of personal technology. These behaviors are increasing in college, as is the frustration of college instructors who witness them, so be sure not to engage in them.

Using Cell Phones

Keeping a cell phone on in class is a clear example of classroom incivility because if it rings, it will interfere with the right of others to learn. In a study of college students who were exposed to a cell phone ringing during a class session and were later tested for their recall of information presented in class, they scored approximately 25 percent worse when attempting to recall information that was presented at the time a cell phone rang. This attention loss occurred even though the material was covered by the professor before the cell phone rang and was projected on a slide during the call. This study also showed that students were further distracted when classmates frantically searched through handbags or pockets to find and silence a ringing (or vibrating) phone (Shelton, Elliot, Eaves, & Exner, 2009). These findings clearly suggest that the civil thing to do is turn your cell phone off before entering the classroom or keep it out of the classroom altogether.

Sending and Receiving Text Messages

Just as answering a cell phone during class is a violation of civility because it interferes with the learning of other members of the classroom community, so too is text messaging. Although messaging is often viewed as a quick and soundless way to communicate, it can momentarily disrupt learning if it takes place when the instructor is covering critical or complex information. Text messaging while driving a car can take your eyes and mind off the road, thereby putting yourself and others in danger. Similarly, messaging in the classroom takes your eyes and mind off the instructor and any visual aids being displayed at the time. It's also discourteous or disrespectful to instructors when you put your head down and turn your attention from them while they're speaking to the class. Finally, it can be distracting or disturbing to classmates who see you messaging instead of listening and learning.

Correct Use of the Internet

There are common rules for the use of the Internet (see Snapshot Summary 1.4), colloquially referred to as *netiquette* [nétti kèt]. These rules hold true for social media sites such as Facebook, LinkedIn, Twitter, Instagram, Snapchat or others.

Plagiarism: A Violation of Academic Integrity

What Is Plagiarism?

Plagiarism is deliberate or unintentional use of someone else's work without acknowledging it, giving the reader the impression that it's your own work.

Student Perspective

"My intent was not to plagiarize. I realize I was unclear [about] the policy and am actually thankful for now knowing exactly what I can and cannot do on assignments and how to prevent academic dishonesty in the future."

—First-year student's reflection on a plagiarism violation

Various Forms of Plagiarism

1. Submitting an entire paper, or portion thereof, that was written by someone else
2. Copying sections of someone else's work and inserting it into your own work
3. Cutting paragraphs from separate sources and pasting them into the body of your own paper
4. Paraphrasing (rewording) someone else's words or ideas without citing that person as a source.

Snapshot Summary

1.4 Top 20 Rules to Follow for Appropriate Netiquette

1. The Internet is not private. What goes out on the airwaves stays on the airwaves! Do not post pictures to the Internet that you would not want your mom or younger cousin to see.
2. Avoid saying anything that could be interpreted as derogatory (e.g., no cursing).
3. Do not say harsh or mean things to someone over e-mail or text (this could be considered cyber bullying) and do not post nasty, mean, or insulting items about someone.
4. Do not respond to nasty e-mails sent to you.
5. Do not break up with a significant other via text or e-mail.
6. When you receive an e-mail that says to forward it to everyone you know, please don't.
7. Do not use ALL CAPITALS. IT IMPLIES YOU ARE SHOUTING!!!
8. When you send messages online, make sure you proofread and correct mistakes before sending.
9. Do not forward other people's e-mails without their permission.
10. Do not forward virus warnings. They are generally hoaxes.
11. Ask before you send huge attachments.
12. Keep your communications short and to the point.
13. Do not leave the subject field blank in e-mails.
14. Avoid posting personal messages to a listserv.
15. Avoid using texting language for e-mails or social media sites (use correct spellings and correct language mechanics).
16. Remember to treat others online as you would like to be treated.
17. Use the Internet in ways that do not take away from your learning, but add to it.
18. Allow an appropriate amount of time for a person to respond to a message (24–48 business hours).
19. Be sure to have an appropriate salutation (i.e., *good morning, hello*) and closing (i.e., *goodbye, see you tomorrow*, etc.) in your e-mails.
20. Avoid slang (i.e., *wha's up, yo*, etc.) and acronyms (*btw, lol*, etc.)

"To err is human. To really foul things up requires a computer."

—Unknown

"The best thing about the Internet is that it makes everyone a publisher. The worst thing about the Internet is that it makes everyone a publisher."

—Unknown

Student *Perspective*

"When a student violates an academic integrity policy no one wins, even if the person gets away with it. It isn't right to cheat and it is an insult to everyone who put the effort in and did the work, and it cheapens the school for everyone. I learned my lesson and have no intention of ever cheating again."

—First-year student's reflection on an academic integrity violation

5. Not placing quotation marks around someone else's exact words that appear in the body of your paper
6. Failing to cite the source of factual information included in your paper that's not common knowledge
7. Submitting a paper for more than one class

Note: If the source for information included in your paper is listed at the end of your paper in your reference (works cited) section but is not cited in the body of your paper, this still qualifies as plagiarism.*

Sources: Academic Integrity at Princeton (2003); Pennsylvania State University (2005); Purdue University Online Writing Lab (2004).

Think About It — Journal Entry 1.6

*Look back at the definition and forms of plagiarism. List any form of plagiarism contained in that box that you were not already aware of.

____

____

____

____

____

____

People with integrity have the courage to admit when they're wrong and when they haven't done what they should have done. They don't play the role of victim and look for something or someone else to blame; they're willing to accept the blame and "take the heat" when they're wrong and to take responsibility for making it right. They feel remorse or guilt when they haven't lived up to their own ethical standards, and they use this guilt productively to motivate them to do what's right in the future.

Student Perspective

"I understood what I did was morally wrong and now I have to overcome it and move on living morally and ethically. It's really amazing that integrity is in everything we do in our lives."

—First-year student's reflection on an academic integrity violation

Summary and Conclusion

Research reviewed in this chapter points to the conclusion that successful students are able to:

1. Understand the differences between high school and college;
2. Understand responsible classroom personal behaviors;
3. Understand the dos and don'ts of Internet usage; and
4. Understand the syllabus and class policies.*

Chapter 1 Exercises

1.1 Personal Traits of a Responsible Student

*Construct a master list of personal traits you need to be a responsible student.

1. ______________________________

2. ______________________________

3. ______________________________

4. ______________________________

5. ______________________________

1.2 Is It or Is It Not Plagiarism?

Following are four incidents that were actually brought to a judicial review board to determine if plagiarism had occurred and, if so, what the penalty should be. After you read each case, answer the questions listed below it.

Case 1. A student turned in an essay that included substantial material copied from a published source. The student admitted that he didn't cite the sources properly, but argued that it was because he misunderstood the directions, not because he was attempting to steal someone else's ideas.

Is this plagiarism?

How severe is it? (Rate it on a scale from 1 = low to 10 = high)

What might the consequence or penalty be for the student?

How could the suspicion of plagiarism have been avoided in this case?

Case 2. A student turned in a paper that was identical to a paper submitted by another student for a different course.

Is this plagiarism?

How severe is it? (Rate it on a scale from 1 = low to 10 = high)

What might the consequence or penalty be for the student?

How could the suspicion of plagiarism have been avoided in this case?

Case 3. A student submitted a paper he wrote in a previous course as an extra-credit paper for a course.

Is this plagiarism?

How severe is it? (Rate it on a scale from 1 = low to 10 = high)

What might the consequence or penalty be for the student?

How could the suspicion of plagiarism have been avoided in this case?

Case 4. A student submitted a paper in an art history course that contained some ideas from art critics that she read about and whose ideas she agreed with. The student claimed that not citing these critics' ideas wasn't plagiarism because their ideas were merely their own subjective judgments or opinions, not facts or findings, and, furthermore, they were opinions that she agreed with.

Is this plagiarism?

How severe is it? (Rate it on a scale from 1 = low to 10 = high)

What might the consequence or penalty be for the student?

Looking back at these four cases, which of them do you think are the most severe and least severe violations of academic integrity? Why?

Crime and Punishment: Plagiarism and Its Consequences

In an article that appeared in an Ohio newspaper, titled "Plagiarism Persists in Classrooms," an English professor is quoted as saying, "Technology has made it easier to plagiarize because students can download papers and exchange information and papers through their computers. But technology has also made it easier to catch students who plagiarize." This professor's college subscribes to a Web site that matches the content of students' papers with content from books and online sources. Many professors now require students to submit their papers through this Web site. If students are caught plagiarizing, for a first offense, they typically receive an F for the assignment or the course. A second offense can result in dismissal or expulsion from college, which has already happened to a few students.

Source: Mariettatimes.com (March 22, 2006).

Discussion Questions

1. Why do you think students plagiarize? What do you suspect are the primary motives, reasons, or causes?
2. What do you think is a fair or just penalty for those found guilty of a first plagiarism violation? What is fair for those who commit a second violation?
3. How do you think plagiarism could be most effectively reduced or prevented from happening in the first place?

Chapter 1 Reflection

Name: ________________________

List and describe at least five principles discussed in this chapter that you can use to be a successful college student.

1.

2.

3.

4.

5.

Now explain HOW you can put these principles into practice.*

For Further Consideration

Game Plan Specifics for Success with Instructors and Classes

***The Top Ten**

1. Attend all your classes because . . .
   - Attendance is a predictor of success
   - New information is shared in class that you may not get anywhere else, and the information will probably be on the test
   - In-class activities and participation may be assigned points
   - You can stay on task and not get behind

2. Be on time because . . .
   - Tardiness can quickly become a habit
   - Late arrivals interrupt the instructor, the class, and the learning environment
   - You will gather all the information covered by the instructor

3. Monitor your cell phone usage because . . .
   - A ringing cell phone disrupts the class and learning environment
   - Texting in class disrupts your learning and is a distraction to others

4. Read your chapter before class time because . . .
   - If you know something about the material before the class begins, you will relate better to the discussions and activities
   - Prior review enhances memory, learning, and recall

5. Stay engaged, participate in discussions, and use respectful language and tone because . . .
   - You will learn the material by processing and using the new information in several ways
   - What comes around goes around, and the respect you show others will come back to you; plus, it's a great way to prepare for the work environment

6. Keep conversations directed to the entire class and instructor not the person sitting next to you because . . .
   - The entire class may be interested in your subject related comments, so raise your hand and share instead of talking to the person sitting next to you
   - Side conversations distract the learning environment for you and others

7. Always do your best and produce high quality work because . . .
   - Developing your work ethic now and practicing while you can will serve you well in the work environment
   - High quality work leads to better grades and a greater understanding of the material

8. Correctly cite your work to avoid plagiarism because . . .
   - Failure to cite the work of others may lead to a failing grade, removal from class, or even expulsion from the college depending on college policies
   - Authors deserve the credit for their original material, so if you don't know how to correctly cite material used in a research or term paper talk with someone in the Academic Achievement Center or the Library

9. Turn assignments in on time; seek assistance through the Academic Achievement Center, as needed because . . .
   - Turning in late work can quickly become a detrimental habit
   - Instructors often fail to accept late work
   - Instructors may accept late work within a time parameter but may reduce the points by 50%
   - Learning to adhere to deadlines is a skill you will use in your career

10. Learn your instructors' names and communicate with them as needed. Visit your instructor during office hours for academic help because . . .
   - They will answer questions for you and help you learn the material
   - Instructors want to see you succeed . . . it makes them happy
   - Instructors can serve as references for college applications, scholarships, or jobs, so it's important to communicate effectively with them and be a contributing student in class

How to Address Major Concerns and Academic Issues with Instructors and College Personnel

Learning to appropriately resolve conflict without becoming overly emotional is a life skill that you will need at college, home, and on the job. Problems and conflicts can and do arise in our lives, and our responses to these conflicts impact our academic, professional, and personal relationships. An overly emotional response to conflict may lead to serious consequences and outcomes.

Each environment has its own set of unwritten rules regarding etiquette and protocol with respect for others being the driving force. When meeting with others to address concerns or other issues follow the *Problem Solving Techniques* noted below. You may want to role play or practice some of these strategies.

Problem Solving Techniques

1. Identify the problem and your role in the conflict. Identify how you feel and why.

2. Make yourself aware of the college policies/procedures in the area of your concern. You may want to visit with an advisor or counselor first to determine the correct policy to review.

3. Schedule a time to meet with the instructor or administrator. When you have a serious concern, you should not arrive to discuss the issue without an appointment.

4. Put the scheduled time in your planner and be on time to the appointment.

5. Have a list prepared that includes your concern and what outcome you are seeking.

6. At the scheduled meeting, monitor your behavior and always present a respectful and professional attitude, tone of voice, and demeanor. As noted above, you may want to role play with a family member, friend, or counselor prior to the meeting to ensure that you can respectfully share your concerns.

7. Ask for a short break to step outside and calm yourself if you become upset or angry.

8. Respect the decision made by the instructor or administrator even when disappointed by the decision.

9. If you think the problem has not been resolved, check the policy to see if you may involve another person and hear their opinion. If policy does allow further resolution, then start over with the *Problem Solving Techniques* noted above. If the decision made is final, then treat all with respect and accept the decision. Learn from your experience.

Avoiding Plagiarism

The DMACC Library offers information related to plagiarism at https://www.dmacc.edu/library/Pages/welcome.aspx*

SQ4R Worksheet

*Your Name:

Selection Title/Chapter:

Author(s):

1. **Survey**: Look at the title, visuals, questions, excerpts, headings and sub-headings. Afterward, answer the questions below.

What do I already know about the topics?	What do I expect to learn?

2. **Question**: Create questions based on your survey of the text. If there are headings, turn them into questions. Include *at least three* below to help focus your attention as you read.

A.
B.
C.
D.
E.

3. **Read** and **Record** (Annotate): Read the selection thoroughly, highlight, and make note of important points, associations, and unfamiliar terms. Complete the chart using **your own words**. Provide a sketch and/or explanation of the visuals. Use and attach a separate sheet if needed.

Page and Paragraph #	Vocabulary Terms	Notes and Definitions	Visuals

(*Continued*)

(*Continued*)

4. **Recite**: Answer your questions from step two.

a.
b.
c.
d.
e.

5. **Review and Reflect**: Check your memory by verbalizing the above information. Below, write a summary **in your own words** of what you have read, connecting the content ideas. Additionally, write a brief reflection including your personal response to the reading (use "I" and make connections to your own experiences, ask more questions, respond to the text, and consider anything you were reminded of or visualized while reading).*

Summary:

Reflection:

Adapted from Florida Online Reading Professional Development. (n.d.). *SQ4R*. Retrieved from the Marco Island Charter Middle School website at http://micms.org/SQ4R.pdf

Educational and Career Planning and Decision Making

2

Making Wise Choices about Your Courses, Major, Degree, and Career Plans

THOUGHT STARTER

Journal Entry 2.1

LEARNING GOAL

To develop strategies for exploring different academic fields and for choosing an educational path that will enable you to achieve your personal and career goals.

*1. Are you decided or undecided about a college major?

____

2. If you are undecided, list any subjects that might be possibilities:

____

____

3. If you are decided, what is your choice and why did you choose this major?

____

____

4. Indicate how sure you are about that choice by circling one of the following options:

absolutely sure   fairly sure   not too sure   likely to change

Why?

____

____

____

____

The Importance of Long-Range Educational Planning

College will allow you many choices about what courses to enroll in and what field to specialize in. By looking ahead and developing a tentative plan for your courses beyond the first term of college, you will position yourself to view your college experience as a full-length movie and get a sneak preview of the total picture. In contrast, scheduling your classes one term at a time just before each registration period (when everyone else is making a mad rush to register) forces you to view your academic experience as a series of short, separate snapshots that lack connection or direction.

Long-range educational planning also enables you to take a proactive approach to your future. Being proactive means you are taking early, preventative action that anticipates events before they sneak up on you and force you to react without time to plan your best strategy. As the old saying goes, "If you fail to plan, you plan to fail." Through advanced planning, you can actively take charge of your academic future and make it happen *for* you, rather than waiting and passively letting it happen *to* you.

"When you have to make a choice and don't make it, that is in itself a choice."

—William James, philosopher and one of the founders of American psychology

Remember

Any long-range plan you develop is not set in stone: it can change depending on changes in your academic interests and future plans. The purpose of long-range planning is not to lock you into a particular plan but to free you from shortsightedness, procrastination, or denial about choosing to take charge of your life.

"Education is our passport to the future; for tomorrow belongs to the people who prepare for it today."

—Malcolm X, African American civil rights leader

Don't take the denial and avoidance approach to planning your educational future.

Think About It — *Journal Entry* 2.2

Choosing a major is a life-changing decision because it will determine what you do for the rest of your life. Would you agree or disagree with this statement?

Why?

____

____

____

____

____

____

One important element of long-range educational planning is deciding whether you're going to continue your education beyond your community college experience by transferring to a four-year college or university and when you plan to make that transition. Some community college students plan to transfer to a four-year college before completing their associate degree at their community college. However, we strongly recommend that you complete your general education program before attempting to transfer, because multiple advantages are associated with completing 60 or more units at a two-year college and attaining an associate degree. These advantages are listed in the next section.*

Advantages of Completing an Associate Degree before Transferring to a Four-Year College or University

1. **Many four-year campuses give priority admission to transfer students who have completed an associate degree (CSU Student Transfer, 2015; Washington State Board for Community & Technical Colleges, 2015). Thus, earning an associate degree will increase your transfer chances and options. It also allows you to capitalize on articulation agreements between two- and four-year campuses that grant "block transfer" of all general education credits earned for an associate degree. Research shows that students with more transfer credits at the time they enter a four-year college are more likely to complete a bachelor's degree (CCRC, 2014).

2. **By completing an associate degree, you buy extra time and advising support to reach a final decision about your college major and what four-year college you'll transfer to.** If you're unsure about what major you want to declare, or what four-year college you want to attend, returning to your community college for your sophomore year provides an additional year of time and advising support to reach both of these important decisions.

    What field of study you major in and what four-year college you attend are often interrelated decisions. Some majors may only be offered at certain colleges, and the nature and quality of the same major may vary from one campus to the next. A second year at your community college can provide the time and support you need to reach a well-informed decision about what four-year campus is the best choice for your major.

3. **Research shows that students who complete an associate degree make a smoother academic transition to four-year campuses.** Students who transfer before completing an associate degree tend to experience more "transfer shock"—a sharper drop in GPA after transferring to a four-year institution—than do students who transfer after completing an associate degree (Laanan, 2001). The superior post-transfer performance of students who complete an associate degree may be due to the fact that they (a) develop a stronger set of transferable skills by completing more academic skill-building courses (writing, math, oral communication) prior to transfer and (b) acquire a broader base of knowledge by completing the wide range of general education courses required for the associate degree. In addition, completing an associate degree allows you to complete all these academic skill-building courses and general education requirements at a community college—where classes are smaller and courses are taught by experienced instructors whose primary responsibility is teaching, not research. (At larger universities, first- and second-year courses are often taught by the least experienced professors or graduate students.)

4. **Earning an associate degree opens up more opportunities for you to obtain internships, part-time employment during the academic year, or full-time**

employment during the summers in between your junior and senior years of college. Having an associate degree increases your chances of being hired and also increases the amount you're paid for the work you're hired to do (Gagliardi & Heimstra, 2013; Mullin & Phillippe, 2013). Employees possessing an associate degree earn substantially more money than individuals with a high school diploma (Ganzglass, 2014; Tinto, 2012). This may be particularly advantageous if, for some reason, you're unable to complete a four-year degree or have to postpone its completion.

5. **Completing an associate degree supplies you with more time and opportunity to accumulate academic awards and honors prior to transfer (e.g., graduating with honors and participating in Phi Theta Kappa—national honor society for two-year college students).** Such awards increase your chances of receiving scholarships and grants from four-year colleges. Furthermore, since these accomplishments remain on your permanent college record after completing a bachelor's degree, they strengthen your job prospects after college graduation, as well as your chances of acceptance to graduate or professional school.
6. **Completing an associate degree provides you with more opportunity for leadership development and recognition during your sophomore year.** As a community college student, you become eligible for a variety of resume-building and character-building leadership opportunities during your second year (e.g., orientation week leader, peer tutor, or peer mentor). At four-year colleges and universities, sophomores are often unable to assume these leadership positions because they may be reserved for more experienced juniors and seniors. At two-year colleges, sophomores are the "seniors" and you can engage in leadership experiences during your sophomore year that will: (a) increase your chances of acceptance at four-year colleges, (b) qualify you for similar leadership positions at the four-year college to which you transfer, and (c) enhance your job prospects during your last two years of college and after completing your four-year degree.
7. **Completing an associate degree gives you the opportunity to participate in your community college's graduation ceremony.** Even if you plan to transfer and graduate from a four-year college with a bachelor's degree, don't underestimate the importance of celebrating your attainment of an associate degree. This is a significant achievement because:
    - It indicates you have survived and thrived during the two most critical years of the college experience. (Research shows that almost 75% of those students who withdraw from college will do so during the freshman and sophomore years [American College Testing, 2015]). Your attainment of an associate degree serves as evidence to four-year colleges and employers that you had the grit to persist and complete these two critical years.
    - It signifies that you've successfully completed the general education component of the college experience. In many ways, this is the most important component of your college career because it represents the acquisition of breadth of knowledge and the development of essential, transferable skills (e.g., writing, speaking, critical thinking, and quantitative reasoning) that spell success in all majors and all careers. Surveys indicate that these are the type of lifelong learning skills that employers look for and value most in employees (AAC&U, 2013).
    - It's an opportunity for you to be recognized publicly—in front of family, friends, faculty, and fellow students. Research indicates that student involvement in college rituals or ceremonial events (such as graduation) reinforces their commitment to continue their education and reach their

educational goal (Kuh, et al., 2005). Thus, participating in your community college's graduation ceremony isn't only an opportunity for you to celebrate achievement of your associate degree; it's also an opportunity to receive a motivational "shot in the arm" that propels you toward completion of a four-year degree. Proof of the power of the graduation experience is illustrated in the following excerpt of a letter written by a student who graduated with an associate degree from a two-year college and transferred to a four-year campus to complete her bachelor's degree.

> *"I just wanted to get in touch and let you know how I am doing. I successfully graduated from USF [a four-year college]. Looking back, the two-year college experience helped me achieve successful habits that brought me to where I am today. Also, during the graduation ceremony for my associate degree, I saw some fellow students wearing the yellow shawl that represented walking with honors. I thought to myself, 'I am going to walk with honors when I get my B.A.' And that I did! Who would have ever thought? [Now] I have decided that I want to go to graduate school."*
>
> —*Letter from a two-year college graduate received by Joe Cuseo***

Snapshot Summary

2.1 Tips for Students Transferring to Four-Year Colleges and Universities

*The following criteria are those that most likely will be used by four-year colleges to evaluate your application and decide on your acceptance:

- **Academic record.** Colleges will look at your overall GPA and grades for courses in your chosen major.
- **Out-of-class experiences.** For example, your involvement in leadership activities and volunteer experience in the community or on campus can play a role in your acceptance to a four-year college.
- **Letters of recommendation.** Letters can come, for example, from course instructors and academic advisors. Provide the following courtesies for those you ask to write letters of recommendation for you:
  - A *fact sheet* about yourself that will enable them to cite concrete examples or evidence of your achievements and contributions (which will make the letter more powerful)
  - Give the person at least two weeks' notice.
  - A *stamped, addressed* envelope (a personal courtesy that makes the job a little easier for your reference)
  - A *thank-you note* close to the date that the letter is due (not only a nice thing to do but also a reminder in case the person has forgotten about your letter or has not yet set aside time to write it)
- **Personal statement.** In your letter of application for admission, which you write when applying to a school, try to demonstrate your knowledge of:
  - *yourself* (e.g., your personal interests, abilities, and values);
  - your intended *major* (e.g., why you're interested in it and what you might do with it after graduation); and
  - the *college* to which you're applying by showing that you know something specific about the school (e.g., its mission, philosophy, and programs—especially the particular program to which you're applying).

To maximize your success at four-year colleges and universities, take the initiative to connect with people who can contribute to your success, including the following:

- **Faculty.** Make sure they know who you are (e.g., sit in front of class, come up to speak with them after class, visit them in their offices, or volunteer to help them with research they're doing that you find interesting or relevant to your career interests).
- **Students in your major.** Connect with them in study groups and major clubs (psychology club, history club, etc.).
- **Career development specialists.** Connect with these professionals on strategies for enhancing your marketability after graduation. Ask them about what graduates (alumni) with your major have gone on to do and whether they can connect you with an alum in a career that you intend to pursue.

To Be or Not to Be Decided about a College Major: What the Research Shows

Studies of student decisions about a college major show that:

- Less than 10 percent of new college students feel they know a great deal about the fields that they intend to major in.
- As students proceed through the first year of college, they grow more uncertain about the majors they chose when they began college.
- More than two-thirds of new students change their minds about their majors during the first year of college.

Snapshot Summary

2.2 A Checklist of Course-Registration Reminders for Community College Students

Achieving your educational goals requires both long- and short-range planning. Your long-range plan involves completing your degree, and your short-range plan involves continuing your enrollment in college from term to term. When planning to register for the next academic term, keep the following list of reminders handy to ensure that your term-to-term transition proceeds smoothly.

- Check the registration dates and be prepared to register at the earliest date that's available to you.
- Check with an academic advisor to be sure that you're planning to take the right classes for your program, major, and any four-year school you plan to transfer to.
- Let your advisor know what your educational goals are and if you've changed your goals since the last time you registered.
- Let your advisor know the total number of hours per week you plan to work so that you create a schedule that will allow you to successfully balance schoolwork and for-pay work.
- If you're receiving financial aid, meet with a financial aid counselor or advisor to be sure that you have adequate funds to cover next term's tuition, book costs, and parking fees.
- Once you've registered, periodically check the status of your courses because last-minute changes can occur in the time and day when courses meet and it's possible that one of your courses might be canceled (e.g., due to insufficient enrollment).

Remember

*Unlike in high school, summer school in college isn't something you do to make up for courses that were failed or should have been taken during the "regular" school year (fall and spring terms). Instead, it's an additional term that you can use to make further progress toward your college degree and reduce the total time it takes to complete your degree.**

- Only one in three college seniors eventually major in the same fields that they chose during their first year of college (Cuseo, 2005; HERI, 2014).

*These findings demonstrate that the vast majority of students entering college are not certain about their college majors. Many students don't reach their final decision about a major *before* starting their college experience; instead, they make that decision *during* their college experience. Being uncertain about a major is nothing to be embarrassed about. Beginning college students may be undecided for very good

"Not all who wander are lost."

—J. R. R. Tolkien, *The Lord of the Rings*

reasons. For instance, you may be undecided simply because you have interests in various subjects; this is a healthy form of indecision because it shows that you have a range of interests and a high level of motivation to learn about different subjects. You may also be undecided simply because you're a careful, reflective thinker whose decision-making style is to gather more information before making a firm and final commitment.

In one study of students who were undecided about a major at the start of college, 43 percent had several ideas in mind but were not yet ready to commit to one of them (Gordon & Steele, 2003). They had some ideas but still wanted to explore them and keep their options open, which is an effective way to go about making decisions.

As a first-year student, it's only natural to be at least somewhat uncertain about your educational goals because you haven't yet experienced the variety of subjects and academic programs that make up the college curriculum, some of which you didn't know existed. In fact, one purpose of general education courses is to help new students develop the critical thinking skills needed to make wise choices and well-informed decisions, such as their choice of a college major.

Similarly, changing your original educational plans is not necessarily a bad thing. It may mean that you have discovered another field that's more interesting to you or that's more compatible with your personal interests and talents. It's okay to start off not knowing what your major will be or whether you want to pursue a four-year degree or a shorter-range educational goal, such as an associate degree or vocational-technical certificate. You still have time to make up your mind and to change your mind. Don't think that you must lock yourself into a particular plan and must either stick with it or drop out of college if your plans change. You can take courses that will count toward graduation, regardless of what major or educational track you end up taking.

Changing your educational plan has one downside: if you make that change late in your college experience, it can result in more time to graduation (and more tuition) because you may need to complete additional courses required for your newly chosen field.

"When you get to a fork in the road, take it."

—Yogi Berra, Hall of Fame baseball player

Think About It — Journal Entry 2.3

If you've already chosen a major or specialized program, what led you to this choice?

____

____

____

____

Remember

As a rule, you should reach a fairly firm decision about your major during your second (sophomore) year in college. However, to reach a good decision within this time frame, the process of exploring and planning should begin now—during your first term in college.

Myths about the Relationship between Majors and Careers

Good decisions are based not on misconceptions or myths, but on accurate information. Effective planning for a college major requires accurate information about the relationship between majors and careers. Unfortunately, several popular myths about the relationship between majors and careers can lead to uninformed or unrealistic choices of a college major.

Myth 1. When you choose your major, you're choosing your career. While some majors lead directly to a particular career, most do not. Majors leading directly to specific careers are called preprofessional or prevocational majors, and they include such fields as accounting, engineering, and nursing. However, most college majors don't channel you directly down one particular career path: they leave you with various career options. All physics majors don't become physicists, all philosophy majors don't become philosophers, all history majors do not become historians, and all English majors do not become Englishmen (or Englishwomen). The career paths of most college graduates are not straight lines that run directly from their majors to their careers. The trip from college to career or careers is more like climbing a tree. As illustrated in Figure 2.1, you begin with the tree's trunk—the foundation of general education (courses required of all college students, whatever their major may be)—which grows into separate limbs (different college majors) that, in turn, lead to different branches (different career paths or options).

Note that the career branches grow from the same limb. Likewise, the same major leads to a "family" of related careers. For example, an English major often leads to careers that involve use of the written language (e.g., editing, journalism, and publishing), while a major in art leads to careers that involve use of visual media (e.g., illustration, graphic design, and art therapy). (Note that the Web site

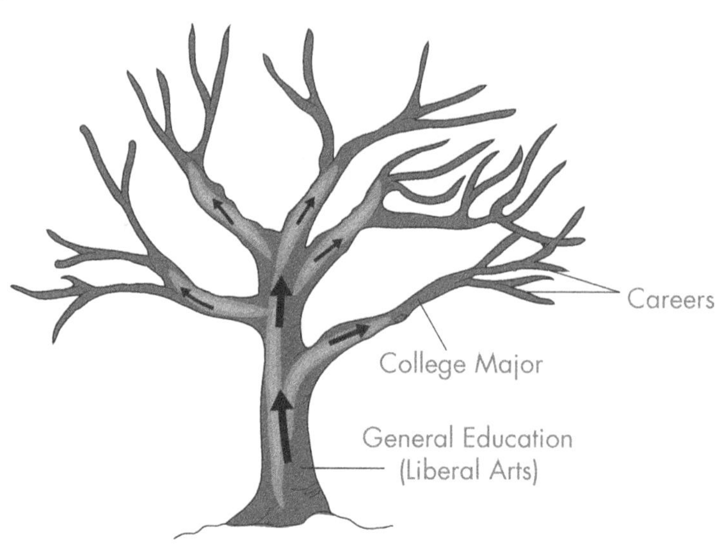

The Relationship between General Education (Liberal Arts), College Majors, and Careers

www.mymajors.com provides useful and free information on groups or families of jobs that tend to be related to different majors).

Also, different majors can lead to the same career. For instance, many majors can lead a student to law school and to an eventual career as a lawyer; there is no undergraduate major in law or prelaw. Similarly, premed isn't a major. Although most students interested in going to medical school after college major in some field in the natural sciences (e.g., biology or chemistry), it's possible for students to go to medical school with majors in other fields, particularly if they take and do well in certain science courses that are emphasized in medical school (e.g., general biology, general chemistry, and organic and inorganic chemistry).

Thus, don't presume that your major is your career or that your major automatically turns into your career. This is one reason some students procrastinate about choosing a major; they think they are making a lifelong decision and fear that if they make the "wrong" choice they'll be stuck doing something they hate for the rest of their lives. The belief that your major becomes your career may also account for 58 percent of college graduates choosing to major in a preprofessional or prevocational field such as nursing, accounting, or engineering (Association of American Colleges & Universities, 2007). These majors have careers obviously connected to them, which reassures students (and their family members) that they will have jobs after graduation. However, although students in prevocational majors may be more likely to be hired immediately after graduation, tracking college graduates with other college majors has shown that six months after graduation they too have jobs; thus, they are not more likely to be unemployed (Pascarella & Terenzini, 2005).

Remember

Don't assume that choosing your college major means you're choosing what you'll be doing for as long as you'll be living.

Student *Perspective*

"Things like picking majors and careers really scare me a lot! I don't know exactly what I want to do with my life."

—First-year student

Research on college graduates indicates that they change careers numerous times, and the further they continue along their career paths, the more likely they are to work in fields unrelated to their college majors (Millard, 2004). Remember that the general education curriculum is a significant part of a college education. It allows students to acquire knowledge in diverse subjects and to develop durable, transferable skills (e.g., writing, speaking, and organizing) that qualify college graduates for a diversity of careers, regardless of what their particular majors happened to be.

The order in which decisions about majors and careers are covered in this book reflects the order in which they are likely to be made in your life. For most college majors, students first decide on their majors; later, they decide on their careers. Although it is important to think about the relationship between your choice of major and your choice of career or careers, these are different choices that are usually made at different times. Both choices relate to your future goals, but they involve different time frames: choosing your major is a short-range goal, whereas choosing your career is a long-range goal.

Remember

Choosing a major and choosing a career are not always the same decision: they are often separate decisions that don't have to be made at the same time.

Myth 2. After a bachelor's degree, any further education must be in the same field as your college major. After college graduation, you have two main options or alternative paths available to you:

1. You can enter a career immediately.
2. You can continue your education in graduate school or professional school. (See Figure 2.2 for a visual map of the signposts or stages in the college experience and the basic paths available to you after college graduation.)

Once you complete a bachelor's degree, it's possible to continue your education in a field that's not directly related to your college major. This is particularly true for students who are majoring in preprofessional careers that funnel them directly into a particular career after graduation (Pascarella & Terenzini, 2005). For example, if you major in English, you can still go to graduate school in a subject other than English; you could go to law school or get a master's degree in business administration. It's common to find graduate students in masters of business administration programs who were not business majors in college In fact, most students who attend graduate school in the field of business (e.g., MBA programs) were not business majors when they were in college (Zlomek, 2012).*

Think About It — *Journal Entry* 2.4

Reflect on the preceding timeline and Figure 2.2, which suggests that it will take you two years to complete an associate degree and four years to complete a bachelor's degree.

1. Do you see yourself completing an associate degree in two years? A bachelor's degree in four years? Why or why not?

____

____

2. Do you plan to transfer after completing an associate degree?

____

If yes, to what college or university?

____

If no, do you ever see yourself eventually returning to college to complete your bachelor's degree?

____

3. Do you see any possible interfering factors or potential obstacles that might prolong the time you need to reach your educational goals?

____

____

____

"We should not underestimate the ability of people to eventually obtain their college degrees. Nor should we minimize the diversity of behaviors which lead individuals to leave and eventually to return to complete their college degree programs."

—Vincent Tinto, nationally known researcher and scholar on college student success

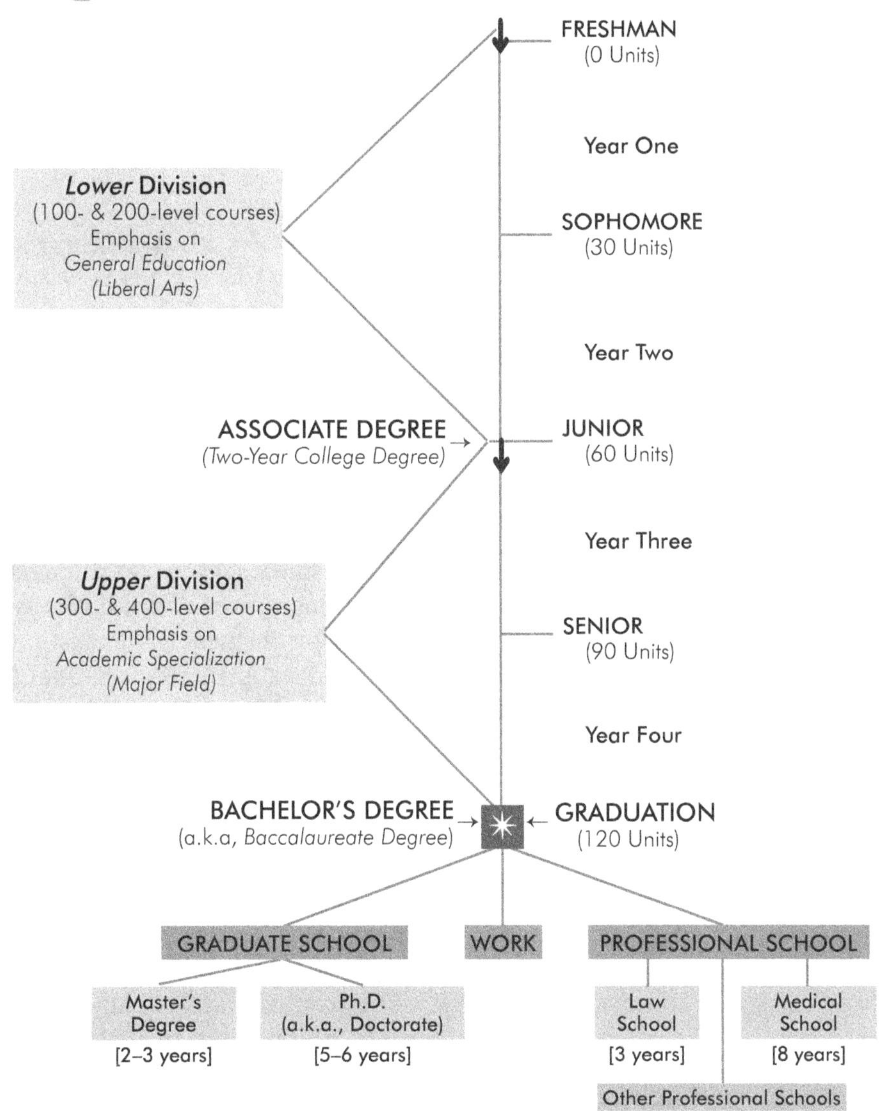

Notes

1. The total number of *general education* units and the total number of units needed to **graduate** with a bachelor's degree may vary somewhat from school to school. Also, the total number of units required for a *major* will vary somewhat from major to major and from school to school.
2. It often takes college students longer than four years to graduate due to a variety of reasons, such as working part-time and taking fewer courses per term, needing to repeat courses that were failed or dropped, or making a late change to a different major and needing to fulfill additional requirements for the new major.
3. *Graduate* and *professional* schools are options for continuing to higher levels of education after completion of an undergraduate (college) education.
4. Compared to graduate school, *professional* school involves advanced education in more "applied" professions (e.g., pharmacy or public administration).

Timeline to the Future: A Snapshot of the College Experience and Beyond

Author's Experience

My undergraduate degree was in political science and sociology. When I graduated from college, I spent the first eight years of my professional life becoming a corporate manager. I did not major in business, but found that my liberal arts background gave me the problem-solving and communication skills that were crucial in working with a variety of people in my profession. You do not need to major in business to be a successful business person. Indeed, employers are telling us that they are looking for those who can problem solve, critically think, write and speak well, and work with a diversity of people and thought.

Aaron Thompson

"Employers are far more interested in the prospect's ability to think and to think clearly, to write and speak well, and how (s)he works with others than in his major or the name of the school (s)he went to. Several college investigating teams found that these were the qualities on which all kinds of employers, government and private, base their decisions."

—Lauren Pope, *Looking beyond the Ivy League* (1990)*

**Myth 3. Most college graduates are employed in business settings, so students (and their parents) often conclude that if students are going to work for a business, they better major in business. This belief likely explains why business is the most popular major among college students (National Center for Education Statistics, 2014). However, college graduates now working in business settings have majored in variety of fields besides business, and many CEOs of today's most profitable companies did not major in business (Elliot, 2015). Certainly, if you have an interest in and passion for majoring in business, by all means major in business; however, don't choose a business major because you think it's the only major that will qualify you to work for and succeed in a business organization after graduation.

Myth 4. A commonly held myth is that all you can do with a major in a liberal arts subject is to teach the subject you majored in (e.g., math majors become math teachers; history majors become history teachers). The truth is that students majoring in different liberal arts fields go on to enter, advance, and prosper in a wide variety of careers. College graduates with degrees in the liberal arts who went on to achieve professional success in careers other than teaching include:

- Jill Barad (English major), CEO, Mattel Toys
- Willie Brown (liberal studies major), Mayor of San Francisco
- Ken Chenault (History major), CEO, American Express
- Christopher Connor (Sociology major), CEO, Sherwin Williams
- Robert Iger (Communications major), CEO, Walt Disney Company

Student Perspective

"They asked me during my interview why I was right for the job and I told them because I can read well, write well and I can think. They really liked that because those were the skills they were looking for."

—English major hired by a public relations firm (*Los Angeles Times*, April 4, 2004)

Significant numbers of liberal arts majors are also employed in positions relating to marketing, human resources, and public affairs (Bok, 2006; Useem, 1989). An experienced career counselor once tracked the majors of college graduates working in the insurance industry. She found an art history major working at a major insurance firm whose job was to value oriental carpets and art holdings. She found a geology major working for an insurance company whose job was to evaluate beach properties and determine the odds of hurricanes or other natural phenomena causing property damage. This former geology major spent much of her work time traveling to beachfront communities to review new developments and assessing damages after hurricanes or other tragic events (Brooks, 2009).

Research also reveals that the career mobility and career advancement of liberal arts majors working in the corporate world are comparable to business majors. For example, liberal arts majors are just as likely to advance to the highest levels of corporate leadership as majors in such preprofessional fields as business and engineering (Pascarella & Terenzini, 2005). The point we're making here is that if you have a passion for and talent in a liberal arts field, don't dismiss it as being "impractical," and don't be dismayed or discouraged by those who challenge your choice by asking: "What are you going to do with a degree in that major?" (Brooks, 2009).**

Think About It — Journal Entry 2.5

*In what ways do you think your general education courses will improve your work performance in the career field you may pursue?

____

____

____

____

____

Factors to Consider When Choosing Your Major or Field of Study

Gaining self-awareness is the critical first step in making decisions about a college major, or any other important decision. You must know yourself before you can know what choice is best for you. While this may seem obvious, self-awareness and self-discovery are often overlooked aspects of the decision-making process. In particular, you need awareness of:

- Your *interests*, what you like doing;
- Your *abilities*, what you're good at doing; and
- Your *values*, what you feel good about doing.

Research indicates that students are more likely to continue in college and graduate when they choose majors that reflect their personal interests and talents (Leuwerke, et al., 2004; Pascarella & Terenzini, 2005).*

"I try to do more to please myself, and making good grades and doing well in school helps my ego. It gives me confidence, and I like that feeling."

—First-year student (Franklin, 2002)

*Multiple Intelligences: Identifying Personal Abilities and Talents

One element of the self that you should be aware of when choosing a major is your mental strengths, abilities, or talents. Intelligence was once considered to be one general trait that could be detected and measured by a single intelligence test score. The singular word *intelligence* has now been replaced by the plural word *intelligences* to reflect the fact that humans can display intelligence (mental ability) in many forms other than performance on an IQ test.

Listed in Snapshot Summary 2.3 are forms of intelligence identified by Howard Gardner (1999, 2006) based on studies of gifted and talented individuals, experts in different lines of work, and various other sources. As you read through the types of intelligence, place a checkmark next to the type that you think represents your strongest ability or talent. (You can possess more than one type.) Keep your type(s) of intelligence in mind when you're choosing a college major because different majors emphasize different thinking skills. Ideally, you want to select an academic field that allows you to utilize your strongest skills and talents. Choosing a major that's compatible with your abilities should enable you to master the concepts and skills required by your major more easily and more deeply. If you follow your academic talents, you're also more likely to succeed or excel in what you do, which will bolster your academic self-confidence and motivation.

Snapshot Summary

2.3 Multiple Forms of Intelligence

- **Linguistic intelligence.** Ability to communicate through language—e.g., verbal skills in the areas of speaking, writing, listening, and reading.
- **Logical-mathematical intelligence.** Ability to reason logically and succeed in tasks that involve mathematical problem solving—e.g., making logical arguments and following logical reasoning, or ability to work well with numbers and make quantitative calculations.
- **Spatial intelligence.** Ability to visualize relationships among objects arranged in different spatial positions and the ability to perceive or create visual images—e.g., forming mental images of three-dimensional objects; detecting detail in objects or drawings; artistic talent for drawing, painting, sculpting, and graphic design; and skills related to sense of direction and navigation.
- **Musical intelligence.** Ability to appreciate or create rhythmical and melodic sounds—e.g., playing, writing, and arranging music.
- **Interpersonal (social) intelligence.** Ability to relate to others, to accurately identify others' needs, feelings, or emotional states of mind, and to effectively express emotions and feelings to others—e.g., interpersonal communication skills, ability to accurately "read" the feelings of others, and ability to meet their emotional needs.
- **Intrapersonal (self) intelligence.** Ability to introspect and understand one's own thoughts, feelings, and behavior—e.g., capacity for personal reflection, emotional self-awareness, and self-insight.
- **Bodily-kinesthetic (psychomotor) intelligence.** Ability to use one's own body skillfully and learn through bodily sensations or movements—e.g., skilled at tasks involving physical coordination, ability to work well with hands, mechanical skills, talent for building models, assembling things, and using technology.

Student Perspective

"I used to operate a printing press. In about two weeks I knew how to run it and soon after I could take the machine apart in my head and analyze what each part does, how it functioned, and why it was shaped that way."

—Response of college sophomore to the questions "What are you really good at? What comes easily or naturally to you?"

- **Naturalist intelligence.** Ability to carefully observe and appreciate features of the natural environment—e.g., keen awareness of nature or natural surroundings, and ability to understand causes and consequences of events occurring in the natural world.
- **Existential.** Ability to conceptualize phenomena and experiences that require one to go beyond sensory or physical evidence, such as questions and issues involving the origin of the universe and human life, and the purpose of human existence.

Source: Gardner (1993, 1999, 2006).

Think About It — Journal Entry 2.6

Which types of intelligence listed in Snapshot Summary 2.3 are your strongest areas? Which majors or fields of study do you think may be the best match for your natural talents?

____

____

____

____

____

____

Author's Experience

I first noticed that students in different academic fields may have different learning styles when I was teaching a psychology course that was required for students majoring in nursing and social work. I noticed that some students in class seemed to lose interest (and patience) when we got involved in lengthy class discussions about controversial issues or theories, while others seemed to love it. On the other hand, whenever I lectured or delivered information for an extended period, some students seemed to lose interest (and attention), while others seemed to get into it and took great notes. After one class period that involved quite a bit of class discussion, I began thinking about which students seemed most involved in the discussion and which seemed to drift off or lose interest. I suddenly realized that the students who did most of the talking and seemed most enthused during the class discussion were the students majoring in social work. On the other hand, most of the students who appeared disinterested or a bit frustrated were the nursing majors.

When I began to think about why this happened, it dawned on me that the nursing students were accustomed to gathering factual information and learning practical skills in their major courses and were expecting to use that learning style in my psychology course. The nursing majors felt more comfortable with structured class sessions in which they received lots of factual, practical information from the professor. On the other hand, the social work majors were more comfortable with unstructured class discussions because courses in their major often emphasized debating social issues and hearing viewpoints or perspectives.

As I left class that day, I asked myself: Did the nursing students and social work students select or gravitate toward their major because the type of learning emphasized in the field tended to match their preferred style of learning?

Joe Cuseo

To sum up, the most important factor to consider when reaching decisions about a major is whether it is compatible with four characteristics of your self: (1) your learning style, (2) your abilities, (3) your personal interests, and (4) your values (see Figure 2.3). These four pillars provide the foundation for effective decisions about a college major.

Strategies for Discovering a Major Compatible with Your Interests, Talents, and Values

If you're undecided about a major, there's no need to feel anxious or guilty. You're at an early stage in your college experience. Just be sure that you don't put all thoughts about your major on the back burner. Start exploring and developing a game plan now that will lead you to a wise decision about your major.

Similarly, if you've already chosen a major, this doesn't mean that you'll never have to give any more thought to that decision. Instead, you should continue the exploration process by carefully testing your first choice, making sure it's a choice that is compatible with your abilities, interests, and values. In other words, take the approach that it's your *current* choice; whether it becomes your firm and *final* choice will depend on how well you perform, and how interested you are, in the first courses you take in the field.

To explore and identify majors that are compatible with your personal strengths and interests, use the following strategies:

1. **Use past experience to help you choose a major.** Think about the subjects that you experienced during high school and your early time in college. As the old saying goes, "Nothing succeeds like success itself." If you have done well and continue to do well in a certain field of study, this may indicate that your natural abilities and learning style correspond well with the academic skills required by that particular field. This could translate into future success and satisfaction in the field if you decide to pursue it as a college major.

   You can enter information about your academic performance in high school courses at the Web site mymajors.com, which will analyze it and provide you with college majors that may be a good match for you (based on your academic experiences in high school).
2. **Use your elective courses to explore your interests and abilities in subjects that you might consider as majors.** As the name implies, "elective" courses are those that you elect or choose to take. *Electives* are courses that you may elect (choose) to enroll in; they count toward your college degree but are not required for general education or your major. For example, your campus may have a general education requirement in social or behavioral sciences that requires you to take two courses in this field, but you're allowed to choose what those two courses are from a menu of options in the field, such as anthropology, economics, political science, psychology, or sociology. If you're considering one of these subjects as a possible major, you can take an introductory course in that subject to test your interest in it while simultaneously fulfilling a general education requirement needed for graduation. This strategy will allow you to use general education as the main highway for travel toward your final destination (a college degree) while using your electives to explore side roads (potential majors) along the way. If you find one that's compatible with your talents and interests, you may have found yourself a major.

3. **Be sure you know the courses that are required for the major you're considering.** In college, it's expected that students may know the requirements for the major they've chosen. These requirements vary considerably from one major to another. Be sure to review your college catalog carefully to determine what courses are required for the major you're considering. If you have trouble tracking down the requirements in your college catalog, don't become frustrated. These catalogs are often written in a technical manner that can sometimes be hard to interpret. If you need help identifying and understanding the requirements for a major that you are considering, don't be embarrassed about seeking assistance from an advisor.

Author's Experience

As an academic advisor, I often see students who are confused about what they want to major in, especially traditionally aged (18 to 24 years old) students. I can relate to these students because I changed my major multiple times before I reached a final decision. The first piece of advice I give students about choosing majors is to use their resources (e.g., academic advisement) and to do some research on the courses required for the majors they're considering. Over the last few years, I've seen many students who want to major in forensic science—largely due to the popularity of the *CSI* shows. I then ask them how they feel about science and math, and many of these students tell me they hate those subjects. When I inform them that becoming a forensic scientist often involves a minimum of a master's in chemistry, they decide to look at other majors. Fewer surprises like this would occur if students did at least some research on what courses are required for the majors and careers they're considering.

Julie McLaughlin

Keep in mind that college majors often require courses in fields outside of the major. Such courses are designed to support the major. For instance, psychology majors are often required to take at least one course in biology, and business majors are often required to take calculus. If you are interested in majoring in a particular subject area, be sure you are fully aware of such outside requirements and are comfortable with them.

Once you've accurately identified all courses required for the major you're considering, ask yourself the following two questions:

- Do the course titles and descriptions appeal to my interests and values?
- Do I have the abilities or skills needed to do well in these courses?

You don't want to be surprised by unexpected requirements after you have already committed to a major, particularly if these unanticipated requirements do not match your personal abilities, interests, or learning styles.

4. **Talk with students majoring in the field you are considering and ask them about their experiences.** Try to speak with several students in the field so that you get a balanced perspective that goes beyond the opinion of one individual. A good way to find students in the major you're considering is to visit student clubs on campus related to the major (e.g., psychology club or history club). The following questions may be good ones to ask students in a major that you're considering:

- What first attracted you to this major?
- What would you say are the advantages and disadvantages of majoring in this field?
- Knowing what you know now, would you choose the same major again?

5. **Sit in on some classes in the field you are considering as a major.** If the class you want to visit is large, you probably could just slip into the back row and listen. However, if the class is small, you should ask the instructor's permission. When visiting a class, focus on the content or ideas being covered in class rather than the instructor's personality or teaching style. (Keep in mind that you're trying to decide whether you will major in the subject, not in the teacher.)
6. **Discuss the major you're considering with an academic advisor.** It's probably best to speak with an academic advisor who advises students in various majors rather than to someone who advises only students in their particular academic department or field. You want to be sure to discuss the major with an advisor who is neutral and will give you unbiased feedback about the pros and cons of majoring in that field.
7. **Speak with some faculty members in the department that you're considering as a major.** Consider asking them the following questions:
   - What academic skills or qualities are needed for a student to be successful in your field?
   - What are the greatest challenges faced by students majoring in your field?
   - What do students seem to like most and least about majoring in your field?
   - What can students do with a major in your field after college graduation?
   - What types of graduate programs or professional schools would a student in your major be well prepared to enter?
8. **Visit your Career Development Center.** See whether information is available on college graduates who've majored in the field you're considering and what they've gone on to do with that major after graduation. This will give you an idea about the types of careers the major can lead to or what graduate and professional school programs students often enter after completing a major in the field that you're considering.
9. **Surf the Web site of the professional organization associated with the field that you're considering as a major.** For example, if you're thinking about becoming an anthropology major, check out the Web site of the American Anthropological Association. If you're considering history as a major, look at the Web site of the American Historical Association. The Web site of a professional organization often contains useful information for students who are considering that field as a major. For example, the Web site of the American Philosophical Association contains information about nonacademic careers for philosophy majors, and the American Sociological Association's Web site identifies various careers that sociology majors are qualified to pursue after college graduation. To locate the professional Web site of the field that you might want to explore as a possible major, ask a faculty member in that field or complete a search on the Web by simply entering the name of the field followed by the word *association*.
10. **Be sure you know what academic standards must be met for you to be accepted for entry into a major.** Because of their popularity, certain college majors may be impacted or oversubscribed, which means that more students are interested in majoring in these fields than there are openings for them. Preprofessional majors that lead directly to a particular career are often the ones that become oversubscribed (e.g., accounting, education, engineering, premed, nursing, or physical therapy). On some campuses, these majors are called restricted majors, meaning that departments control their enrollment by limiting the number of students they let into the major. For example, departments may restrict entry to their major by admitting only students who have achieved an overall GPA of 3.0 or higher in certain introductory courses required by the majors, or they may

take all students who apply for the major, rank them by their GPA, and then count down until they have filled their maximum number of available spaces (Strommer, 1993).

Be sure you know whether the major you're considering is impacted or oversubscribed and whether it requires you to meet certain academic standards before you can be admitted. As you complete courses and receive grades, check to see whether you are meeting these standards. If you find yourself failing to meet these standards, you may need to increase the amount of time and effort you devote to your studies and seek assistance from your campus Learning Center. If you're working at your maximum level of effort and are regularly using the learning assistance services available on your campus but are still not meeting the academic standards of your intended major, consult with an academic advisor to help you identify an alternative field that may be closely related to the restricted major you were hoping to enter.

Think About It — Journal Entry 2.7

Do you think that the major you're considering is likely to be oversubscribed (i.e., there are more students wanting to major in the field than there are openings in the courses)? Explain.

____

____

____

____

____

____

11. **Consider the possibility of a college minor in a field that complements your major.** A college minor usually requires about one-half the number of credits (units) required for a major. Most campuses allow you the option of completing a minor with your major. Check with your academic advisor or the course catalog of the school you're considering transferring to; if the school offers a minor that interests you, find out what courses are required to complete it.

    If you have strong interests in two different fields, a minor will allow you to major in one of these fields while minoring in the other. Thus, you can pursue two fields that interest you without having to sacrifice one for the other. Furthermore, a minor can be completed at the same time as most college majors without delaying your time to graduation. (In contrast, a double major will typically lengthen your time to graduation because you must complete the separate requirements of two different majors.) You can also pursue a second field of study alongside your major without increasing your time to graduation by completing a cognate area—a specialization that requires fewer courses to complete than a minor (e.g., four to five courses instead of seven to eight courses). A concentration area may have even fewer requirements (only two to three courses).

Taking a cluster of courses in a field outside your major can be an effective way to strengthen your resume and increase your employment prospects because it demonstrates your versatility and allows you to gain experience in areas that may be missing or underemphasized in your major. For example, students majoring in the fine arts (e.g., music or theater) or humanities (e.g., English or history) may take courses in the fields of mathematics (e.g., statistics), technology (e.g., computer science), and business (e.g., economics)—none of which are emphasized by their majors.

12. **Join a professional organization as a student.** Many professional organizations offer discounted rates for students. These organizations offer opportunities for networking with those already in the profession as well as educational experiences through local, regional, and national conferences.

Think About It — Journal Entry 2.8

Before you start to dig into this chapter, take a moment to answer the following questions:

1. Have you decided on a career, or are you leaning strongly toward one?

____

2. If yes, why have you chosen this career? (Was your decision influenced by anybody or anything?)

____

____

____

3. If no, are there any careers you're considering as possibilities? What are they?

____

____

____

The Importance of Career Planning

College graduates in the 21st century are likely to continue working until age 75 (Herman, 2000). Once you enter the workforce full time, you'll spend most of the remaining waking hours of your life working. The only other single activity that you'll spend more time doing in your lifetime is sleeping. When you consider that such a sizable portion of your life is spent working and that your career can strongly influence your sense of personal identity and self-esteem, it becomes apparent that career choice is a critical process that should begin early in your college experience.

Remember

When you're doing career *planning, you're also doing* life *planning because you are planning how you will spend most of the waking hours of your future.*

Even if you've decided on a career that you were dreaming about since you were a preschooler, the process of career exploration and planning is not complete because you still need to decide on what specialization within that career you'll pursue. For example, if you're interested in pursuing a career in law, you'll need to eventually decide what branch of law you wish to practice (e.g., criminal law, corporate law, or family law). You'll also need to decide what employment sector or type of industry you would like to work in, such as nonprofit, for-profit, education, or government. Thus, no matter how certain or uncertain you are about your career path, you'll need to begin exploring career options and start taking your first steps toward formulating a career development plan.

Strategies for Career Exploration and Development

Reaching an effective decision about a career involves four steps:

1. **Awareness of yourself.** Your personal abilities, interests, needs, and values.

↓

2. **Awareness of your options.** The variety of career fields available to you.

↓

3. **Awareness of what best "fits" you.** The careers that best match your personal abilities, interests, needs, and values.

↓

4. **Awareness of the process.** How to prepare for and gain entry into the career of your choice.

Step 1. Self-Awareness

The more you know about yourself, the better your choices and decisions will be. Self-awareness is a particularly important step to take when making career decisions because the career you choose says a lot about who you are and what you want from life. Your personal identity and life goals should not be based on or built around your career choice: it should be the other way around.

Remember

Your personal attributes and goals should be considered first because they provide the foundation on which you build your career choice and future life.

One way to gain greater self-awareness of your career interests is by taking psychological tests or assessments. These assessments allow you to see how your interests in certain career fields compare with those of other students and professionals who've experienced career satisfaction and success. These comparative perspectives can give you important reference points for assessing whether your level of interest in a career is high, average, or low relative to other students and working professionals. Your Career Development Center or Counseling Center is the place on campus where you can find these career-interest tests, as well as other instruments that allow you to assess your career-related abilities and values.

When making choices about a career, you may have to consider one other important aspect of yourself: your personal needs. A "need" may be described as something stronger than an interest. When you satisfy a personal need, you are doing something that makes your life more satisfying or fulfilling. Psychologists have identified several important human needs that vary in strength or intensity from person to person. Listed in Do It Now! 2.1 are personal needs that are especially important to consider when making a career choice.

2.1 DO IT NOW

Personal Needs to Consider When Making Career Choices

As you read the needs listed here, make a note after each one indicating how strong the need is for you (high, moderate, or low).

1. **Autonomy.** The need to work independently without close supervision or control. Individuals high in this need may experience greater satisfaction working in careers that allow them to be their own bosses, make their own decisions, and control their own work schedules. Individuals low in this need may experience greater satisfaction working in careers that are more structured and involve working with a supervisor who provides direction, assistance, and frequent feedback.
2. **Affiliation.** The need for social interaction, a sense of belonging, and the opportunity to collaborate with others. Individuals high in this need may experience greater satisfaction working in careers that involve frequent interpersonal interaction and teamwork with colleagues or co-workers. Individuals low in this need may be more satisfied working alone or in competition with others.

Student Perspective

"To me, an important characteristic of a career is being able to meet new, smart, interesting people."

—First-year student

3. **Achievement.** The need to experience challenge and a sense of personal accomplishment. Individuals high in this need may be more satisfied working in careers that push them to solve problems, generate creative ideas, and continually learn new information or master new skills. Individuals low in this need may be more satisfied with careers that don't continually test their abilities and don't repeatedly challenge them to stretch their skills with new tasks and different responsibilities.

Student Perspective

"I want to be able to enjoy my job and be challenged by it at the same time. I hope that my job will not be monotonous and that I will have the opportunity to learn new things often."

—First-year student

4. **Recognition.** The need for high rank, status, and respect from others. Individuals high in this need may crave careers that are prestigious in the eyes of friends, family, or society. Individuals with a low need for recognition would feel comfortable working in a career that they find personally fulfilling, without being concerned about how impressive or enviable their career appears to others.
5. **Sensory stimulation.** The need to experience variety, change, and risk. Individuals high in this need may be more satisfied working in careers that involve frequent changes of pace and place (e.g., travel), unpredictable events (e.g., work tasks that vary considerably), and moderate stress (e.g., working under pressure of competition or deadlines). Individuals with a low need for sensory stimulation may feel more comfortable working in careers that involve regular routines, predictable situations, and minimal amounts of risk or stress.

Student Perspective

"For me, a good career is very unpredictable and interest-fulfilling. I would love to do something that allows me to be spontaneous."

—First-year student

"Don't expect a recluse to be motivated to sell, a creative thinker to be motivated to be a good proofreader day in and day out, or a sow's ear to be happy in the role of a silk purse."

—Pierce Howard, *The Owner's Manual for the Brain* (2000)

Think About It — *Journal Entry* 2.9

1. Which of the five needs in Do It Now! 2.1 did you indicate as being strong personal needs? Why?

____

____

____

____

2. What career or careers do you think would best match your strongest needs?

____

____

____

____

Author's Experience

While enrolled in my third year of college with half of my degree completed, I had an eye-opening experience. I wish this experience had happened in my first year, but better late than never. Although I had chosen a career during my first year of college, my decision-making process was not systematic and didn't involve critical thinking. I chose a major based on what sounded prestigious and would pay me the most money. Although these are not necessarily bad factors, my failure to use a systematic and reflective process to evaluate these factors was bad. In my junior year of college I asked one of my professors why he decided to get his Ph.D. and become a professor. He simply answered, "I wanted autonomy." This was an epiphany for me. He explained that when he looked at his life he determined that he needed a career that offered independence, so he began looking at career options that would offer that. After that explanation, *autonomy* became my favorite word, and this story became a guiding force in my life. After going through a critical self-awareness process, I determined that autonomy was exactly what I desired and a professor is what I became.

Aaron Thompson

Taken altogether, four aspects of yourself should be considered when exploring careers: your personal abilities, interests, values, and needs. As illustrated in Figure 2.3, these four pillars provide a solid foundation for effective career choices and decisions. You want to choose a career that you're good at, interested in, and passionate about and that fulfills your personal needs.

Lastly, since a career choice is a long-range decision that involves life beyond college, self-awareness should involve not only reflection on who you are now but also self-projection—reflecting on how you see yourself in the future. When you engage in the process of self-projection, you begin to see a connection between where you are now and where you want or hope to be.

Student *Perspective*

"I think that a good career has to be meaningful for a person. It should be enjoyable for the most part [and] it has to give a person a sense of fulfillment."

—First-year student

FIGURE 2.3

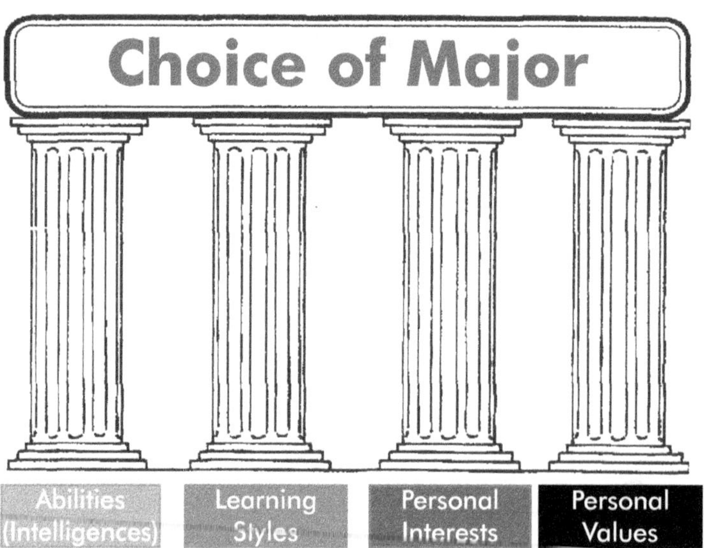

Personal Characteristics Providing the Foundation for Effective Career Choice

Think About It — *Journal Entry* 2.10

Project yourself 10 years into the future and visualize your ideal career and life.

1. What are you spending most of your time doing during your typical workday?

____

____

2. Where and with whom are you working?

____

3. How many hours are you working per week?

____

4. Where are you living?

____

5. Are you married? Do you have children?

____

6. How does your work influence your home life?

____

____

Ideally, your choice of a career should be one that leads to the best-case future scenario in which your typical day goes something like this: You wake up in the morning and hop out of bed enthusiastically, eagerly looking forward to what you'll be doing at work that day. When you're at work, time flies by, and before you know it, the day's over. When you return to bed that night and look back on your day, you feel good about what you did and how well you did it.

For this ideal scenario to have any chance of becoming a reality, or even coming close to reality, you have to select a career path that is true to yourself—a path that leads you to a career that closely matches your abilities (what you do well), your interests (what you like to do), your values (what you feel good about doing), and your needs (what brings you satisfaction and fulfillment in life).

Step 2. Awareness of Your Options

To make effective decisions about your career path, you need to have accurate knowledge about the nature of different careers and the realities of the work world. The Career Center is the first place to go for this information and help with career exploration and planning. In addition to helping you explore your personal career interests and abilities, the Career Center is your key campus resource for learning about the nature of different careers and for strategies on locating career-related work experiences.

If you were to ask people to name as many careers as they can, they wouldn't come close to naming the 900 career titles listed by the federal government in its Occupational Information Network. Many of these careers you may have never heard of, but some of them may represent good career options for you. You can learn about careers through nine major routes or avenues:

- Reading about them in books or online
- Becoming involved in cocurricular programs on campus related to career development
- Taking career development courses
- Interviewing people in different career fields
- Observing (shadowing) people at work in different careers
- Interning
- Participating in a co-op program
- Volunteering
- Working part-time

Author's Experience

When my sister was in the last year of her nursing degree, she decided she wanted to be a pediatric nurse and work at one of the top 10 pediatric hospitals in the country. At the time, I lived in a city with an excellent pediatric hospital. My sister decided to come visit me for an extended weekend and made appointments to shadow different units in that hospital on her visit. She fell in love with the place and decided she definitely wanted to work there! A few months later, when she was in her last semester of school, that hospital called her and asked if she wanted to come and interview for jobs on all four units. They'd been just as impressed with her when she shadowed as she was with them, and they made a note on her resume to call her when she was close to graduating. She interviewed and was offered all four jobs! It turned out her shadowing experience actually ended up being a "pre-interview," and she had a job before she even graduated!

Julie McLaughlin

Resources on Careers

Your Career Center and your College Library are campus resources where you can find a wealth of reading material on careers, either in print or online. Listed here are some of the most useful sources of written information on careers:

- ***Dictionary of Occupational Titles* (www.occupationalinfo.org).** This is the largest printed resource on careers; it contains concise definitions of over 17,000 jobs. It also includes information on:
  - work tasks that people in the career typically perform regularly;
  - types of knowledge, skills, and abilities that are required for different careers;
  - interests, values, and needs of individuals who find working in particular careers to be personally rewarding; and
  - background experiences of people working in different careers that qualified them for their positions.
- ***Occupational Outlook Handbook* (https://www.bls.gov/ooh/).** This is one of the most widely available and used resources on careers. It contains descriptions of approximately 250 positions, including information on the nature of work, work conditions, places of employment, training or education required for career entry and advancement, salaries, careers in related fields, and additional sources of information about particular careers (e.g., professional organizations and governmental agencies). A distinctive feature of this resource is that it contains information about the future employment outlook for different careers.
- ***Encyclopedia of Careers and Vocational Guidance* (Chicago: Ferguson Press).** As the name suggests, this is an encyclopedia of information on qualifications, salaries, and advancement opportunities for various careers.
- **Occupational Information Network (O*NET) Online (online.onetcenter.org).** This is America's most comprehensive source of online information about careers. It contains an up-to-date set of descriptions for almost 1,000 careers, plus lots of other information similar to what you would find in the *Dictionary of Occupational Titles.*

In addition to these general sources of information, your Career Center and College Library should have books and other published materials related to specific careers or occupations (e.g., careers for English majors).

You can also learn a lot about careers by simply reading advertisements for position openings in your local newspaper or online, such as at www.careerbuilder.com. When reading position descriptions, make special note of the tasks, duties, or responsibilities they involve and ask yourself whether these positions are compatible with your personal profile of abilities, interests, needs, and values.

Career Planning and Development Programs

Periodically during the academic year, cocurricular programs devoted to career exploration and career preparation are likely to be offered on your campus. For example, the Career Center may sponsor career exploration or career planning workshops that you can attend for free. Also, the Career Center may organize a career fair on campus, at which professionals working in different career fields are given booths on campus where you can visit with them and ask questions about their careers. Research indicates that career workshops offered on campus are effective in helping students plan for and decide on a career (Brown & Krane, 2000; Hildenbrand & Gore, 2005).

Career Development Courses

Many colleges offer career development courses for elective credit. These courses typically include self-assessment of your career interests, information about different careers, and strategies for career preparation. You should be doing career planning, so why not do it by taking a career development course that rewards you with college credit for doing it? Studies show that students who participate in career development courses experience significant benefits in terms of their career choice and career development (Pascarella & Terenzini, 2005).

Informational Interviews

One of the best and most overlooked ways to get accurate information about careers is to interview professionals who are working in career fields. Career development specialists refer to this strategy as informational interviewing. Don't assume that working professionals would not be interested in taking time out of their day to speak with a student. Most are willing to be interviewed about their careers; they often enjoy it (Crosby, 2002).

Informational interviews provide you inside information about what careers are like because you're getting that information directly from the horse's mouth. It also helps you gain experience and confidence in interview situations, which may help you prepare for future job interviews. Furthermore, if you make a good impression during informational interviews, the people you interview may suggest that you contact them again after graduation in case there are position openings. If there are openings, you might find yourself being the interviewee instead of the interviewer (and you might find yourself a job).

Think About It — Journal Entry 2.11

If you were to observe or interview a working professional in a career that interests you, what position would that person hold?

____

____

____

____

____

____

Career Observation (Shadowing)

In addition to learning about careers from reading and interviews, you can experience careers more directly by placing yourself in workplace situations or work environments that allow you to observe workers performing their daily duties. Two college-sponsored programs may be available on your campus that would allow you to observe working professionals:

- **Job Shadowing Programs.** These programs allow you to follow ("shadow") and observe a professional during a typical workday.
- **Career Center.** Learn about what job shadowing programs may be available on your college campus. If none are available in a career field that interests you, consider finding one on your own by using strategies similar to those we recommend for informational interviews at the end of this chapter. The only difference is that instead of asking the person for an interview, you'd be asking whether you could observe that person at work. The same person who gave you an informational interview might be willing to allow such observation. Keep in mind that one or two days of observation will give you some firsthand information about a career, but will not give you firsthand experience in that career.

Internships and Co-Ops

In contrast to job shadowing, where you observe someone at work, an internship program immerses you in the work itself and gives you the opportunity to perform career-related work duties. A distinguishing feature of internships is that you can receive academic credit and sometimes financial compensation for the work you do. An internship usually totals 120 to 150 work hours, which may be completed at the same time you're enrolled in a full schedule of classes or when you're not taking classes (e.g., during summer term).

An advantage of an internship is that it enables college students to avoid the classic catch-22 situation they often run into when interviewing for their first career positions after graduation. The interview scenario usually goes something like this: The potential employer asks the college graduate, "What work experience have you had in this field?" The recent graduate replies, "I haven't had any work experience because I've been a full-time college student." This scenario can be avoided if you complete an internship during your college experience, which allows you to say, "Yes, I do have work experience in this field." We encourage you to participate in an internship while in college because it will enable you to beat the "no experience" rap after graduation and distinguish yourself from many other college graduates. Research shows that students who have internships while in college are more likely to develop career-relevant work skills and find employment immediately after college graduation (Pascarella & Terenzini, 2005).

Internships are typically available to college students during their junior or senior year; however, there may be internships available to first- and second-year students on your campus. You can also pursue internships on your own. Published guides describe various career-related internships, along with information on how to apply for them (e.g., *Peterson's Internships* and the *Vault Guide to Top Internships*). You could also search for internships on the Web (e.g., www.internships.com). Another good resource for possible information on internships is the local chamber of commerce in the town or city where your college is located or in your hometown.

Another option for gaining firsthand work experience is enrolling in courses that allow you to engage in hands-on learning related to your career interest. For instance, if you're interested in working with children, courses in child psychology or early childhood education may offer experiential learning opportunities in a preschool or daycare center on campus.

A co-op is similar to an internship, but involves work experience that lasts longer than one academic term and often requires students to stop their coursework temporarily to participate in the program. However, some co-op programs allow you to continue to take classes while working part time at a co-op position; these are sometimes referred to as parallel co-ops. Students are paid for participating in co-op programs (Smith, 2005).

The value of co-ops and internships is strongly supported by research, which indicates that students who have these experiences during college:

- Are more likely to report that their college education was relevant to their career;
- Receive higher evaluations from employers who recruit them on campus;
- Have less difficulty finding initial positions after graduation;
- Are more satisfied with their first career positions after college;
- Obtain more prestigious positions after graduation; and
- Report greater job satisfaction (Gardner, 1991; Knouse, Tanner, & Harris, 1999; Pascarella & Terenzini, 1991, 2005).*

When employers are asked to rank various factors they consider important when hiring new college graduates, internships or cooperative education programs receive the highest ranking (National Association of Colleges & Employers, 2012, 2014). Employers also report that when full-time positions open up in their organization or company, they usually turn first to their own interns and co-op students (National Association of Colleges & Employers, 2013).

Volunteer Service

*Engaging in volunteerism not only helps your community, but also helps you by giving you the opportunity to explore different work environments and gain work experience in career fields that relate to your area of service. For example, volunteer service to different age groups (e.g., children, adolescents, or the elderly) and service in different environments (e.g., hospital, school, or laboratory) can provide you with firsthand work experience and simultaneously give you a chance to test your interest in possibly pursuing future careers related to these different age groups and work environments.

Author's Experience

As an academic advisor, I was once working with two first-year students, Kim and Christopher. Kim was thinking about becoming a physical therapist, and Chris was thinking about becoming an elementary school teacher. I suggested to Kim that she visit the hospital near our college to see whether she could do volunteer work in the physical therapy unit. The hospital did need volunteers, so she volunteered in the physical therapy unit and loved it. That volunteer experience confirmed for her that physical therapy was what she should pursue as a career. She completed a degree in physical therapy and is now a professional physical therapist.

I suggested to Chris, the student who was thinking about becoming an elementary school teacher, that he visit some local schools to see whether they could use a volunteer teacher's aide. One of the schools did need his services, and Chris volunteered as a teacher's aide for about 10 weeks. At the halfway point during his volunteer experience, he came into my office to tell me that the kids were just about driving him crazy and that he no longer had any interest in becoming a teacher. He ended up majoring in communications.

Kim and Chris were the first two students I advised to get involved in volunteer work to test their career interests. Their volunteer experiences proved so valuable for helping both of them make a career decision that I now encourage all students I advise to get volunteer experience in the fields they're considering for future careers.

Joe Cuseo

Volunteer service also enables you to network with professionals outside of college who may serve as excellent references and resources for letters of recommendation for you. Furthermore, if these professionals are impressed with your volunteer work, they may become interested in hiring you part-time while you're still in college or full time when you graduate.

It may be possible to do volunteer work on campus by serving as an informal teaching assistant or research assistant to a faculty member. Such experiences are particularly valuable for students intending to go to graduate school. If you have a good relationship with any faculty members who are working in an academic field that interests you, consider asking them whether they would like some assistance (e.g., with their teaching or research responsibilities). Your volunteer work for a college professor could lead to making a presentation with your professor at a professional conference or even result in your name being included as a coauthor on an article published by the professor.

Think About It — Journal Entry 2.12

Have you done volunteer work? If you have, did you learn anything from your volunteer experiences that might help you decide which types of work best match your interests or talents?

Jobs that you hold during the academic year or during summer break should not be overlooked as potential sources of career information and as resume-building experience. Part-time work can provide opportunities to learn or develop skills that may be relevant to your future career, such as organizational skills, communication skills, and the ability to work effectively with co-workers from diverse backgrounds or cultures.

Also, work in a part-time position may eventually turn into a full-time career. The following personal story illustrates how this can happen.

Author's Experience

One student of mine, an English major, worked part-time for an organization that provides special assistance to mentally handicapped children. After he completed his English degree, he was offered a full-time position in this organization, which he accepted. While working at his full-time position with handicapped children, he decided to go to graduate school part time and eventually completed a master's degree in special education, which qualified him for a promotion to a more advanced position in the organization, which he also accepted.

Joe Cuseo

It might also be possible for you to obtain part-time work experience on campus through your school's work-study program. A work-study job allows you to work at your college in various work settings, such as the Financial Aid Office, College Library, Public Relations Office, or Computer Services Center, and often allows you to build your employment schedule around your academic schedule. On-campus work can provide you with valuable career-exploration and resume-building experiences, and the professionals for whom you work can serve as excellent references for letters of recommendation to future employers. To see whether you are eligible for your school's work-study program, visit the Financial Aid Office on your campus.

Learning about careers through firsthand experience in actual work settings (e.g., shadowing, internships, volunteer services, and part-time work) is critical to successful career exploration and preparation. You can take a career-interest test, or you can test your career interest through actual work experiences. There is simply no substitute for direct, hands-on experience for gaining knowledge about careers. These firsthand experiences represent the ultimate career-reality test. They allow you direct access to information about what careers are really like, as opposed to how they are portrayed on TV or in the movies, which often paint an inaccurate or unrealistic picture of careers, making them appear more exciting or glamorous than they are.

In summary, firsthand experiences in actual work settings equip you with five powerful career advantages:

- Learn about what work is like in a particular field;
- Test your interest and skills for certain types of work;
- Strengthen your resume by adding experiential learning to academic (classroom) learning;
- Acquire contacts for letters of recommendation; and
- Network with employers who may refer or hire you for a position after graduation.

Be sure to use your campus resources (e.g., the Career Center, Counseling Center, and Financial Aid Office), your local resources (e.g., chamber of commerce), and your personal contacts (family and friends) to locate and participate in work experiences that relate to your career interests. When you land an internship, work hard at it, learn as much as you can from it, and build relationships with as many people as possible at your internship site, because these are the people who can provide you with future contacts, references, and referrals.

"Give me a history major who has done internships and a business major who hasn't, and I'll hire the history major every time."

—William Ardery, senior vice president, investor communications company (quoted in *The New York Times*)

Think About It — Journal Entry 2.13

1. Have you learned anything from your firsthand work experiences that may influence your future career plans?

____

____

____

____

2. If you could get firsthand work experience in any career field right now, what career would it be? Why?

____

____

____

____

Step 3. Awareness of What Best Fits You

When considering career options, don't buy into either of the following common myths about careers, which can lead students to poor career decisions.

Myth 1. Once you've decided on a career, you have decided on what you'll be doing for the rest of your life. This is simply and totally false. The term *career* derives from the same root word as *racecourse*. Like a racecourse, a career involves movement that typically takes different turns and twists, and as in any race, it's not how fast you start but how strong you finish that matters most. This ability to move and change direction is what distinguishes a professional career from a dead-end job. Americans average four careers in a lifetime; it's also estimated that today's college graduates will change jobs 12 to 15 times, which will span three to five career fields (U.S. Bureau of Labor Statistics, 2005). These statistics may be surprising because you're probably going to college with the idea that you're preparing for a particular career. However, these results become less surprising when you consider that the general education component of your college experience provides you with versatile, transferable skills that can qualify you for different positions in various career fields.

Myth 2. You need to pick a career that's in demand and that will get you a job with a good starting salary right after graduation. Looking only at careers that are "hot" now and have high starting salaries can distract you from looking at yourself and cause you to overlook a more important question: are these careers truly compatible with your personal abilities, interests, needs, and values? Starting salaries and available job openings are external factors that can be easily seen and counted; thus, they may get more attention and receive more weight in the decision-making process than qualities that are harder to see and put a number on, such as inner characteristics. In the case of career decision making, this can result in college students choosing careers based exclusively on external factors (salaries and openings) without giving equal (or any) attention to such internal factors as personal abilities, interests, and values. This can lead some college graduates to enter careers that eventually leave them bored, frustrated, or dissatisfied.

The number of job offers you receive immediately after graduation and the number of dollars you earn as a starting salary in your first position are short-term (and shortsighted) standards for judging whether you've made a good career choice. Remember that there's a critical difference between career *entry* and career *advancement.* Some college graduates may not bolt out of the starting gate and begin their career paths with well-paying first positions, but they will steadily work their way up the career ladder and be promoted to more advanced positions than graduates who start out with higher salaries.

Student Perspective

"I would rather make little money doing something I love than be rich doing something that makes me miserable."

—First-year student

Criteria (Standards) to Consider When Evaluating Career Options

Effective decision making requires you to identify all important factors that should be considered when evaluating your options and determine how much weight (influence) each of these factors should carry. As we emphasize throughout this chapter, the factor that should carry the greatest weight in career decision making is the match between your choice and your personal abilities, interests, needs, and values.

Suppose you discover more than one career option that's compatible with these four dimensions of yourself. What other aspects of a career should be considered to help you reach a decision and make a selection? Many people would probably say salary, but as the length of the following list suggests, other important aspects or characteristics of careers should be factored into your decision-making process.

Student Perspective

"A big paycheck is a plus but it is not necessary. I would rather be inspired."

—First-year student

- **Work conditions.** Work conditions include such considerations as:
  - the nature of the work environment (e.g., physical and social environment);
  - the geographical location of the work (e.g., urban, suburban, or rural);
  - the work schedule (e.g., number of hours per week and flexibility of hours); and
  - work-related travel (e.g., opportunities to travel, frequency of travel, and locations traveled to).
- **Career entry.** Can you enter into the career without much difficulty, or does the supply of people pursuing the career far exceed the demand (e.g., professional acting or athletes)? If a career is highly competitive and difficult to gain entry into, it doesn't mean you should automatically give up on it; however, it does mean you should have an alternative career to fall back on until you can (or in case you can't) catch a break that will allow you to break into your ideal career.
- **Career advancement (promotion).** An ideal first job educates and prepares you to advance to an even better one. Will the career you're considering provide you with opportunities for promotion to more advanced positions?
- **Career mobility.** Is it easy to move out of the career and into a different career path? This may be an important factor to consider because careers may rise or fall in demand; furthermore, your career interests or values may change as you gain more work and life experience.
- **Financial benefits.** Financial considerations include salary—both starting salary and expected salary increases with greater work experience or advancement to higher positions. However, they also include fringe benefits, such as health insurance, paid vacation time, paid sick-leave time, paid maternity- or paternity-leave time, paid tuition for seeking advanced education, and retirement benefits.

"The French work to live, but the Swiss live to work."
—French proverb

- **Impact of the career on your personal life.** How would the career affect your family life, your physical and mental health, and your self-concept or self-esteem? Remember that your life should not be built around your career: your career should be built around your life. Your means of making a living and other important aspects of yourself need to be considered simultaneously when making career choices, because the nature of your work will affect the nature (and quality) of your life.

"Money is a good servant but a bad master."
—French proverb

Remember

A good career decision should involve more than salary and should take into consideration how the career will affect all dimensions of your self (social, emotional, physical, etc.) throughout all stages of your adult life: young adulthood, middle age, and late adulthood. It's almost inevitable that your career will affect your identity, the type of person you become, how you will balance the demands of work and family, and how well you will serve others beyond yourself. An effective career decision-making process requires you to make tough and thoughtful decisions about what matters most to you.

Think About It — Journal Entry 2.14

Answer the following questions about a career that you're considering or have chosen:

1. What is the career?

____

2. Why are you considering this career? (What led or caused you to become interested in it?)

____

____

3. Would you say that your interest in this career is motivated primarily by intrinsic factors—that is, factors "inside" of you, such as your personal abilities, interests, needs, and values? Or, would you say that your interest in the career is influenced more heavily by extrinsic factors—that is, factors "outside" of you, such as starting salary, pleasing parents, meeting family expectations, or meeting an expected role for your gender (male role or female role)? Why?

____

____

____

4. If money was not an issue and you could earn a comfortable living in any career, would you choose the same career? Why or why not? What career would you choose?

____

____

____

____

Step 4. Awareness of the Process

Whether you're keeping your career options open or you've already decided on a particular career, you can start preparing for career success by using the following strategies.

Self-Monitoring: Watching and Tracking Your Personal Skills and Positive Qualities

Don't forget that *learning* skills are also *earning* skills. The skills you're acquiring in college may appear to be just *academic* skills, but they're also *career* skills. For instance, when you're in the process of completing academic tasks such as taking tests and writing papers, you're using various career-relevant skills (e.g., analyzing, organizing, communicating, and problem solving).

Many students think that a college degree or certificate is an automatic passport to a good job and career success (Ellin, 1993; Sullivan, 1993). However, for most employers of college graduates, what matters most is not only the credential but also the skills and personal strengths an applicant brings to the position (Figler & Boles, 2007). You can start building these skills and strengths by self-monitoring (i.e., watching yourself and keeping track of the skills you're using and developing during your college experience). Skills are mental habits, and like all other habits that are repeatedly practiced, their development can be so gradual that you may not even notice how much growth is taking place—perhaps somewhat like watching grass grow. Thus, career development specialists recommend that you consciously track your skills to remain aware of them and to put you in a position to "sell" them to potential employers (Lock, 2004).

One strategy you can use to track your developing skills is to keep a career-development journal in which you note academic tasks and assignments you've completed, along with the skills you used to complete them. Be sure to record skills in your journal that you've developed in nonacademic situations, such as those skills used while performing part-time jobs, personal hobbies, cocurricular activities, or volunteer services. Since skills are actions, it's best to record them as action verbs in your career-development journal.

The key to discovering career-relevant skills and qualities is to get in the habit of stepping back from your academic and out-of-class experiences to reflect on what skills and qualities these experiences entailed and then get them down in writing before they slip your mind. You're likely to find that many personal skills you develop in college will be the same ones that employers will seek in the workforce.

Author's Experience

After class one day, I had a conversation with a student (Max) about his personal interests. He said he was considering a career in the music industry and was now working part-time as a disc jockey at a nightclub. I asked him what it took to be a good disc jockey, and in less than five minutes of conversation, we discovered many more skills were involved in doing his job than either of us had realized. He was responsible for organizing three to four hours of music each night he worked; he had to read the reactions of his audience (customers) and adapt or adjust his selections to their musical tastes; he had to arrange his selections in a sequence that periodically varied the tempo (speed) of the music he played throughout the night; and he had to continually research and update his music collection to track the latest trends in hits and popular artists. Max also said that he had to overcome his fear of public speaking to deliver announcements that were a required part of his job.

Although we were just having a short, friendly conversation after class about his part-time job, Max wound up reflecting on and identifying multiple skills he was using on the job. We both agreed that it would be a good idea to get these skills down in writing so that he could use them as selling points for future jobs in the music industry or in any industry.

Joe Cuseo

2.2 DO IT NOW

Personal Skills Relevant to Successful Career Performance

The following behaviors represent a sample of useful skills that are relevant to success in various careers (Bolles, 1998). As you read these skills, underline or highlight any of them that you have performed, either inside or outside of school.

advising	assembling	calculating	coaching	coordinating
creating	delegating	designing	evaluating	explaining
initiating	mediating	measuring	motivating	negotiating
operating	planning	producing	proving	researching
resolving	sorting	summarizing	supervising	synthesizing
translating				

In addition to tracking your developing skills, track your positive traits or personal qualities. While it's best to record your skills as action verbs because they represent actions that you can perform for anyone who hires you, it may be best to track your attributes as adjectives because they describe who you are and what personal qualities you can bring to the job. Do It Now! 2.3 gives a sample of personal traits and qualities that are relevant to success in multiple careers. As you read these traits, underline or highlight any of them that you feel you possess or will soon possess.*

2.3 DO IT NOW

**Personal Traits and Qualities Relevant to Successful Career Performance

collaborative	conscientious	considerate	curious	dependable
determined	energetic	enthusiastic	ethical	flexible
imaginative	industrious	loyal	observant	open-minded
outgoing	patient	persuasive	positive	precise
prepared	productive	prudent	punctual	reflective
sincere	tactful	team player	thorough	thoughtful

Remember

*Keeping track of your developing skills and your positive qualities is as important to your successful entry into a future career as completing courses and compiling credits.***

Self-Marketing: Packaging and Presenting Your Personal Strengths and Achievements

*To convert your college experience into immediate employment, it might be useful to view yourself (a college graduate) as a product and employers as intentional customers who may be interested in making a purchase (of your skills and attributes). As a first-year student, it could be said that you're in the early stages of the product-development process. Now is the time to begin the process so that by the time you graduate, your finished product (you) will be one that employers notice and become interested in purchasing.

An effective self-marketing plan is one that gives employers a clear idea of what you can bring to the table and do for them. This should increase the number of job offers you receive and increase your chances of finding a position that best matches your interests, talents, and values.

You can effectively advertise or market your personal skills, qualities, and achievements to future employers through the following channels:

- College transcript
- Cocurricular experiences
- Personal portfolio
- Personal resume
- Letters of application (a.k.a. cover letters)
- Letters of recommendation (a.k.a. letters of reference)
- Networking
- Personal interview

These are the primary tools you will use to showcase yourself to employers and employers will use to evaluate you. Here's how you can strategically prepare for and sharpen these tools to maximize their effectiveness.

College Transcript

A college transcript is a listing of all courses you enrolled in and the grades you earned in those courses. Two pieces of information included on your college transcript can influence employers' hiring decisions or admissions committee decisions about your acceptance to a four-year college, graduate, or professional school: (1) the grades you earned in your courses, and (2) the types of courses you completed.

Simply stated, the better your grades in college, the better your employment prospects after college. Research on college graduates indicates that the higher their grades, the higher:

- The prestige of their first job;
- Their total earnings; and
- Their job mobility.

This relationship between college grades and career success exists for students at all types of colleges and universities, regardless of the reputation or prestige of the institution they attend (Pascarella & Terenzini, 1991, 2005).

The particular types of courses listed on your college transcript can also influence employment and acceptance decisions. Listed here are the types of courses that should strengthen your college transcript.

- **Honors courses.** If you achieve excellent grades during your first year, you may apply or be recommended for the honors program at your campus and take more academically challenging courses. If you qualify for the honors program, we recommend that you accept the challenge. Even though A grades may be more difficult to achieve in honors courses, the presence of these courses on your college transcript clearly shows that you were admitted to the honors program and were willing to accept this academic challenge.
- **Leadership courses.** Many employers hire college graduates with the hope or expectation that they will advance and eventually assume important leadership positions in the company or organization. Although a leadership course is not likely to be required for general education, or for your major, it is an elective course that will develop your leadership skills and the impressiveness of your college transcript.
- **International and cross-cultural courses.** Courses whose content crosses national and cultural boundaries are often referred to as international and cross-cultural courses. These courses are particularly pertinent to success in today's world, in which there is more international travel, more interaction among citizens from different countries, and more economic interdependence among nations than at any other time in world history (Office of Research, 1994). As a result of these developments, employers now place higher value on employees with international knowledge and foreign language skills (Fixman, 1990; Office of Research, 1994). Taking courses that have an international focus, or that focus on cross-cultural comparisons, helps you develop a global perspective that can improve the quality of your college degree and increase the attractiveness of your college transcript to potential employers.
- **Diversity (multicultural) courses.** America's workforce is more ethnically and racially diverse today than at any other time in the nation's history, and it will grow even more so in the years ahead (U.S. Bureau of Labor Statistics, 2005). Successful career performance in today's diverse workforce requires sensitivity to human differences and the ability to relate to people from different cultural backgrounds (National Association of Colleges & Employers, 2003; Smith, 1997). College courses relating to diversity awareness and appreciation, or courses emphasizing multicultural interaction and communication, can be valuable additions to your college transcript that should strengthen your career preparation, placement, and advancement.*

Co-Curricular Experiences

Participation in student clubs, campus organizations, and other types of co-curricular activities can be a valuable source of experiential learning that can complement classroom-based learning and contribute to your career preparation and development. A sizable body of research supports the value of co-curricular experiences for career success (Astin, 1993; Hart Research Associates, 2006, 2014; Kuh, 1993; Pascarella & Terenzini, 1991, 2005). Strongly consider getting involved in co-curricular life on your campus, especially involvement with co-curricular experiences that:

- *Allow you to develop leadership and helping skills (e.g., leadership retreats, student government, college committees, peer counseling, or peer tutoring);
- Enable you to interact with others from diverse ethnic and racial groups (e.g., multicultural club or international club), and
- Provide you with out-of-class experiences related to your academic major or career interests (e.g., student clubs in your college major or intended career field).

Keep in mind that co-curricular experiences are also resume-building experiences that provide solid evidence of your commitment to the college community outside the classroom. Be sure to showcase these experiences to prospective employers.

Also, the campus professionals with whom you may interact while participating in co-curricular activities (e.g., the director of student activities or dean of students) can serve as valuable references for letters of recommendation to future employers or graduate and professional schools.

Personal Portfolio

You may have heard the word *portfolio* used to mean a collection of artwork that professional artists put together to showcase or advertise their artistic talents. However, a portfolio can be a collection of any materials or products that illustrates an individual's skills and talents or demonstrates an individual's educational and personal development. For example, a portfolio could include such items as:

- Outstanding papers, exam performances, research projects, or lab reports;
- Artwork, photos from study abroad, service learning, or internships experiences;
- Video footage of oral presentations or theatrical performances;
- CDs of musical performances;
- Assessments from employers or coaches; and
- Letters of recognition or commendation.

You can start the process of portfolio development right now by saving your best work and performances. Store them in a traditional portfolio folder, or save them on a computer disc to create an electronic portfolio. Another option would be to create a Web site and upload your materials there. Eventually, you should be able to build a well-stocked portfolio that documents your skills and demonstrates your development to future employers or future schools.

Letters of Application (a.k.a. Cover Letters)

You write a letter of application when applying for a position opening or for acceptance to a school. When writing these letters, be sure that you demonstrate awareness and knowledge of:

- Yourself (e.g., your personal interests, abilities, and values);
- The organization or institution to which you are applying (e.g., showing that you know something specific about its purpose, philosophy, programs, and the position you are applying for); and
- The match or fit between you and the organization (e.g., between the skills and qualities you possess and those that the position requires).

Focusing on these three major points should make your letter complete and will allow the letter to flow sequentially from a focus on *you,* to a focus on *them,* to a focus on the *relationship* between you and them. Here are some suggestions for developing each of these three points in your letter of application.

- **Organize information about yourself into a past-present-future sequence of personal development.** For instance, point out the following:
    - Where you have been—your past history or background experiences that qualify you to apply for the position (academic, co-curricular, and work experiences).
    - Where you are now—why you've decided to apply for the position today.
    - Where you intend to go—what you hope to do or accomplish for the employer once you get there.

Taking this past-present-future approach to organizing your letter should result in a smooth, well-sequenced flow of information about you and your development. Also, by focusing on where you've been and where you're going, you demonstrate your ability to reflect on the past and project to the future.

When describing yourself, try to identify specific examples or concrete illustrations of your positive qualities and areas in which you have grown or improved in recent years. While it is important to highlight all your major strengths, this doesn't necessarily mean you should ignore or cover up areas in which you feel you still need to improve or develop. No human is perfect; one indication of someone with a healthy self-concept is that person's ability to recognize and acknowledge both personal strengths and areas in which further improvement or development is needed. Including a touch of honest self-assessment in your letter of application demonstrates both sincerity and integrity. It should also reduce the risk that your letter will be perceived as a "snow job" that pours on mounds and pounds of self-flattery without an ounce of personal humility.

- **Do some advance research about the particular organization to which you're applying.** In your letter of application, mention some aspects or characteristics of the organization that you've learned about, such as one of its programs that impressed you or attracted your interest. This sends the message that you have taken the time and initiative to learn something about the organization, which says something positive about you.
- **Make it clear why you feel there is a good fit or match between you and the organization to which you've applied.** When applying for a position, your first objective is to focus on what you can do for the organization rather than what it can do for you or what's in it for you. Point out how your qualities, skills, interests, or values are in line with the organization's needs or goals. By doing some research on the particular institution or organization that you're applying to, and by including this information in your letter of application, you also distinguish your application from the swarms of standard "form letters" that companies receive from other applicants.

Letters of Recommendation (a.k.a. Letters of Reference)

Personal letters of recommendation can be a powerful way to document your strengths and selling points. To maximize the power of your personal recommendations, give careful thought to:

- Who should serve as your references;
- How to approach them; and
- What to provide them.

Strategies for improving the quality of your letters of recommendation are suggested in Do It Now! 2.4.

2.4 DO IT NOW

The Art and Science of Requesting Letters of Recommendation: Effective Strategies and Common Courtesies

1. **Select recommendations from people who know you well.** Think about individuals with whom you've had an ongoing relationship, who know your name, and who know your strengths: for example, an instructor who you've had for more than one class, an academic advisor whom you see often, or an employer whom you've worked for over an extended period.
2. **Seek a balanced blend of letters from people who have observed you perform in different settings or situations.** The following are settings in which you may have performed well and people who may have observed your performance in these settings:
   - The classroom—a professor who can speak to your academic performance.
   - On campus—a student life professional who can comment on your contributions outside the classroom.
   - Off campus—a professional for whom you've performed volunteer service, part-time work, or an internship.
3. **Pick the right time and place to make your request.** Be sure to make your request well in advance of the letter's deadline date (e.g., at least two weeks). First ask whether the person is willing to write the letter, and then come back with forms and envelopes. Do not approach the person with these materials in hand, because this may send the message that you have assumed or presumed the person will automatically say "yes." (This is not the most socially sensitive message to send someone whom you're about to ask for a favor). Lastly, pick a place where the person can give full attention to your request. For instance, make a personal visit to the person's office, rather than making the request in a busy hallway or in front of a classroom full of students.
4. **Waive your right to see the letter.** If the school or organization to which you're applying has a reference-letter form that asks whether or not you want to waive (give up) your right to see the letter, waive your right—as long as you feel reasonably certain that you will be receiving a good letter of recommendation. By waiving your right to see your letter of recommendation, you show confidence that the letter to be written about you will be positive, and you assure the person who reads the letter that you didn't inspect or screen it to make sure it was a good one before sending it.
5. **Provide your references with a fact sheet about yourself.** Include your experiences and achievements—both inside and outside the classroom. This will help make your references' job a little easier by providing points to focus on. More importantly, it will help you because your letter becomes more powerful when it contains concrete examples or illustrations of your positive qualities and accomplishments. On your fact sheet, be sure to include any exceptionally high grades you may have earned in certain courses, as well as volunteer services, leadership experiences, special awards or forms of recognition, and special interests or talents that relate to your academic major and career choice. Your fact sheet is the place and time for you to "toot your own horn," so don't be afraid of coming across as a braggart or egotist. You're not being conceited—you're just showcasing your strengths.
6. **Provide your references with a stamped, addressed envelope.** This is a simple courtesy that makes their job a little easier and demonstrates your social sensitivity.
7. **Follow up with a thank-you note.** Thank your references at about the time when your letter of recommendation should be sent.

   This is the right thing to do because it shows your appreciation; it's also the smart thing to do because if the letter hasn't been written yet, the thank-you note serves as a gentle reminder for your reference to write the letter.
8. **Let your references know the outcome of your application** (e.g., your admission to a school or acceptance of a job offer). This is the courteous thing to do, and your references are likely to remember your courtesy, which could strengthen the quality of any future letters they may write for you.

Think About It — *Journal Entry* 2.15

1. Have you met a faculty member or other professional on campus who knows you well enough to write a personal letter of recommendation for you?

2. If yes, who is this person, and what position does he or she hold on campus?

Networking

Would it surprise you to learn that 80 percent of jobs are never advertised? Almost one-half of all job hunters find employment through people they know or have met, such as friends, family members, and casual acquaintances. When it comes to locating positions, *whom* you know can be as important as *what* you know or how good your resume looks. Consequently, it's important to continually expand the circle of people who are aware of your career interests and abilities, because they can be a valuable source of information about employment opportunities.

Also, be sure to share copies of your resume with friends and family members, just in case they come in contact with employers who are looking for somebody with your career interests and qualifications.

Personal Interview

A personal interview is your opportunity to make a positive in-person impression. You can make a strong first impression during any interview by showing that you've done your homework and have come prepared. In particular, you should come to the interview with knowledge about yourself and your audience.

You can demonstrate knowledge about yourself by bringing a mental list of your strongest selling points to the interview and being ready to speak about them when the opportunity arises. You can demonstrate knowledge of your audience by doing some homework on the organization you are applying to, the people who are likely to be interviewing you, and the questions they are likely to ask you. Try to acquire as much information about the organization and its key employees as is available to you online and in print. When you know your audience (who your interviewers are likely to be and what they're likely to ask), and when you know yourself well (what about yourself you're going to say), you should then be ready to answer what probably is the most important interview question of all: "What can *you* do for *us?*"

To prepare for interviews, visit your Career Development Center and inquire about questions that are commonly asked during personal interviews. You might also try to speak with seniors who have interviewed with recruiters and ask them whether certain questions tended to be frequently asked. Once you begin to participate in actual interviews, make note of the questions you are asked. Although you may be able to anticipate some of the more general questions that are asked in almost any interview, there likely will be unique questions asked of you that relate specifically to your personal qualifications and experiences. If these questions are asked in one of your interviews, there's a good chance they'll be asked in a future interview. As soon as you complete an interview, mentally review it and attempt to recall the major questions you were asked before they slip your mind. Consider developing an index-card catalog of questions that you've been asked during interviews, with the question on one side and your prepared response on the reverse side. By being better prepared for personal interviews, you'll increase the quality of your answers and decrease your level of anxiety. You should also have a list of questions to ask at the interview. This shows that you are interested and did your homework. Finally, remember to dress appropriately for an interview. If you are unsure how to dress, consult a professional you trust on campus.

Lastly, remember to send a thank-you note to the person who interviewed you. This is not only the courteous thing to do, but also the smart thing to do because it demonstrates your interpersonal sensitivity and reinforces the person's memory of you.

Technology and Career Placement

Once you start looking for a job, internship, or co-op, it is very important to consider how you use technology:

1. **Your e-mail address.** Make sure it is professional and would not offend anyone.
2. **Your cell phone.** Consider your "ringback tone." If it is music that has offensive language, remove it. Also, make sure your voice mail message is short and professional. Time is precious and people don't want to listen to a two-minute voice mail message, no matter what it is about.
3. **Facebook, Twitter, etc.** Make sure anything you post would not turn off any potential employers. Even if your page is marked "private," employers are hiring people to get all the dirt on you!

It is important when you are looking for a job to put your best self out there; this includes your digital self.

Summary and Conclusion

Here is a snapshot of the points that were made in this chapter:

- Changing your educational goal is not necessarily a bad thing; it may represent your discovery of another field that's more interesting to you or that's more compatible with your personal interests and talents.
- Several myths exist about the relationship between college majors and careers that need to be dispelled:
  - **Myth 1.** When you choose your major, you're choosing your career.
  - **Myth 2.** After a bachelor's degree, any further education must be in the same field as your college major.
  - **Myth 3.** You should major in business because most college graduates work in business settings.
  - **Myth 4.** If you major in a liberal arts field, the only career available is teaching.

- You should be aware of two important elements when choosing your major: your form or forms of multiple intelligence (your mental strengths or talents) and your learning style (your preferred way of learning).
- Strategically select your courses in a way that contributes most to your educational, personal, and professional development. Choose your elective courses with one or more of the following purposes in mind:
  - Choose a major or confirm whether your first choice is a good one.
  - Acquire a minor or build a concentration that will complement your major.
  - Broaden your perspectives on the world around you.
  - Become a more balanced or complete person.
  - Handle the practical life tasks that face you now and in the future.
  - Strengthen your career development and employment prospects after graduation.

With higher education comes more freedom of choice and a greater opportunity to determine your own academic course of action. Employ it and enjoy it—use your freedom strategically to make the most of your college experience and college degree.*

Chapter 2 Exercises

2.1 Planning General Education

- Look at your online college catalog. Use the index in the catalog to find the general education requirements. You will find that general education requirements are organized into academic divisions of knowledge that make up the college curriculum, such as humanities, fine arts, and natural sciences. Within each of these academic divisions, you'll see courses listed that fulfill the general education requirement for that particular division. In some cases, you'll have no choice about what courses you must take to fulfill the general education requirement, but in most cases, you'll have the freedom to choose from a group of courses. Read the course descriptions to get an idea about what each course covers, and choose those courses that are most relevant to your educational and career plans or to your interests in fields that you might consider choosing as a major.
- Record the courses you plan to take to fulfill your general education requirements on the following form. (Remember that courses you are taking this term may be fulfilling certain general education requirements, so be sure to include them on the form.)

General Education Planning Form

Academic Division: ________________

General education courses you plan to take to fulfill requirements in this division:

(Record the course number and course title)

Academic Division: ________________

General education courses you plan to take to fulfill requirements in this division:

Academic Division: ________________

General education courses you plan to take to fulfill requirements in this division:

Academic Division: ________________

General education courses you plan to take to fulfill requirements in this division:

Academic Division: ______________

General education courses you plan to take to fulfill requirements in this division:

Academic Division: ______________

General education courses you plan to take to fulfill requirements in this division:

2.2 Planning for a College Major and Transfer to a Four-Year College

In the preceding exercise, you made a plan for the general education component of your college experience. Now consider developing a tentative plan for a college major or specialized field of study. Even if you don't think you're going to transfer to a four-year college and complete a bachelor's degree, it's still a good idea to complete this exercise because it'll give you an idea about what it would take to get such a degree. It's possible that when you see it all laid out in a plan, you might be motivated to pursue a bachelor's degree—if not right now, then perhaps at a later point in your life.

1. Go to your college catalog and use its index to locate pages containing information related to the major you have chosen or are considering. If you are undecided, select a field that you might consider as a possibility. To help you identify possible majors, you can use your catalog or go online and complete the short interview at the www.mymajors.com Web site.

   The point of this exercise is not to force you to commit to a major now, but to familiarize you with the process of developing a plan, thereby putting you in a position to apply this knowledge when you reach a final decision about the major you intend to pursue. Even if you don't yet know what your final destination may be with respect to a college major, creating this educational plan will keep you moving in the right direction.

2. Once you've selected a major for this assignment, look at the catalog of the four-year college to which you plan to transfer to identify the courses that are required for the major you have selected.

   You'll find that you must take certain courses for the major; these are often called core requirements. For instance, at most colleges, all business majors must take microeconomics. You will likely discover that you can choose other required courses from a menu or list of options (e.g., "choose any three courses from the following list of six courses"). Such courses are often called restricted electives in the major. When you find restricted electives in the major you've selected, read the course descriptions and choose those courses from the list that appeal most to you.

   College catalogs can sometimes be tricky to navigate or interpret, so if you run into any difficulty, don't panic. Seek help from an academic advisor.

Notes

1. If you have not decided on a major, a good strategy might be to concentrate on taking liberal arts courses to fulfill your general education requirements during your first year of college. This will open more slots in your course schedule during your sophomore year. By that time, you may have a better idea of what you want to major in, and you can fill these open slots with courses required by your major. This may be a particularly effective strategy if you choose to major in a field that has many lower-division (freshman and sophomore) requirements that have to be completed before you can be accepted as a transfer student in that major.
2. Keep in mind that the course number indicates the year in the college experience that the course is usually taken. Courses numbered in the 100s (or below) are typically taken in the first year of college, 200-numbered courses in the sophomore year, 300-numbered courses in the junior year, and 400-numbered courses in the senior year. Also, be sure to check whether the course you're planning to take has any prerequisites—courses that need to be completed before you can enroll in the course you're planning to take. For example, if you are planning to take a course in literature, it is likely that you cannot enroll in it until you have completed at least one prerequisite course in writing or English composition.
3. To complete a college degree in four years, you should complete about 30 credits each academic year. Summer term is considered part of an academic year, and we encourage you to use that term to help keep you on a four-year timeline.
4. Check with an academic advisor to see whether your college and the four-year college to which you're planning to transfer have developed a projected plan of scheduled courses, which indicates the academic term when courses listed in the catalog are scheduled to be offered (e.g., fall, spring, or summer) for the next two to three years. If such a long-range plan of scheduled courses is available, take advantage of it because it will enable you to develop a personal educational plan that includes not only what courses you will take but also when you will take them. This can be an important advantage because some courses you may need for graduation will not be offered every term. We strongly encourage you to inquire about and acquire any long-range plan of scheduled courses that may be available and use it when developing your long-range graduation plan.
5. Don't forget to include out-of-class learning experiences as part of your educational plan, such as volunteer service, internships, and study abroad.

Your long-range graduation plan is not something set in stone that can never be modified. Like clay, its shape can be molded and changed into a different form as you gain more experience with the college curriculum. Nevertheless, your creation of this initial plan will be useful because it will provide you with a blueprint to work from. Once you have created slots specifically for your general education requirements, your major courses, and your electives, you have accounted for all the categories of courses you will need to complete to graduate. Thus, if changes need to be made to your plan, they can be easily accommodated by simply substituting different courses into the slots you've already created for these three categories.

Case Studies

General Education versus Career Specialization

Joe was looking forward to college because he thought he would have freedom to select the courses he wanted and the opportunity to get into the major of his choice (computer science). However, he is disappointed with his first-term schedule of classes because it consists mostly of required general education courses that do not seem to relate to his major, and some of these courses are about subjects that he already took in high school (English, history, and biology). He's beginning to think he would be better off moving off the transfer track and getting a technical degree so that he could finish sooner, get into the computer industry, and start earning money.

Discussion Questions

1. What do you see as the potential advantages and disadvantages of Joe pursuing a technical degree instead of a four-year college degree?
2. Can you relate to Joe, or do you know of students who feel as he does?
3. Do you see any way Joe might strike a balance between pursuing his career interest and obtaining his college degree so that he can pursue both goals at the same time?

Career Choice: Conflict and Confusion

Jennifer is a first-year student whose family has made a great financial sacrifice to send her to college. She deeply appreciates the tremendous commitment her family has made to her education and wants to pay them back as soon as possible. Consequently, she has been looking into careers that offer the highest starting salaries to college students immediately after graduation. Unfortunately, none of these careers seem to match Jennifer's natural abilities and personal interests. She knows she'll have to make a decision soon because the careers with high starting salaries involve majors that have many course requirements, and if she expects to graduate in a reasonable period, she'll have to start taking some of these courses during her first year.

Discussion Questions

1. If you were Jennifer, what would you do?
2. Do you see any way that Jennifer might balance her desire to pay back her parents as soon as possible with her desire to pursue a career that's compatible with her interests and talents?
3. What other questions or factors do you think Jennifer should consider before making her decision?

Chapter 2 Reflection

Name: ______________________

What is your ideal career?

What would your work day be like?

Make a detailed plan for how you can get to this career.

What are some things you can utilize from this chapter to make it happen?*

Transfer Planning at DMACC

Is it best to complete my two-year degree at DMACC before transferring to a four-year college? And, if so, what are the advantages?

Yes, complete your degree before transferring. You will have a credential to place on your resume to help with job searches and internships.

Many of Iowa's four-year colleges will allow a DMACC AA degree to transfer as a "whole package" for most majors. This degree transfer means you will have satisfied the college's general education requirements by completing an AA degree, even if the courses do not match up exactly to that college's specific general education requirements. This acceptance allows you to transfer as a junior and focus on your chosen major once you arrive at the four-year college. However, the AA degree is not appropriate for all majors, so you should discuss your transfer plans with an advisor. Also, some colleges provide scholarships for transfer students who have completed their two-year degrees.

When should I start planning my transfer?

Start planning now. If you are planning to transfer from DMACC to a four-year college, it is important to begin preparing for your transfer as early as possible to ensure a smooth transition. The decisions you make today will affect your transfer to the four-year college, which is why it is crucial to begin planning now. For example, your transfer college may prefer specific courses as part of your major, and you may be able to complete some of those courses as part of your AA degree saving yourself time and money.

How should I begin?

- Meet with an Advisor. You are strongly encouraged to meet with an advisor to discuss your transfer options. Advisors are available on every campus to assist you throughout the planning process.
- Choose a Major. Many majors require you to complete specific coursework prior to your acceptance. It is, therefore, important to have a college major selected before you transfer. If you are undecided about your future career or major, you should begin exploring your options early in your college career. Career counselors are available to guide you through self-assessment and career exploration activities.
- Select a College. It is beneficial to have a transfer college in mind early on in the planning process. Research your options and make sure the college you choose offers your intended major. A *School Comparison Worksheet* is available at the end of this section to help you compare and contrast the colleges you are considering.

What courses should I take?

- The Liberal Arts AA degree usually provides the best transfer. The general education or "core" courses are generally equivalent to the first two years at a four-year college; however, an AA degree is not the best route for all majors. Once you have decided on a major, you should talk with an advisor to determine the best transfer plan.
- Take the prerequisite courses for your major. Your transfer college or a DMACC advisor can help you identify the prerequisites you need. Transfer plans are available for many different majors. These plans are a great resource in helping you select appropriate courses for your major.
- Start taking courses in subject areas that interest you, but reserve the bulk of your major coursework for your transfer college. Upper-level courses don't necessarily transfer into your major; and most colleges require that you complete upper-level courses on their campus.

- Complete course sequences when required. For example, your major might require a sequence of two semesters of chemistry. This requirement could mean you will need to complete both CHM 122 and CHM 132 (for example) in order for the courses to transfer.

What if I plan to transfer to an out-of-state college?

DMACC has articulation agreements with a few out-of-state colleges, and these agreements can help you with course selection. However, it is important for you to visit with an advisor at the college you plan to attend, because the four-year college will determine if and how your credits will transfer. In most cases, liberal arts courses are still the most appropriate for you to take.

When should I apply?

Deadlines vary from college to college. It is important that you check with your transfer institution about their specific deadlines. The Career Center & Transfer Resource Center provides admission and scholarship information for most Iowa four-year colleges, but the best resource for this information is your four-year college transfer admission counselor. The college *Admission Checklist* (available at the end of this section) can help you keep track of all important deadlines.

How do I transfer my credits?

Your transfer college will require you to provide official transcripts from each college you have attended. Transcripts must be sent directly from one college to another to be considered "official." Transcript requests must be submitted to the DMACC Registration Office; the Transcript Request Form is available online. Each college has its own policies regarding the acceptance and application of transfer credit.

What questions should I ask the four-year colleges?

- Do you offer my major?
- Is admission into my major competitive?
- What are the admission requirements?
- Is there a deadline for admission?
- Is there an admission fee or deposit required?
- How will my DMACC courses transfer?
- What courses do I need to take before I transfer?
- How many credits can I transfer into your college?
- What is your college's foreign language requirement?
- How much is tuition?
- What payment options are available?
- Are there deadlines for financial aid?
- What scholarships are available for transfer students?
- What are my options for on-campus housing?
- When do I need to apply for housing?
- How much does it cost for housing and meal plans?
- Do you offer fast track or evening courses?
- What student activities and organizations are available?

What else should I know?

- DMACC has articulation agreements and transfer plans with many four-year colleges and universities. These are valuable tools that can assist you in selecting appropriate transfer courses.
- Many colleges offer scholarships for transfer students. Scholarship information is usually available on the college's website.
- Our *Cross Enrollment* agreement allows DMACC students to take a class for free at Drake, Grand View, or Iowa State. This is an excellent way to sample another college.
- DMACC has several special programs and 2 + 2 degree programs with four-year colleges. See an advisor for additional information.
- Students transferring to Iowa and UNI are encouraged to participate in the Admissions Partnership Program (APP).
- Visit a DMACC advisor for more information on these opportunities.

Tips for a Successful Transfer

- Start planning your transfer to a four-year college as early as possible while you are a student at DMACC. Planning well in advance will increase your preparation and success in transferring your credits.
- Consider what your major will be at the four-year college. Choosing a major early is beneficial because many majors have prerequisite courses or specific admission criteria. This will help you plan your DMACC courses. If you are undecided about your major, you should begin the planning process now.
- If you are uncertain where you will transfer after DMACC, start researching four-year colleges now. No two colleges are the same. Requirements, majors, and practices will vary. A good place to start is by using the Internet to look at different college websites. Attend a DMACC college fair to visit with representatives from different four-year colleges. At the Ankeny Campus, you may also use the information resources in the Career Center in Building 5 to learn about different four-year colleges and majors.
- Meet with a DMACC advisor. Discuss your transfer plans with each advisor who assists you with your academic planning. Talk to your advisor about transfer agreements or special programs that may be available with the four-year colleges you are considering, such as course articulation, cross enrollment, admission partnership programs, etc.
- Request a college catalog, an admission application, financial aid, scholarship, and housing information from the four-year colleges you are considering. Request information that may be specific to transfer students.
- To help you finalize your decision as to where you will transfer after DMACC, set up a campus visit to colleges you are interested in attending. Campus visits are important because they provide first-hand information that you simply won't get by talking to friends, looking at a website, or in a catalog.
- When you schedule your visit, ask for an appointment with an advisor. Be prepared. Take a list of questions with you about admission, major requirements, transfer credits, or anything else you are unsure about. Take a student copy of your DMACC transcript with you. You can log in and print a student copy of your transcript from the DMACC Web Information System. Take notes and document the names of the people you talk with during your visit in case you have questions in the future.
- Keep important assignments and research papers from your DMACC classes, and your DMACC catalog. Some four-year colleges may require a portfolio of your college coursework or may need additional course information to award transfer credit.

- Complete an application for admission to the college of your choice. Research the college admission deadlines and application fees early on in the process. Also, scholarship and housing opportunities may be limited and can be dependent upon an offer for admission, so apply early!
- Request to have your official college transcript sent to your transfer college. You will need to request a transcript from each college you have attended. Students may request transcripts through MyDMACC/Web Info.
- Complete financial aid, scholarship, and housing applications. Be aware of deadlines and complete all materials as early as possible. Stay in touch with your transfer school. Attend an orientation/registration day. Some colleges hold early registration sessions for transfer students.
- You are ready to start classes. Good luck!

School Comparison Worksheet

Name: ____________________

Date: ____________________

	School #1	School #2	School #3
University/College Name			
Type: Public/Private Religious affiliation; tech, liberal arts, etc.			
Philosophy: Educational focus Have there been changes in last 10 yrs?			
Major: Intended major available? Geared in the right direction for me?			
Size: Average class size (Gen Ed and major) Total Populations			
Ratios: Faculty to student (Gen Ed and major) Number who continue to grad school			
Demos: On-campus to commuter Diversity; undergrads in major			
Costs: Annual Tuition and Fees Books, housing, etc.			
Location: Rural/Urban setting; city/town size Distance from home			
Scholarships: Transfer specific			
Credits: Will credits transfer and how many? In the correct sequence for major?			
Housing: Types available on campus Off-campus options and contacts			
Facilities: Classrooms and buildings Computer labs; Student Center and Rec			
Flexibility: Times and Presentation options "Fast Track"; multiple locations			
Major: Needed at time of transfer? Most popular and why; new majors?			
Completion: Average years (overall and major) Average for transfer student			
Campus: Most popular activities Substance policies			
Insurance: Student option available? Restrictions/limitations/costs			
Accreditation: Regionally accredited Accreditation/Certification in major			
Family: Childcare options Discounts for relatives/dependents			
Security: Local law enforcement/contract Special services (e.g. car walk)			
Overall impression: People Campus, community			
Other Notes:			
Unanswered Questions:			

Admission Checklist

Name: ____________________

Date: ____________________

	School #1	School #2	School #3
University/College Name			
Admission Deadline			
Date Admission Application Sent			
Date Preliminary Transcripts Sent			
Date ACT/SAT Scores Sent			
Date Accepted to College			
Date Transfer Credit Evaluation Received			
Free Application for Federal Student Aid (FAFSA) priority deadline			
Date FAFSA Sent/Submitted			
Date Student Aid Report Received (SAR)			
Scholarship Application Deadline			
Date Scholarship Applications Sent			
Date Award Letter Received			
Award Letter Acceptance Deadline			
Tuition/Housing Deposit Deadline			
Date Tuition/Housing Deposit Sent			
Tuition/Housing Deposit Refund Deadline			
Date Final College Transcripts Sent			
Minimum # of transferable credits to apply			
Minimum # of transferable credits for admission			
Minimum course grade for transferability			
Foreign Language requirement			
Letters of recommendation and/or Portfolio			
Need minimum GPA from high school course(s)			
Need ACT/SAT scores; if yes, minimum scores			
Need high school/GED completion			

SQ4R Worksheet

Your Name:

Selection Title/Chapter:

Author(s):

1. **Survey**: Look at the title, visuals, questions, excerpts, headings and sub-headings. Afterward, answer the questions below.

What do I already know about the topics?	What do I expect to learn?

2. **Question**: Create questions based on your survey of the text. If there are headings, turn them into questions. Include *at least three* below to help focus your attention as you read.

A.
B.
C.
D.
E.

3. **Read** and **Record** (Annotate): Read the selection thoroughly, highlight, and make note of important points, associations, and unfamiliar terms. Complete the chart using **your own words**. Provide a sketch and/or explanation of the visuals. Use and attach a separate sheet if needed.

Page and Paragraph #	Vocabulary Terms	Notes and Definitions	Visuals

(*Continued*)

(*Continued*)

4. **Recite**: Answer your questions from step two.

a.
b.
c.
d.
e.

5. **Review and Reflect**: Check your memory by verbalizing the above information. Below, write a summary **in your own words** of what you have read, connecting the content ideas. Additionally, write a brief reflection including your personal response to the reading (use "I" and make connections to your own experiences, ask more questions, respond to the text, and consider anything you were reminded of or visualized while reading).

Summary:

Reflection:

Adapted from Florida Online Reading Professional Development. (n.d.). *SQ4R*. Retrieved from the Marco Island Charter Middle School website at http://micms.org/SQ4R.pdf

Managing Time and Preventing Procrastination

3

THOUGHT STARTER | *Journal Entry* 3.1

LEARNING GOAL

To help you appreciate the significance of managing time and supply you with a powerful set of time-management strategies that can be used to promote your success in college and beyond.

*Complete the following sentence with the first thought that comes to your mind.

For me, time is . . .

____

____

____

____

The Importance of Time Management

For many first-year students, the beginning of college means the beginning of more independent living and self-management. Even if you've lived on your own for some time, managing time is an important skill to possess because you're likely juggling multiple responsibilities, including school, family, and work. Studies show that most first-year community college students are attending classes while working either part-time or full-time (American Association of Community Colleges, 2009). In college, the academic calendar and your class schedule will differ radically from those during high school. You will have less "seat time" in class each week and more "free time" outside of class, which you will have the freedom to self-manage; it will not be closely monitored by school authorities or family members, and you will be expected to do more academic work on your own outside of class. Personal time-management skills grow in importance when a person's time is less structured or controlled by others, leaving the individual with more decision-making power about how personal time will be spent. Thus, it is no surprise that research shows the ability to manage time effectively as playing a crucial role in college success (Erickson, Peters, & Strommer, 2006).

Student *Perspective*

"The major difference [between high school and college] is time. You have so much free time on your hands that you don't know what to do for most of the time."

—First-year college student (Erickson & Strommer, 1991)

Simply stated, college students who have difficulty managing their time have difficulty managing college. In one study, sophomores who had an outstanding first year in college (both academically and socially) were compared with another group of sophomores who struggled during their freshman year. Interviews conducted with these students revealed one key difference between the two groups: The sophomores who experienced a successful first year repeatedly brought up the topic of time during the interviews. The successful students said they had to think carefully about how they spent their time and budget their time because it was a scarce resource. In contrast, the sophomores who experienced difficulty in their first year of

Student *Perspective*

"I cannot stress enough that you need to intelligently budget your time."

—Words written by a first-year student in a letter of advice to students who are about to begin college

college hardly talked about the topic of time during their interviews, even when they were specifically asked about it (Light, 2001).

Studies also indicate that managing time plays a pivotal role in the lives of working adults. Setting priorities and balancing multiple responsibilities (work, family, and school) that compete for limited time and energy can be a juggling act and a source of stress for people of all ages (Harriott & Ferrari, 1996).

For these reasons, time management should be viewed not only as a college-success strategy but also as a life-management and life-success skill. Studies show that people who manage their time well report being more in control of their lives and happier (Myers, 1993). In short, when you gain greater control of your time, you become more satisfied with your life.

Author's Experience

I started the process of earning my doctorate a little later in life than other students. I was a married father with a preschool daughter (Sara). Since my wife left for work early in the morning, it was always my duty to get up and get my daughter's day going in the right direction. In addition, I had to do the same for me—which was often harder than doing it for my daughter. Three days of my week were spent on campus in class or in the library. (We did not have quick access to research on computers then as you do now.) The other two days of the workweek and the weekend were spent on household chores, family time, and studying. I knew that if I was going to have any chance of finishing my Ph.D. in a reasonable amount of time and have a decent family life, I had to adopt an effective schedule for managing my time. Each day of the week, I held to a very strict routine. I got up in the morning, drank coffee while reading the paper, took a shower, got my daughter ready for school, and took her to school. Once I returned home, I put a load of laundry in the washer, studied, wrote, and spent time concentrating on what I needed to do to be successful from 8:30 a.m. to 12:00 p.m. every day. At lunch, I had a pastrami and cheese sandwich and a soft drink while rewarding myself by watching *Perry Mason* reruns until 1:00 p.m. I then continued to study until it was time to pick up my daughter from school. Each night I spent time with my wife and daughter and prepared for the next day. I lived a life that had a preset schedule. By following this schedule, I was able to successfully complete my doctorate in a decent amount of time while giving my family the time they needed. (By the way, I still watch *Perry Mason* reruns.)

Aaron Thompson

Strategies for Managing Time

Effective time management involves three key mental processes:

1. **Analysis.** Breaking down time into specific segments and work into smaller tasks;
2. **Itemizing.** Identifying all key tasks that need to be done and by what dates; and
3. **Prioritizing.** Organizing and attacking tasks in order of their importance.

The following steps can help you apply these skills to find more time in your schedule and use this time more productively.

1. **Break down your time and become more aware of how it's spent.** Have you ever asked yourself, "Where did all the time go?" or told yourself, "I just can't seem to find the time"? One way to find out where your time went is by taking a time inventory (Webber, 1991). To do this, you conduct a time analysis by breaking down and tracking your time, recording what you do and when you do it. By mapping out how you spend time, you become more aware of how much total time you have available to you and how its component parts are used up, including patches of wasted time in which you get little or nothing accomplished. You don't have to do this time analysis for more than a week or two. This should be long enough to give you some sense of where your time is going and allow you to start developing strategies for using your time more effectively and efficiently.

Think About It — *Journal Entry* 3.2

1. What is your greatest time waster?

____

____

____

____

____

____

2. Is there anything you can do right now to stop or eliminate it?

____

____

____

____

____

____

"Dost thou love life? Then do not squander time, for that is the stuff life is made of."

—Benjamin Franklin, 18th-century inventor, newspaper writer, and signer of the *Declaration of Independence*

2. **Identify which key tasks you need to accomplish and when you need to accomplish them.** We make lists to be sure we don't forget items we need from the grocery store or people we want to be sure are invited to a party. We can use the same list-making strategy for work tasks so that we don't forget to do them or forget to do them on time. Studies of effective people show that they are list makers and they write out lists not only for grocery items and wedding invitations, but also for things they want to accomplish each day (Covey, 2004).

   You can itemize your tasks by listing them in one of the following time-management tools:

   - **Cell phone.** Use the calendar tools on your phone or a calendar app to record due dates and set up the alert functions to remind yourself of deadlines. You can set up task lists or "To Do" lists and set priorities for each item you enter.
   - **Small, portable planner.** List all your major assignments and exams for the term, along with their due dates. If you pull all work tasks from different courses into one place, it is easier to keep track of what you have to do and when you have to do it.

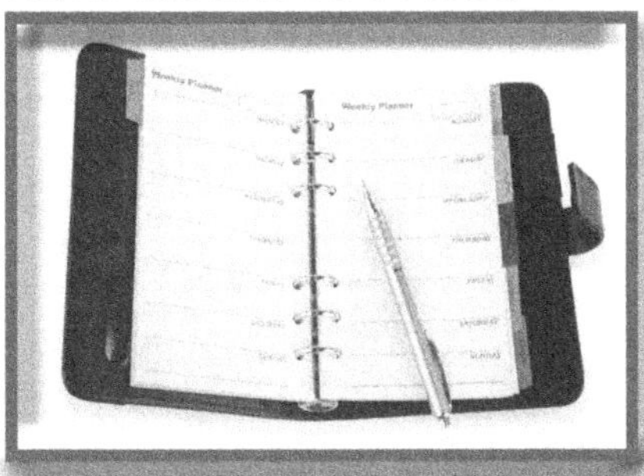

Using a personal planner is an effective way to itemize your academic commitments.

- **Large, stable calendar.** Record in the calendar's date boxes your major assignments for the academic term and when they are due. Place the calendar in a position or location where it's in full view and you can't help but see it every day (e.g., on your bedroom or refrigerator door). If you regularly and literally "look" at the things you have to do, you're less likely to "overlook" them, forget about them, or subconsciously push them out of your mind.

Think About It — *Journal Entry* 3.3

1. Do you have a calendar for the current academic term that you carry with you?

____

____

2. If yes, why? If no, what do you use instead?

____

____

____

____

____

____

3. How does that work for you?

____

____

____

____

____

____

Author's Experience

My mom was the person who ensured I got up for school on time. Once I got to school, the bell would ring to let me know to move on to the next class. When I returned home, I had to do my homework and chores. My daily and weekly schedules were dictated by others.

When I entered college, my mom quickly realized that I needed to develop my own system for being organized, focused, and productive without her assistance. Since I came from a modest background, I had to work my way through college. Juggling schedules became an art and science for me. I knew the things that I could not miss, such as work and school, and the things I could miss—TV and girls. (OK, TV, but not girls.)

After college, I spent 10 years in business—a world where I was measured by being on time and a productive "bottom line." It was during this time that I discovered a scheduling book. When I became a professor, I had other mechanisms to make sure I did what I needed to do when I needed to do it. This was largely based on when my classes were offered. Other time was dedicated to working out and spending time with my family. Now, as an administrator, I have an assistant who keeps my schedule for me. She tells me where I am going, how long I should be there, and what I need to accomplish while I am there. Unless you take your parents with you or have the luxury of a personal assistant, it's important to determine which activities are required and to allow time in your schedule for fun. Use a planner!

Aaron Thompson

3. **Rank your tasks in order of their importance.** Once you've itemized your work by listing all tasks you need to do, prioritize them—determine the order in which you will do them. Prioritizing basically involves ranking your tasks in terms of their importance, with the highest-ranked tasks appearing at the top of your list to ensure that they are tackled first. How do you determine which tasks are most important and should be ranked highest? Two key criteria or standards of judgment can be used to help determine which tasks should be your priorities:
   - **Urgency.** Tasks that are closest to their deadline or due date should receive high priority. For example, finishing an assignment that's due tomorrow should receive higher priority than starting an assignment that's due next month.
   - **Gravity.** Tasks that carry the heaviest weight (count the most) should receive highest priority. For example, if an assignment worth 100 points and another worth 10 points are due at the same time, working on the 100-point task should receive higher priority. You want to be sure you invest your work time on work tasks that matter most. Just like investing money, you want to invest your time on tasks that yield the greatest dividends or payoff.

One strategy for prioritizing your tasks is to divide them into A, B, and C lists (Lakein, 1973; Morgenstern, 2004). The A list is for *essential* tasks—what you *must* do now. The B list is for *important* tasks—what you *should* do soon. Finally, the C list is for *optional* tasks—what you *could* or *might* do later if there is time remaining after you've completed the tasks on the A and B lists. Organizing your tasks in this fashion can help you decide how to divide your labor in a way that ensures you put first things first. What you don't want to do is waste time on unimportant things and deceive yourself into thinking that you're keeping busy and getting things done when actually you're doing things that just take your time (and mind) away from the more important things.

Student *Perspective*

"I like to get rid of my stress by doing what I have to do first, like if it's a paper."

—First-year college student's response to the question "What do you do to reduce your stress level?"

At first glance, itemizing and prioritizing may appear to be rather boring chores. However, if you look at these mental tasks carefully, they require many higher-level thinking skills, such as:

1. **Analysis.** Breaking down time into its component elements or segments and breaking down work into specific tasks;

2. **Evaluation.** Critically evaluating the relative importance or value of tasks; and
3. **Synthesis.** Organizing individual tasks into classes or categories based on their level of priority.

Thus, developing self-awareness about how you spend time is more than a menial clerical task: when done with thoughtful reflection, it's an exercise in higher-level thinking. It's also a good exercise in values clarification, because what people choose to spend their time on is a more accurate indicator of what they truly value than what they *say* they value.

Develop a Time-Management Plan

"Time = Life. Therefore waste your time and waste your life, or master your time and master your life."

—Alan Lakein, international expert on time management and author of the bestselling book *How to Get Control of Your Time and Your Life* (1973)

Humans are creatures of habit. Regular routines help us organize and gain control of our lives. Doing things by design, rather than leaving them to chance or accident, is the first step toward making things happen for us rather than allowing them to happen to us by chance or accident. By developing an intentional plan for how you're going to spend your time, you're developing a plan to gain greater control of your life.

Don't buy into the myth that you don't have time to plan because it takes too much time that could be spent on getting started and getting things done. Time-management experts estimate that the amount of time you spend planning your work reduces your total work time by a factor of three (Goldsmith, 2010; Lakein, 1973). In other words, for every one unit of time you spend planning, you save three units of work time. Thus, five minutes of planning time will typically save you 15 minutes of total work time, and 10 minutes of planning time will save you 30 minutes of work time. This saving of work time probably occurs because you develop a clearer game plan or plan of attack for identifying what needs to be done and the best order in which to get it done. A clearer sense of direction reduces the number of mistakes you may make due to false starts—starting the work but then having to restart it because you started off in the wrong direction. If you have no plan of attack, you're more likely to go off track and in the wrong direction; when you discover this at some point after you've started, you're then forced to retreat and start over.

As the old proverb goes, "A stitch in time saves nine." Planning your time represents the "stitch" (in time) that saves you nine additional stitches (units of time). Like successful chess players, successful time managers plan ahead and anticipate their next moves.

Elements of a Comprehensive Time-Management Plan

Once you've accepted the notion that taking the time to plan your time saves you time in the long run, you're ready to design a time-management plan. The following are the key elements of a comprehensive, well-designed plan for managing time:

1. **A good time-management plan should have several time frames.** Your academic time-management plan should include:
   - A *long-range* plan for the entire academic term that identifies deadline dates for reports and papers that are due toward the end of the term;
   - A *mid-range* plan for the upcoming month and week; and
   - A *short-range* plan for the following day.

The preceding time frames may be integrated into a total time-management plan for the term by taking the following steps:

a. Identify deadline dates of all assignments, or the time when each of them must be completed (your long-range plan).
b. Work backward from these final deadlines to identify dates when you plan to begin taking action on these assignments (your short-range plan).
c. Identify intermediate dates when you plan to finish particular parts or pieces of the total assignment (your mid-range plan).

This three-stage plan should help you make steady progress throughout the term on college assignments that are due later in the term. At the same time, it will reduce your risk of procrastinating and running out of time.

Here's how you can put this three-stage plan into action this term. Develop a long-range plan for the academic *term*.

- Review the *course syllabus (course outline)* for each class you are enrolled in this term, and highlight all major exams, tests, quizzes, assignments, and papers and the dates on which they are due.

Remember

College professors are more likely than high school teachers to expect you to rely on your course syllabus to keep track of what you have to do and when you have to do it. Your instructors may not remind you about upcoming papers, tests, quizzes, assignments, etc.

- Obtain a *large calendar* for the academic term and record all your exams, assignments, and so on, for all your courses in the calendar boxes that represent their due dates. To fit this information within the calendar boxes, use creative abbreviations to represent different tasks, such as E for exam and TP for term paper. When you're done, you'll have a centralized chart or map of deadline dates and a potential master plan for the entire term.
- Use the calendar and task list function on your cell phone. Enter your schedule, important dates, and deadlines, and set alert reminders. Since you carry your cell phone with you regularly, you will always have this information at your fingertips.
- **Plan your *week*.**
  a. Make a map of your *weekly schedule* that includes times during the week when you are in class, when you typically eat and sleep, and if you are employed, when you work.
  b. If you are a full-time college student, find *at least 25 total hours per week* when you can do academic work outside the classroom. (These 25 hours can be pieced together in any way you like, including time between daytime classes and work commitments, evening time, and weekend time.) When adding these 25 hours to the time you spend in class each week, you will end up with a 40-hour workweek, similar to any full-time job. If you are a part-time student, you should plan on spending at least two hours on academic work outside of class for every hour that you're in class.
  c. Make good use of your *free time between classes* by working on assignments and studying in advance for upcoming exams. See Do It Now! 3.1 for a summary of how you can make good use of your out-of-class time to improve your academic performance and course grades.

Student Perspective

"The amount of free time you have in college is much more than in high school. Always have a weekly study schedule to go by. Otherwise, time slips away and you will not be able to account for it."

—First-year college student (Rhoads, 2005)

- **Plan your *day*.**
  a. Make a *daily to-do list*.

Remember

If you write it out, you're less likely to block it out and forget about it.

"In high school we were given a homework assignment every day. Now we have a large task assigned to be done at a certain time. No one tells [us] when to start or what to do each day."

—First-year college student (Rhoads, 2005)

  b. Attack daily tasks in *priority order*.

Remember

"First things first." Plan your work by placing the most important and most urgent tasks at the top of your list, and work your plan by attacking tasks in the order in which you have listed them.

Student *Perspective*

"I was constantly missing important meetings during my first few weeks because I did not keep track of the dates and times. I thought I'd be told again when the time was closer, just as had been done in high school. Something I should have done to address that would have been to keep a well-organized planner for reference."

—Advice to new students from a college sophomore (Walsh, 2005)

- Carry a *small calendar, planner, or appointment book* with you at all times. This will enable you to record appointments that you may make on the run during the day and will allow you to jot down creative ideas or memories of things you need to do, which sometimes pop into your mind at the most unexpected times.
- Carry *portable work* with you during the day—that is, work you can take with you and do in any place at any time. This will enable you to take advantage of "dead time" during the day. For example, carry material with you that you can read while sitting and waiting for appointments or transportation, allowing you to resurrect this dead time and convert it to "live" work time.
- Wear a *watch* or carry a cell phone that can accurately and instantly tell you what time it is and what date it is. You can't even begin to manage time if you don't know what time it is, and you can't plan a schedule if you don't know what date it is. Set the time on your watch or cell phone slightly ahead of the actual time; this will help ensure that you arrive to class, work, or meetings on time.

Think About It — *Journal Entry* 3.4

1. Do you make a to-do list of things you need to get done each day?

   never seldom often almost always

2. If you selected "never" or "seldom," why don't you?

____

____

____

____

____

____

3.1 DO IT NOW

Making Productive Use of Free Time Outside the Classroom

Unlike in high school, homework in college often does not involve turning things in to your instructor daily or weekly. The academic work you do outside the classroom may not even be collected and graded. Instead, it is done for your own benefit to help prepare yourself for upcoming exams and major assignments (e.g., term papers or research reports). Rather than formally assigning work to you as homework, your professors expect that you will do this work on your own and without supervision. Listed below are strategies for working independently and in advance of college exams and assignments. These strategies will increase the quality of your time management in college and the quality of your academic performance.

Working Independently in Advance of Exams

Use the following strategies to use out-of-class time wisely to prepare for exams:

- **Complete reading assignments** relating to lecture topics before the topic is discussed in class. This will make lectures easier to understand and will prepare you to participate intelligently in class (e.g., ask meaningful questions of your instructor and make informed comments during class discussions).
- **Review your class notes** between class periods so that you can construct a mental bridge from one class to the next and make each upcoming lecture easier to follow. When reviewing your notes before the next class, rewrite any class notes that may be sloppily written the first time. If you find notes related to the same point all over the place, reorganize them by combining them into one set of notes. Lastly, if you find any information gaps or confusing points in your notes, seek out the course instructor or a trusted classmate to clear them up before the next class takes place.
- **Review information** you highlighted in your reading assignments to improve your retention of the information. If certain points are confusing to you, discuss them with your course instructor during office hours or with a fellow classmate outside of class.
- **Integrate key ideas** in your class notes with information that you have highlighted in your assigned reading that relates to the same major point or general category. In other words, put related information from your lecture notes and your reading in the same place (e.g., on the same index card).
- **Use a part-to-whole study method** whereby you study material from your class notes and assigned reading in small pieces during short, separate study sessions that take place well in advance of the exam; then make your last study session before the exam a longer review session during which you restudy all the small parts together as a whole. It's a myth that studying in advance is a waste of time because you'll forget it all anyway by test time. As you'll see in Chapter 5, information studied in advance of an exam remains in your brain and is still there when you later review it. Even if you cannot recall the previously studied information when you first start reviewing it, you will relearn it faster than you did the first time, thus proving that some memory of it was retained from your earlier study sessions.

Work Independently Well in Advance of Due Dates for Term Papers and Research Reports

Work on large, long-range assignments by breaking them into the following smaller, short-term tasks:

- Search for and select a topic.
- Locate sources of information on the topic.
- Organize the information obtained from these sources into categories.
- Develop an outline of the report's major points and the order or sequence in which you plan to discuss them.
- Construct a first draft of the paper (and, if necessary, a second draft).
- Write a final draft of the paper.
- Proofread the final draft of your paper for minor mechanical mistakes, such as spelling and grammatical errors, before submitting it to your instructor.

Murphy's Laws:
1. Nothing is as simple as it looks.
2. Everything takes longer than it should.
3. If anything can go wrong, it will.

—Author unknown; named after Captain Edward Murphy, naval engineer, in 1949

2. **A good time-management plan should include reserve time to take care of the unexpected.** You should always hope for the best but should always be prepared for the worst. Your time-management plan should include a buffer zone or safety net, building in extra time that you can use to accommodate unforeseen developments or unexpected emergencies. Just as you should plan to save money in your bank for unexpected extra costs (e.g., emergency medical expenses), you should plan to save time in your schedule for unexpected events that cost you time (e.g., dealing with unscheduled tasks or taking longer than expected to complete already-planned tasks).
3. **A good time-management plan should capitalize on your biological rhythms.** When you plan your daily schedule, be aware of your natural peak periods and down times. Studies show that individuals differ in terms of the time of day when their bodies naturally tire and prefer to sleep or become energized and prefer to wake up. Some people are "early birds" who prefer to go to sleep early and wake up early; others are "night owls" who prefer to stay up late at night and get up late in the morning (Natale & Ciogna, 1996). Individuals also vary with respect to the times of day when they are at their highest and lowest levels of energy. Naturally, early birds are more likely to be morning people whose peak energy period occurs before noon; night owls are likely to be more productive in the late afternoon and evening. Also, most people experience a post-lunch dip in energy in the early afternoon (Monk, 2005).

   Be aware of your most productive hours of the day and schedule your highest-priority work and most challenging tasks for when you tend to work at peak performance levels. For example, schedule out-of-class academic work so that you're tackling academic tasks that require intense thinking (e.g., technical writing or complex problem solving) when you are most productive; schedule lighter work (e.g., light reading or routine tasks) at the times when your energy level tends to be lower. Also, keep your natural peak and down times in mind when you schedule your courses. Try to arrange your class schedule in such a way that you experience your most challenging courses at the times of the day when your body (brain) is most ready and able to accept that challenge.
4. **A good time-management plan should include a balance of work and recreation.** Don't only plan work time: plan time to relax, refuel, and recharge. Your overall plan shouldn't turn you into an obsessive-compulsive workaholic. Instead, it should represent a balanced blend of work and play, which includes activities that promote your mental and physical wellness, such as relaxation, recreation, and reflection. You could also arrange your schedule of work and play as a self-motivation strategy by using your play time to reward your work time.

Student *Perspective*

"It is just as important to allow time for things you enjoy doing because this is what will keep you stable."

—Words written by a first-year college student in a letter of advice to new students

Remember

A good time-management plan should help you stress less, learn more, and earn higher grades while leaving you time for other important aspects of your life. A good plan not only enables you to get your work done on time, but also enables you to attain and maintain balance in your life.

A good time-management plan includes a balanced blend of time planned for both work and recreation.

Author's Experience

My mom is a schoolteacher, and when my sister and I were growing up she had a strict policy: when we came home from school we could have a snack, but after that we were not allowed to do anything else until our homework was finished. I remember that on days when it was really nice outside, I would beg and plead (and sometimes even argue) with my mom about going outside to play. She always won, and often I had wasted so much time arguing that I completely missed out on the opportunity to play at all. At the time I thought my mom was really mean. As I grew older (in high school and college), though, it became easy to put my homework first. My mom had taught me the importance of prioritizing and completing important things (like homework) before things that were not as important.

—*Julie McLaughlin*

Think About It — *Journal Entry* 3.5

1. What activities do you engage in for fun or recreation?

____

____

____

2. What do you do to relax or relieve stress?

____

____

____

3. Brainstorm a list of activities you could do to relieve stress:

____

____

"Some people regard discipline as a chore. For me, it is a kind of order that sets me free to fly."

—Julie Andrews, Academy Award-winning English actress who starred in the Broadway musicals *Mary Poppins* and *The Sound of Music*

5. **A good time-management plan should have some flexibility.** Some people are immediately turned off by the idea of developing a schedule and planning their time because they feel it overstructures their lives and limits their freedom. It's only natural for you to prize your personal freedom and resist anything that appears to restrict your freedom in any way. A good plan preserves your freedom by helping you get done what must be done, reserving free time for you to do what you want and like to do.
6. **A good time-management plan shouldn't be a rigid work schedule.** It should be flexible enough to allow you to occasionally bend it without having to break it. Just as work commitments and family responsibilities can crop up unexpectedly, so, too, can opportunities for fun and enjoyable activities. Your plan should allow you the freedom to modify your schedule so that you can take advantage of these enjoyable opportunities and experiences. However, you should plan to make up the work time you lost. In other words, you can borrow or trade work time for play time, but don't "steal" it; you should plan to pay back the work time you borrowed by substituting it for a play period that existed in your original schedule.

Remember

When you create a personal time-management plan, remember that it is your *plan—you own it and you run it. It shouldn't run you.*

Converting Your Time-Management Plan into an Action Plan

Once you've planned the work, the next step is to work the plan. A good action plan is one that gives you a preview of what you intend to accomplish and an opportunity to review what you actually accomplished. You can begin to implement an action plan by constructing a daily to-do list, bringing that list with you as the day begins, and checking off items on the list as you get them done. At the end of the day, review your list and identify what was completed and what still needs to be done. The uncompleted tasks should become high priorities for the next day.

At the end of the day, if you find yourself with many unchecked items still remaining on your daily to-do list, this could mean that you're are spreading yourself too thin by trying to do too many things in a day. You may need to be more realistic about the number of things you can reasonably expect to accomplish per day by shortening your daily to-do list.

Being unable to complete many of your intended daily tasks may also mean that you need to modify your time-management plan by adding work time or subtracting activities that are drawing time and attention away from your work (e.g., taking cellphone calls during your planned work times).

Think About It — *Journal Entry* 3.6

1. By the end of a typical day, how often do you find that you accomplished most of the important tasks you hoped to accomplish?

   never seldom often almost always

2. Why?

____

____

____

____

____

____

Dealing with Procrastination

Procrastination Defined

The word *procrastination* derives from two roots: *pro* (meaning "forward") plus *crastinus* (meaning "tomorrow"). As these roots suggest, procrastinators don't abide by the proverb "Why put off to tomorrow what can be done today?" Their philosophy is just the opposite: "Why do today what can be put off until tomorrow?" Adopting this philosophy promotes a perpetual pattern of postponing what needs to be done until the last possible moment, which results in rushing frantically to get it done (and compromising its quality), getting it only partially done, or not finishing it.

Research shows that 80 to 95 percent of college students procrastinate (Steel, 2007) and almost 50 percent report that they procrastinate consistently (Onwuegbuzie, 2000). Furthermore, the percentage of people reporting that they procrastinate is on the rise (Kachgal, Hansen, & Nutter, 2001).

Procrastination is such a serious issue for college students that some colleges and universities have opened "procrastination centers" to provide help exclusively for students who are experiencing problems with procrastination (Burka & Yuen, 2008).

Student *Perspective*

"I believe the most important aspect of college life is time management. DO NOT procrastinate because, although this is the easy thing to do at first, it will catch up with you and make your life miserable."

—Advice from a first-year student to new college students

A procrastinator's idea of planning ahead and working in advance often boils down to this scenario.

Author's Experience

During my early years in college, I was quite a procrastinator. During my sophomore year, I waited to do a major history paper until the night before it was due. Back then, I had a word processor that was little more than a typewriter; it allowed you to save your work to a floppy disk before printing. I finished writing my paper around 3:00 a.m. and hit "print," but about halfway through the printing I ran out of paper. I woke up my roommate to ask if she had paper, but she didn't. So, at 3:00 a.m. I was forced to get out of my pajamas, get into my street clothes, get into my car, and drive around town to find someplace open at three in the morning that sold typing paper. By the time I found a place, got back home, printed the paper, and washed up, it was time to go to class. I could barely stay awake in any of my classes that day, and when I got my history paper back, the grade wasn't exactly what I was hoping for. I never forgot that incident. My procrastination on that paper caused me to lose sleep the night before it was due, lose attention in all my other classes on the day it was due, and lose points on the paper that I managed to do. Thereafter, I was determined not to let procrastination get the best of me.

Julie McLaughlin

Procrastination is by no means limited to college students. It is a widespread problem that afflicts people of all ages and occupations (Harriott & Ferrari, 1996). This is why you'll find many books on the subject of time management in the self-help section of any popular bookstore. It's also why you see so many people at the post office on April 15 every year, mailing their tax returns at the last possible moment ("Haven't Filed Yet," 2003).

Myths That Promote Procrastination

Before there can be any hope of putting a stop to procrastination, procrastinators need to let go of two popular myths (misconceptions) about time and performance.

Myth 1. "I work better under pressure" (e.g., on the day or night before something is due). Procrastinators often confuse desperation with motivation. Their belief that they work better under pressure is often just a rationalization to justify or deny the truth, which is that they *only* work when they're under pressure—that is, when they're running out of time and are under the gun to get it done just before the deadline.

It's true that some people will only start to work and will work really fast when they're under pressure, but that does not mean they're working more *effectively* and producing work of better *quality*. Because they're playing "beat the clock," procrastinators' focus is no longer on doing the job *well* but on doing the job *fast* so that it gets done before they run out of time. This typically results in a product that turns out to be incomplete or inferior to what could have been produced if the work process began earlier.

"Haste makes waste."

—Benjamin Franklin, 18th-century inventor, newspaper writer, and signer of the *Declaration of Independence*

Confusing rapidity with quality is a mistake. It's an indisputable fact that it takes more time to do higher-quality work, particularly if that job requires higher-level thinking skills such as thinking critically and creatively (Ericsson & Charness, 1994). Academic work in college often requires deep learning and complex thinking, which require time for reflection. Deep thoughts and creative ideas take time to formulate, incubate, and eventually "hatch," which is not likely to happen under time pressure (Amabile, Hadley, & Kramer, 2002). Working under pressure on tasks that require higher-level thinking would be similar to trying to complete a long, challenging test within a short time frame. What happens is people have less time to think, to attend to fine details, to double-check their work, and to fine-tune their final product. Research indicates that most procrastinators admit that the work they produce is of poorer quality because they procrastinate (Steel, Brothen, & Wambach, 2001; Wesley, 1994) and that they experience considerable anxiety and guilt about their procrastination habit (Tice & Baumeister, 1997).

Myth 2. "Studying in advance is a waste of time because you will forget it all by test time." This misconception is commonly used to justify procrastinating with respect to preparing for upcoming exams. As will be discussed in Chapter 5, studying that is distributed (spread out) over time is more effective than massed (crammed) studying. Furthermore, last-minute studying that takes place the night before exams often results in lost sleep time due to the need to pull late-nighters or all-nighters. This fly-by-night strategy interferes with retention of information that has been studied and elevates test anxiety because of lost dream (a.k.a. rapid eye movement, or REM) sleep, which enables the brain to store memories and cope with stress (Hobson, 1988; Voelker, 2004). Research indicates that procrastinators experience higher rates of stress-related physical disorders, such as insomnia, stomach problems, colds, and flu (McCance & Pychyl, 2003).

Working under time pressure adds to performance pressure because procrastinators are left with no margin of error to correct mistakes, no time to seek help on their work, and no chance to handle random catastrophes that may arise at the last minute (e.g., an attack of the flu or a family emergency).

Think About It — Journal Entry 3.7

Have you ever put off work for so long that getting it done turned into an emergency situation?

Explain:

Psychological Causes of Procrastination

Sometimes, procrastination has deeper psychological roots. People may procrastinate for reasons related not directly to poor time-management habits but more to emotional issues involving self-esteem or self-image. For instance, studies show that procrastination is sometimes used as a psychological strategy to protect one's self-esteem, which is referred to as self-handicapping. This strategy may be used by some procrastinators (consciously or unconsciously) to give themselves a "handicap" or disadvantage. Thus, if their performance turns out to be less than spectacular, they can conclude (rationalize) that it was because they were performing under a handicap—lack of time (Chu & Cho, 2005).

"We didn't lose the game; we just ran out of time."

—Vince Lombardi, legendary football coach

For example, if the grade they receive on a test or paper turns out to be low, they can still "save face" (self-esteem) by concluding that it was because they waited until the last minute and didn't put much time or effort into it. In other words, they had the ability or intelligence to earn a good grade; they just didn't try very hard. Better yet, if they happened to luck out and get a good grade despite doing it at the last minute, then the grade just shows how intelligent they are! Thus, self-handicapping creates a fail-safe scenario that's guaranteed to protect the procrastinator's self-image. If the work performance or product is less than excellent, it can be blamed on external factors (e.g., lack of time); if it happens to earn them a high grade, they can attribute the result to their extraordinary ability, which enabled them to do so well despite doing it all at the last minute.

"Procrastinators would rather be seen as lacking in effort than lacking in ability."

—Joseph Ferrari, professor of psychology and procrastination researcher

In addition to self-handicapping, other psychological factors have been found to contribute to procrastination, including the following:

- **Fear of failure.** Feeling that it's better to postpone the job, or not do it, than to fail at it (Burka & Yuen, 1983; Soloman & Rothblum, 1984).
- **Perfectionism.** Having unrealistically high personal standards or expectations, which leads to the belief that it's better to postpone work or not do it than to risk doing it less than perfectly (Flett, Blankstein, Hewitt, & Koledin, 1992; Kachgal et al., 2001).

"Striving for excellence motivates you; striving for perfection is demoralizing."

—Harriet Braiker, psychologist and bestselling author

- **Fear of success.** Fearing that doing well will show others that the procrastinator has the ability to achieve success and others will expect the procrastinator to maintain those high standards by doing "repeat performances" (Beck, Koons, & Milgram, 2000; Ellis & Knaus, 2002; Steel, 2007).
- **Indecisiveness.** Having difficulty making decisions, including decisions about what to do or how to begin doing it (Anderson, 2003; Steel, 2003).
- **Thrill seeking.** Enjoying the adrenaline rush triggered by rushing to get things done just before a deadline (Szalavitz, 2003).

If these or any other issues are involved, their underlying psychological causes must be dealt with before procrastination can be overcome. Because they have deeper roots, it may take some time and professional assistance to uproot them.

Think About It — *Journal Entry* 3.8

1. How often do you procrastinate?

   rarely occasionally frequently consistently

2. When you do procrastinate, what is the usual reason?

   ____

   ____

   ____

   ____

   ____

   ____

Self-Help Strategies for Beating the Procrastination Habit

Once inaccurate beliefs or emotional issues underlying procrastination have been identified and dealt with, the next step is to move from gaining self-insight to taking direct action on the procrastination habit itself. Listed here are our top strategies for minimizing or eliminating the procrastination habit.

1. **Continually practice effective time-management strategies.** If effective time-management practices, such as those previously cited in this chapter, are implemented consistently, they can turn into a habit. Studies show that when people repeatedly practice effective time-management strategies, they gradually become part of their routine and develop into habits. For example, when procrastinators repeatedly practice effective time-management strategies with respect to tasks that they procrastinate on, their procrastination tendencies begin to fade and are gradually replaced by good time-management habits (Ainslie, 1992; Baumeister, Heatherton, & Tice, 1994).

For many procrastinators, getting started *is often their biggest obstacle.*

"Just do it!"

—Commercial slogan of a popular athletic equipment company, named after the Greek goddess of victory: Nike

2. **Make the start of work as inviting or appealing as possible.** Getting started can be a key stumbling block for many procrastinators. They experience what's called "start-up stress" when they're about to begin a task they expect will be unpleasant, difficult, or boring (Burka & Yuen, 2008). If you have trouble starting your work, one way to give yourself a jump-start is to arrange your work tasks in an order that allows you to start on tasks that you're likely to find most interesting or most likely to experience success with. Once you overcome the initial inertia and get going, you can ride the momentum you've created to attack the tasks that you find less appealing and more daunting.

You're also likely to discover that the dreaded work wasn't as difficult, boring, or time-consuming as it appeared to be. When you sense that you're making some progress toward getting work done, your anxiety begins to decline. As with many experiences in life that are dreaded and avoided, the anticipation of the event turns out to be worse than the event itself. Research on students who hadn't started a project until it was about to be due indicates that these students experience anxiety and guilt about delaying their work, but once they begin working, these negative emotions decline and are replaced by more positive feelings (McCance & Pychyl, 2003).

Student Perspective

"Did you ever dread doing something, then it turned out to take only about 20 minutes to do?"

—Conversation overheard in a coffee shop between two college students

3. **Make the work manageable.** Work becomes less overwhelming and less stressful when it's handled in small chunks or pieces. You can conquer procrastination for large tasks by using a "divide and conquer" strategy: divide the large task into smaller, more manageable units, and then attack and complete them one at a time.

"There is nothing to fear but fear itself."

—Franklin D. Roosevelt, 32nd president of the United States and the only American to win four presidential elections

Don't underestimate the power of short work sessions. They can be more effective than longer sessions because it's easier to maintain momentum and concentration for shorter periods. If you're working on a large project or preparing for a major exam, dividing your work into short sessions will enable you to take quick jabs and poke small holes in it, reducing its overall size with each successive punch. This approach will also give you the sense of satisfaction that comes with knowing that you're making steady progress toward completing a big task—continually chipping away at it in short strokes.

Author's Experience

The two biggest projects I've had to complete in my life were writing my doctoral thesis and writing this textbook! The strategy that enabled me to keep going until I completed both of these large tasks was to make up short-term deadlines for myself (e.g., complete 5–10 pages each week). I psyched myself into thinking that these were real "drop-dead" deadlines and that if I didn't meet them and complete these small, shorter-term tasks, I was going to drop the ball and fail to get the whole job done. I think these self-imposed deadlines worked for me because they gave me short, more manageable tasks to work on that allowed me to make steady progress toward my larger, long-term task. It was as if I took a huge, hard-to-digest meal and broke it up into small, bite-sized pieces that I could easily swallow and gradually digest over time, as opposed to trying to consume a large meal right before bedtime (the final deadline).

Joe Cuseo

4. **Organization matters.** Research indicates that disorganization is a factor that contributes to procrastination (Steel, 2007). How well we organize our workplace and manage our work materials can reduce our risk of procrastination. Having the right materials in the right place at the right time can make it easier to get to our work and get going on our work. Once we've made a decision to get the job done, we don't want to waste time looking for the tools we need to begin doing it. For procrastinators, this time delay may be just the amount of time they need to change their minds and not start their work.

One simple yet effective way to organize your college work materials is by developing your own file system. You can begin to create an effective file system by filing (storing) materials from different courses in different colored folders or notebooks. This will allow you to keep all materials related to the same course in the same place and give you direct and immediate access to the materials you need as soon as you need them. Such a system helps you get organized, reduces stress associated with having things all over the place, and reduces the risk of procrastination by reducing the time it takes for you to start working.

5. **Location matters.** *Where* you work can influence when or whether you work. Research demonstrates that distraction is a factor that can contribute to procrastination (Steel, 2007). Thus, it may be possible for you to minimize procrastination by working in an environment whose location and arrangement prevent distraction and promote concentration.

Remember

Select a workplace and arrange your workspace to minimize distraction from people and media. Try to remove everything from your work site that's not directly relevant to your work.

Think About It — Journal Entry 3.9

List your two most common sources of distraction while working. Next to each distraction, identify a strategy that you might use to reduce or eliminate it.

Source of Distraction   Strategy for Reducing This Distraction

1. ____________________

2. ____________________

Student *Perspective*

"To reduce distractions, work at a computer on campus rather than using one in your room or home."

—Suggestion for avoiding work distractions from a college student in a first-year seminar class

Lastly, keep in mind that you can arrange your work environment in a way that not only disables distraction, but also enables concentration. You can enable or empower your concentration by working in an environment that allows you easy access to work support materials (e.g., class notes, textbooks, and a dictionary) and social support (e.g., working with a group of motivated students who will encourage you to get focused, stay on task, and keep on track to complete your work tasks).

Student *Perspective*

"I'm very good at starting things but often have trouble keeping a sustained effort."

—First-year college student

6. **Arrange the order or sequence of your work tasks to intercept procrastination when you're most likely to experience it.** While procrastination often involves difficulty starting work, it can also involve difficulty continuing and completing work (Lay & Silverman, 1996). As previously mentioned, if you have trouble starting work, it might be best to first do tasks that you find most interesting or easiest. However, if you have difficulty maintaining or sustaining your work until it's finished, you might try to schedule work tasks that you find easier and more interesting *in the middle or toward the end* of your planned work time. If you're performing tasks of greater interest and ease at a point in your work when you typically lose interest or energy, you may be able to sustain your interest and energy long enough to continue working until you complete them, which means that you'll have completed your entire list of tasks. Also, doing your most enjoyable and easiest tasks later can provide an incentive or reward for completing your less enjoyable tasks first.
7. **If you're close to completing a task, don't stop until you complete it.** It's often harder to restart a task than it is to finish a task that you've already started, because once you've overcome the initial inertia associated with getting started, you can ride the momentum that you've already created. Furthermore, finishing a task can give you a sense of closure—the feeling of personal accomplishment and self-satisfaction that comes from knowing that you "closed the deal." Placing a checkmark next to a completed task and seeing that it's one less thing you have to do can motivate you to continue working on the remaining tasks on your list.

Summary and Conclusion

Mastering the skill of managing time is critical for success in college and in life beyond college. Time is a valuable personal resource; the better you use it, the greater control you have over your life. On the other hand, if you ignore or abuse this resource, you run the risk of reducing the quality of your work and the quality of your life. Once you let go of the pervasive and pernicious procrastination-promoting myth that you work better under pressure (e.g., on the day or night before something is due), you can begin planning how to manage your time and control your future.

Managing time involves three key processes:

1. Analysis of how we spend time, which will allow us to become more consciously aware of our time-spending habits and enable us to know where all our time actually goes.
2. Development of a plan that connects our short-range, mid-range, and long-range tasks (i.e., for the next day, the next week, and the end of the term).
3. Evaluation of our priorities to ensure that we put most of our time into what's most important or matters the most.

These are the three keys to effective time management; they are also likely to be the keys to managing any personal resource, such as your money or your relationships.*

Chapter 3 Exercises

3.1 Who's in Charge?

*You have a paper due tomorrow for your 10:00 a.m. class. You stay up late writing the paper, and then your friends call and ask you to go out. The paper is finished, and you decide you can print it off when you get to school tomorrow. You have a great time with your friends and oversleep, waking at 9:45 a.m. You go straight to the computer lab and experience difficulties printing off your paper. You find a lab technician to help you, but it takes him 40 minutes to retrieve the paper. You run into class (45 minutes late) and give the paper to your instructor, who informs you that she will take the paper for late credit because the class policy states that any papers handed in after the beginning of class are considered late.

1. Who is primarily responsible for this paper being late? Why?

2. How could the situation have been avoided or handled differently?

3.2 Term at a Glance

Review the syllabus (course outline) for each course you're enrolled in this term, and complete the following information for each:

Term ______________________, Year __________

Course ↓	Professor ↓	Exams ↓	Projects & Papers ↓	Other Assignments ↓	Attendance Policy ↓	Late & Makeup Assignment Policy ↓

1. Is the overall workload what you expected? Are you surprised by the amount of work required in any particular course or courses?

2. At this point in the term, what do you see as your most challenging or demanding course or courses? Why?

3. Do you think you can handle the total workload required for the full set of courses you're enrolled in this term?

4. What adjustments or changes could you make to your personal schedule that would make it easier to accommodate your academic workload this term?

3.3 Your Week at a Glance

On the blank grid that follows, map out your typical week for this term. Start by recording what you usually do on these days, including when you have class, when you work, and when you relax or recreate. You can use abbreviations or write tasks out in full if you have enough room in the box (J = job, R&R = rest/relaxation, etc.). List the abbreviations you create at the bottom of the page so that your instructor can follow them.

If you're a *full-time* student, find *25 hours* in your week that you can devote to homework (HW). These 25 hours could be found between classes, during the day, in the evenings, or on the weekends. If you can find 25 hours per week for homework, in addition to your class schedule, you'll have a 40-hour schoolwork week, which research has shown to result in good grades and success in college.

If you're a *part-time* student, find *two hours* you can devote to homework *for every hour* that you're in class (e.g., if you're in class nine hours per week, find 18 hours of homework time).

	Sunday	Monday	Tuesday	Wednesday	Thursday	Friday	Saturday
7:00 a.m.							
8:00 a.m.							
9:00 a.m.							
10:00 a.m.							
11:00 a.m.							
12:00 p.m.							
1:00 p.m.							
2:00 p.m.							
3:00 p.m.							
4:00 p.m.							
5:00 p.m.							
6:00 p.m.							
7:00 p.m.							
8:00 p.m.							
9:00 p.m.							
10:00 p.m.							
11:00 p.m.							

3.4 Personal Time Inventory

1. Go to the Web site provided by your instructor (optional as assigned by the instructor).
2. Complete the time management exercise at this site. The exercise asks you to estimate the number of hours per day or week that you spend doing various activities (e.g., sleeping, employment, and commuting). As you enter the amounts of time you engage in these activities, the total number of remaining hours available in the week for academic work will be automatically computed.
3. After completing your entries, answer the following questions:
   - How many hours per week do you have available for academic work?
   - Do you have two hours available for academic work outside of class for each hour you spend in class?
   - What time wasters do you detect that might be easily eliminated or reduced to create more time for academic work outside of class?

3.5 Ranking Priorities

Look at the tasks below and decide if they are A, B, or C priorities:

_____ Going for a run

_____ Writing a paper that is due tomorrow

_____ Paying your electric bill that is due next week

_____ Checking out what your friends are doing on Facebook

_____ Getting your haircut

_____ Making an appointment with your academic advisor to register for classes

_____ Playing your favorite video game

_____ Making it to your doctor's appointment

_____ Helping your sister plan her wedding

_____ Picking up your child's prescription from the pharmacy

_____ Studying for your final exams

_____ Calling your cousin to catch up on family gossip

_____ Making reservations for your vacation

_____ Going to see the hot new movie that has come out

_____ Getting your oil changed in your car

_____ Getting your car washed

Case Study

Procrastination: The Vicious Cycle

Darcy has a major paper due at the end of the term. It's now past midterm and she still hasn't started to work on her paper. She tells herself, "I should have started sooner."

However, Darcy continues to postpone starting her work on the paper and begins to feel anxious and guilty about it. To relieve her growing anxiety and guilt, she starts doing other tasks instead, such as cleaning her room and returning e-mails. This makes Darcy feel a little better because these tasks keep her busy, take her mind off the term paper, and give her the feeling that at least she's getting something accomplished. Time continues to pass; the deadline for the paper is growing dangerously close. Darcy now finds herself in the position of having lots of work to do and little time in which to do it.

Source: Burka & Yuen (1983)

Discussion Questions

1. What do you predict Darcy will do at this point?

2. Why did you make the above prediction?

3. What grade do you think Darcy will receive on her paper?

4. What do you think Darcy will do on the next term paper she's assigned?

5. Other than starting sooner, what recommendations would you have for Darcy (and other procrastinators like her) to break this cycle of procrastination and prevent it from happening repeatedly?

Chapter 3 Reflection

Name: ______________________

Looking back on suggestions from this chapter, what are three things you can do to start managing your time better?

1.

2.

3.

Explain how you are going to make this happen.*

For Further Consideration

DMACC Technology and Websites

***Use this page to take notes about DMACC Technology

DMACC email address

- Username and password
- Importance of using your DMACC account
- Using Microsoft Outlook
- Sending an attachment to the instructor
- Finding instructors in the address book

Blackboard

- Completing the online orientation
- Finding the syllabus
- Finding materials for the course
- Participating in discussion questions/forums
- Completing tests/quizzes

Course Companion Sites

- Generic discussion

Web Information System

- Taking ALEKS Math assessment and placement
- Locating unofficial transcripts
- Locating grades
- Completing a degree audit using Degree Works
- Viewing Financial Aid
- Registering for courses

Tech Support

- Locating the online site

Accessing the network at DMACC and at home: P-Drive

DMACC Websites: Locating College Information

- Academic Calendar/Finals Schedule
- Advising
- Announcements/Events
- Campus Recreation
- Catalog
- Courses/Programs
- Counseling
- Credit Schedule
- Disability Services
- Financial Aid
- Registrar/Registration Dates
- Security Services
- Student Health Services
- Tobacco Free Campus
- Tuition and Fees

Accessing the online DMACC Handbook

- To locate college procedures
- To locate general information***

SQ4R Worksheet

***Your Name:

Selection Title/Chapter:

Author(s):

1. **Survey**: Look at the title, visuals, questions, excerpts, headings and sub-headings. Afterward, answer the questions below.

What do I already know about the topics?	What do I expect to learn?

2. **Question**: Create questions based on your survey of the text. If there are headings, turn them into questions. Include *at least three* below to help focus your attention as you read.

A.
B.
C.
D.
E.

3. **Read** and **Record** (Annotate): Read the selection thoroughly, highlight, and make note of important points, associations, and unfamiliar terms. Complete the chart using **your own words**. Provide a sketch and/or explanation of the visuals. Use and attach a separate sheet if needed.

Page and Paragraph #	Vocabulary Terms	Notes and Definitions	Visuals

(*Continued*)

(*Continued*)

4. **Recite**: Answer your questions from step two.

a.
b.
c.
d.
e.

5. **Review and Reflect**: Check your memory by verbalizing the above information. Below, write a summary **in your own words** of what you have read, connecting the content ideas. Additionally, write a brief reflection including your personal response to the reading (use "I" and make connections to your own experiences, ask more questions, respond to the text, and consider anything you were reminded of or visualized while reading).***

Summary:

Reflection:

Adapted from Florida Online Reading Professional Development. (n.d.). *SQ4R*. Retrieved from the Marco Island Charter Middle School website at http://micms.org/SQ4R.pdf

Financial Literacy

4

Managing Money and Minimizing Debt: Balancing Saving, Spending, Learning, and Earning

THOUGHT STARTER *Journal Entry* 4.1

*Complete the following sentence with the first thought that comes to your mind:

For me, money is . . .

____

____

____

____

____

____

LEARNING GOAL

To become more self-aware, knowledgeable, and strategic with respect to managing your money and financing your college education.

In addition to managing time, a personal resource you need to manage to be successful in college (and life) is money. Managing time and managing money have a lot in common. Both require self-awareness of how these resources are spent; both can be saved, or else you could run out of either one of them. Poor time management can also cost people money. For example, a report from H & R Block indicates that procrastinating on filing tax returns costs Americans an average of $400 a year due to errors resulting from last-minute rushing to meet the deadline (Kasper, 2004). How you spend your time and money often represents the true test of what really matters to you and what you truly value.

Beginning college often means the beginning of greater personal independence and greater demands for economic self-sufficiency, critical thinking about consumerism, and effective management of personal finances. The importance of money management for college students is growing for two major reasons. One is the rising cost of a college education, which is causing more students to work while in college and to work more hours per week (Levine & Cureton, 1998). The rising cost of a college education is also requiring students to make more complex decisions about what options (or combination of options) they will use to meet their college expenses. Unfortunately, research indicates that many students today are not choosing financial strategies that contribute most effectively to their educational success in college and their long-term financial success after college (King, 2005).

A second reason money management is growing in importance for college students is the availability and convenience of credit cards. For students today, credit cards are easy to get, easy to use, and easy to abuse. College students can do everything right, such as getting solid grades, getting involved on campus, and getting work experience before graduating, but a poor credit history due to over use of credit cards in college can reduce students' chances of obtaining credit after college and their chances of being hired after graduation. Credit reporting agencies or bureaus collect information about how well you make credit card payments and report your credit score to credit card companies and banks. Potential employers will check your credit score as an indicator or predictor of how responsible you will be as an employee because of a statistical relationship between using a credit card responsibly and being a responsible employee. Thus, being irresponsible with credit while you're in college can affect your ability to land a job after (or during) college. Your credit score report will also affect your likelihood of qualifying for car loans and home loans, as well as your ability to rent an apartment (Pratt, 2008).*

"If we command our wealth, we shall be rich and free; if our wealth commands us, we are poor indeed."

—Edmund Burke, 18th-century author, political philosopher, and supporter of the American Revolution

Furthermore, accumulating high levels of debt while in college is associated with higher levels of student stress (Nelson, et al., 2008), lower academic performance (Susswein, 1995), and greater risk of withdrawing from college (Ring, 1997). On the positive side of the ledger, studies show that when college students learn to use effective money management strategies (such as those discussed below), they can reduce unnecessary spending, minimize accumulation of debt, and lower their overall level of stress (Health & Soll, 1996; Kidwell & Turrisi, 2004; Walker, 1996).

Student Perspective

"My money-management skills are poor. If I have money, I will spend it unless somebody takes it away from me. I am the kind of person who lives from paycheck to paycheck."

—First-year student

Strategies for Managing Money Effectively

Developing Financial Self-Awareness

*Developing any good habit begins with the critical first step of self-awareness. Developing the habit of effective money management begins with awareness of your cash flow—the amount of money you have flowing in and flowing out. As illustrated in Figure 4.1, cash flow can be tracked by:

- Watching how much money you have coming in (income) versus going out (expenses or expenditures); and
- Watching how much money you have accumulated but not spent (savings) versus how much money you've borrowed but not paid back (debt).

FIGURE 4.1

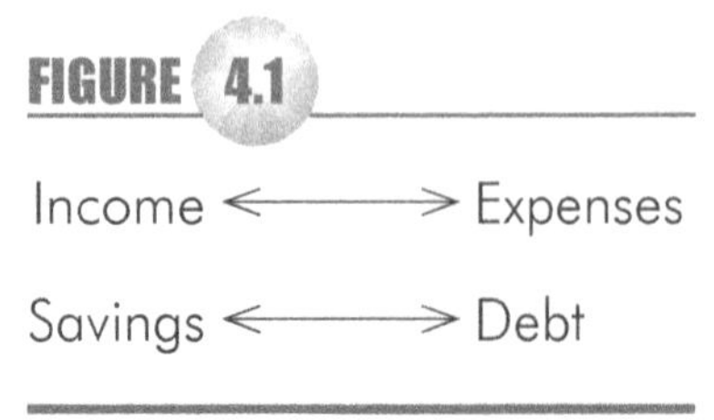

Two Key Avenues of Cash Flow

Income for college students typically comes from one or more of the following sources:

- Scholarships or grants, which don't have to be paid back
- Loans, which must be repaid
- Salary earned from part-time or full-time work
- Personal savings
- Gifts or other forms of monetary support from parents and other family members

Your sources of expenses or expenditures may be classified into three categories:

1. **Basic needs or essential necessities.** Expenses that tend to be fixed because you cannot do without them (e.g., expenses for food, housing, tuition, textbooks, phone, transportation to and from school, and health-related costs).

2. **Incidentals or extras.** Expenses that tend to be flexible because spending money on them is optional or discretionary (i.e., you choose to spend at your own discretion or judgment); these expenses typically include:
   a. Money spent on entertainment, enjoyment, or pleasure (e.g., music, movies, and spring-break vacations); and
   b. Money spent primarily for reasons of promoting personal status or self-image (e.g., buying expensive brand-name products, fashionable clothes, jewelry, and other personal accessories).
3. **Emergency expenses.** Unpredicted, unforeseen, or unexpected costs (e.g., money paid for doctor visits and medicine resulting from illnesses or accidents, your car breaking down).

Think About It — *Journal Entry* 4.2

1. What do you estimate to be your two or three most expensive incidentals (optional purchases)?

   ____

   ____

   ____

2. Do you think you should reduce these expenses or eliminate them altogether? Explain.

   ____

   ____

   ____

3. How can you do this?

   ____

   ____

   ____

Developing a Money-Management Plan

Once you're aware of the amount of money you have coming in (and from what sources) and the amount of money you're spending (and for what reasons), the next step is to develop a plan for managing your cash flow. The bottom line is to ensure that the money coming in (income) is equal to or greater than the money going out (expenses). If the amount of money you're spending exceeds the amount you have coming in, you're "in the red" or have negative cash flow.

Student *Perspective*

"I keep track of my money on Excel."

—First-year student

Strategic Selection and Use of Financial Tools for Tracking Cash Flow

Several financial tools or instruments can be used to track your cash flow and manage your money. These cash-flow instruments include:

- Checking accounts
- Credit cards
- Debit cards

Checking Account

Long before credit cards were created, a checking account was the method most people used to keep track of their money. Checking accounts are now accessed with debit cards; although, checks are often still used to pay rent.

A checking account may be obtained from a bank or credit union; its typical costs include a deposit ($20 to $25) to open the account, a monthly service fee (e.g., $10), and fees for checks. Some banks charge customers a service fee based on the number of checks written, which is a good option if you don't plan to write many checks each month. If you maintain a high enough balance of money deposited in your account, the bank may not charge any extra fees, and if you're able to maintain an even higher balance, the bank may also pay you interest—known as an interest-bearing checking account.

Look for a checking account that does not charge you fees for ATM transactions but provides this as a free service with your account. Also, look for a checking account that doesn't charge you if your balance drops below a certain minimum figure.

Strategies for Using Checking Accounts Effectively

- Whenever you spend money from your account immediately subtract its amount from your balance—i.e., the amount of money remaining in your account—to determine your new balance.
- Keep a running balance or monitor your account to ensure that you know exactly how much money you have in your account at all times. This will reduce the risk that you'll spend more money than you have in your account. If you do overspend, you'll have to pay a charge to the bank and possibly to the business that you attempted to pay.
- Double-check your monthly statement you receive from the bank. Be sure to include the service charges your bank makes to your account that appear on your monthly statement. This practice will make it easier to track errors—on either your part or the bank's part. (Banks can and do make mistakes occasionally.)

Advantages of a Checking Account

A checking account has several advantages:

- You have access to cash at almost any time through an ATM.
- It allows you to review your online bank record of income and expenses.
- A properly managed checking account can serve as a good credit reference for future loans and purchases.

Credit Card (e.g., MasterCard®, Visa®, or Discover®)

A credit card is basically money loaned to you by the credit card company that issues you the card, which you pay back to the company monthly. You can pay the whole bill or a portion of the bill each month—as long as some minimum payment is made. However, for any remaining (unpaid) portion of your bill, you are charged a high interest rate, which is usually about 18 percent. This results in your paying much more for the item than it is actually worth.

Strategies for Selecting a Credit Card

If you decide to use a credit card, pay attention to its annual percentage rate (APR). This is the interest rate you pay for previously unpaid monthly balances, and it can vary depending on the credit card company. Credit card companies also vary in terms of their annual service fees. You will likely find companies that charge higher interest rates tend to charge lower annual fees, and vice versa. As a general rule, if you expect to pay the full balance every month, you're probably better off choosing a credit card that does not charge you an annual service fee. On the other hand, if you think you'll need more time to make the full monthly payments, you may be better off with a credit card company that offers a low interest rate.

Another feature that differentiates one credit card company from another is whether or not you're allowed a "grace period"—i.e., a certain period of time after you receive your monthly statement during which you can pay back the company without paying added interest fees. Some companies may allow you a grace period of a full month, while others may provide none and begin charging interest immediately after you fail to pay on the bill's due date.

Credit cards may also differ in terms of their credit limit (a.k.a. a credit line or line of credit), which refers to the maximum amount of money the credit card company will make available to you. If you are a new customer, most companies will set a credit limit beyond which you will not be granted any additional credit.

Advantages of a Credit Card

If a credit card is used wisely, it has some key advantages as a money-management tool. Its features can provide the following advantages:

- It helps you track your spending habits because the credit card company sends you a monthly statement that includes an itemized list of all your card-related purchases. This list provides you with a paper trail of *what* you purchased that month and *when* you purchased it.
- It provides the convenience of making purchases online, which may save you some time and money that would otherwise be spent traveling to and from stores.
- It allows access to cash whenever and wherever you need it, because any bank or ATM that displays your credit card's symbol will give you cash up to a certain limit, for a transaction fee. Keep in mind that some credit card companies charge a higher interest rate for cash advances than purchases.
- It enables you to establish a personal credit history. If you use a credit card responsibly, you can establish a good credit history that can be used later in life for big-ticket purchases such as a car or home. In effect, responsible use of a credit

card shows others from whom you wish to seek credit (borrow money) that you're financially responsible.

Remember

Do not buy into the belief that the only way you can establish a good credit history is by using a credit card. It's not your only option; you can establish a good credit history through responsible use of a checking account and by paying your bills on time.

Strategies for Using Credit Cards Responsibly

While there may be advantages to using a credit card, you only reap those advantages if you use your card strategically. If not, the advantages of a credit card will be quickly and greatly outweighed by its disadvantages. Listed here are some key strategies for using a credit card in a way that maximizes its advantages and minimizes its disadvantages.

1. **Use a credit card only as a convenience for making purchases and tracking the purchases you make; do not use it as a tool for obtaining a long-term loan.** A credit card's main money-management advantage is that it allows you to make purchases with plastic instead of cash. The credit card allows you the convenience of not carrying around cash and enables you to receive a monthly statement of your purchases from the credit card company, which makes it easier for you to track and analyze your spending habits.

   The "credit" provided by a credit card should be seen simply as a short-term loan that must be paid back at the end of every month.

Remember

Do not use credit cards for long-term credit or long-term loans because their interest rates are outrageously high. Paying such a high rate of interest for a loan represents an ineffective (and irresponsible) money-management strategy.

2. **Limit yourself to one card.** The average college student has 2.8 credit cards (United College Marketing Service, as cited in Pratt, 2008). More than one credit card just means more accounts to keep track of and more opportunities to accumulate debt. You don't need additional credit cards from department stores, gas stations, or any other profit-making business because they duplicate what your personal credit card already does (plus they charge extremely high interest rates and fees for late payments).
3. **Pay off your balance each month in full and on time.** If you pay the full amount of your bill each month, this means that you're using your credit card effectively to obtain an interest-free, short-term (one-month) loan. You're just paying principal—the total amount of money borrowed and nothing more. However, if your payment is late or you do not pay the full balance and you need to pay interest, you end up paying more for the items you purchased than their actual ticket price. For instance, if you have an unpaid balance of $500 on your monthly credit card bill for merchandise purchased the previous month and you are charged the typical 18 percent credit card interest rate, you end up paying $590: $500 (merchandise) + $90 (18 percent interest to the credit card company).

"I need to pay attention to my balance more closely and actually allot certain amounts for certain things."

—First-year student

Credit card companies make their money or profit from the interest they collect from cardholders who do not pay back their credit in full or on time. Just as procrastinating about doing your work is a poor time-management habit, procrastinating about paying your credit card bills is a poor money-management habit that can cost you dearly in the long run because of the high interest rate you pay.

Pay your total balance on time and avoid paying these huge interest rates to credit card companies, which allow them to get rich at your expense. If you cannot pay the total amount owed at the end of the month, pay off as much of it as you possibly can, rather than making the minimum monthly payment. If you keep making only the minimum payment each month and continue using your credit card, you'll begin to pile up huge amounts of debt from the high interest rates.

Student Perspective

"What I don't do that I know I should do is pay my bills on time, i.e., cell phone and credit cards."

—First-year student

"You'll never get your credit card debt paid off if you keep charging on your card and make only the minimum monthly payment. Paying only the minimum is like using a Dixie cup to bail water from a sinking boat."

—Eric Tyson, financial counselor and national bestselling author of *Personal Finance for Dummies* (2003)

Remember

If you keep charging on your credit card while you have an unpaid balance or debt, you no longer have a grace period to pay back your charges: instead, interest is charged immediately on all your purchases.

Snapshot Summary

4.1 Credit Cardholders' Bill of Rights Act of 2009

Congress passed legislation in 2009 that enacted certain protections for consumers who use credit cards. Here are the specific reforms that affect college students:

- Creditors are forbidden from offering credit to consumers under the age of 18 (unless they are emancipated under state law, or the consumer's parent or legal guardian is the primary account holder).
- College students without a cosigner will have their credit line limited to the greater amount of 20 percent of their annual gross income or $500. The collective amount of credit available on all credit cards will be limited to 30 percent of the student's annual gross income.
- Creditors are not allowed to open a credit-card account for a college student who does not have a verifiable annual gross income or already has a credit-card account with that creditor or any of its affiliates (Chan, 2009).

Think About It — Journal Entry 4.3

1. Do you have a credit card? Do you have more than one?

2. If you have at least one credit card, do you pay off your entire balance each month?

3. If you don't pay off your entire balance each month, what would you say is your average unpaid balance per month?

4. What changes would you have to make in your money-management habits to be able to pay off your entire balance each month?

Debit Card

"Never spend your money before you have it."

—Thomas Jefferson, third president of the United States and founder of the University of Virginia

A debit card looks almost identical to a credit card (e.g., it has a MasterCard or Visa logo), but it works differently. When you use a debit card, money is immediately taken out or subtracted from your checking account. Thus, you're only using money that's already in your account (rather than borrowing money), and you don't receive a bill at the end of the month. If you attempt to purchase something with a debit card that costs more than the amount of money you have in your account, your card will not allow you to do so. A debit card will not permit you to pay out any money that is not in your account. Like a check or ATM withdrawal, a purchase made with a debit card should immediately be subtracted from your balance.

Like a credit card, a major advantage of the debit card is that it provides you with the convenience of "plastic"; unlike a credit card, it prevents you from spending beyond your means and accumulating debt. For this reason, financial advisors often recommend using a debit card rather than a credit card (Knox, 2004; Tyson, 2003).

Snapshot Summary

4.2 Financial Literacy: Understanding the Language of Money Management

As you can tell from the number of financial terms used in this chapter, there is a fiscal vocabulary or language that we need to master in order to fully understand our financial options and transactions. In other words, we need to become *financially literate.* As you read the financial terms listed below, place a checkmark next to any term whose meaning you didn't already know.

Account. A formal business arrangement in which a bank provides financial services to a customer (e.g., checking account or savings account).

Annual percentage rate (APR). The interest rate that must be paid when monthly credit card balances are not paid in full.

Balance. The amount of money in a person's account or the amount of unpaid debt.

Bounced check. A check written for a greater amount of money than the amount contained in a personal checking account, which typically requires the person to pay a charge to the bank and possibly to the business that attempted to cash the bounced check.

Budget. A plan for coordinating income and expenses to ensure that sufficient money is available to cover personal expenses or expenditures.

Cash flow. Amount of money flowing in (income) and flowing out (expenses). "Negative cash flow" occurs when the amount of money going out exceeds the amount coming in.

Credit. Money obtained with the understanding that it will be paid back, either with or without interest.

Credit line (a.k.a. credit limit). The maximum amount of money (credit) made available to a borrower.

Debt. Amount of money owed.

Default. Failure to meet a financial obligation (e.g., a student who fails to repay a college loan "defaults" on that loan).

Deferred student payment plan. A plan that allows student borrowers to temporarily defer or postpone loan payments for some acceptable reason (e.g., to pursue an internship or to do volunteer work after college).

Estimated family contribution (EFC). The amount of money the government has determined a family can contribute to the educational costs of the family member who is attending college.

Fixed interest rate. A loan with an interest rate that will remain the same for the entire term of the loan.

Grace period. The amount of time after a monthly credit card statement has been issued during which the credit card holder can pay back the company without paying added interest fees.

Grant. Money received that doesn't have to be repaid.

Gross income. Income generated before taxes and other expenses are deducted.

Insurance premium. The amount paid in regular installments to an insurance company to remain insured.

Interest. The amount of money paid to a customer for deposited money (as in a bank account) or money paid by a customer for borrowed money (e.g., interest on a loan). Interest is usually calculated as a percentage of the total amount of money deposited or borrowed.

Interest-bearing account. A bank account that earns interest if the customer keeps a sufficiently large sum of money in the bank.

Loan consolidation. Consolidating (combining) separate student loans into one larger loan to make the process of tracking, budgeting, and repayment easier. Loan consolidation typically requires the borrower to pay slightly more interest.

Loan premium. The amount of money loaned without interest.

Merit-based scholarship. Money awarded to a student on the basis of performance or achievement that doesn't have to be repaid.

Need-based scholarship. Money awarded to a student on the basis of financial need that doesn't have to be repaid.

Net income. Money earned or remaining after all expenses and taxes have been paid.

Principal. The total amount of money borrowed or deposited, not counting interest.

Variable interest rate. An interest rate on a loan that can vary or be changed by the lender.

Yield. Revenue or profit produced by an investment beyond the original amount invested. For example, the higher lifetime income and other monetary benefits acquired from a college education that exceed the amount of money invested in or spent on a college education.

Think About It — *Journal Entry* 4.4

1. Which of the terms in the above list were new to you?

____

____

2. Do any of these terms apply to your current financial situation or money-management plans? Explain.

____

____

____

____

____

____

Sources of Income for Financing Your College Education

Free Application for Federal Student Aid (FAFSA)

The Free Application for Federal Student Aid (FAFSA) is the application used by the U.S. Department of Education to determine aid eligibility for students. A formula is used to determine each student's estimated family contribution (EFC), which is the amount of money the government has determined a family can contribute to the educational costs of the student. No fee is charged to complete the application, and you should complete it annually to determine your eligibility to receive financial aid, whether you believe you are eligible or not. Apply online at www.fafsa.gov. The DMACC school code is 004589.

Scholarships

Scholarships are available from many sources, including the institution you choose to attend. They are awarded based on various criteria that may include a written essay, ACT or SAT scores, and high school grade point average (GPA). In addition to academic scholarships, scholarships are awarded based on organizations you may have been a part of, race or ethnicity, the region of the country you live in, athletics, artistic talents, and so on. It is important to remember that all scholarships are competitive and deadlines are observed by the awarding agencies or institutions. Be aware of the application material deadlines and submit your materials well in advance of these deadlines.

You should contact the Financial Aid Office to find available scholarships. You can also conduct an Internet search to find many sites that offer scholarship information (like www.fastweb.com), but it is important to remember that you should not enter credit card or bank account information on any site.

Grants

Grants are considered to be gift aid, which typically does not have to be repaid. About two-thirds of all college students receive grant aid, which, on average, reduces their tuition bills by more than half. The Federal Pell Grant is the largest grant program; it provides need-based aid to low-income undergraduate students. The amount of the grant depends on criteria such as: (1) the anticipated contribution of the family to the student's education (EFC), (2) the cost of the postsecondary institution that the student is attending, and (3) the enrollment status of the student (part-time or full-time). Even though grants do not need to be paid back, students must maintain certain academic standards to remain eligible to receive their grant money.

Veterans' Benefits

If you are currently a veteran, you may be eligible for the GI Bill benefits.

What Is the Montgomery GI Bill–Active Duty?

The Montgomery GI Bill–Active Duty, called MGIB for short, provides up to 36 months of education benefits to eligible veterans. Benefits may include, but are not limited to, tuition and fees, a housing allowance, and a books and supplies stipend. Veterans must maintain certain academic standards to receive the benefits. Visit the Office of Veterans Affairs to get more information.

Loans

Student loans need to be repaid once a student graduates from college (or stops out for a certain period of time). To apply for the types of loans listed below, you must complete the FAFSA form.

- **The Federal Subsidized Stafford Loan** is available to students enrolled at least half-time and has a fixed interest rate that's established each year on July 1. The federal government pays the interest on the loan while the student is enrolled. The repayment for this loan begins six months after a student is no longer enrolled half-time.
- **The Federal Unsubsidized Stafford Loan** is a loan that's not based on need and has the same interest rate as the Federal Subsidized Stafford Loan. Students are responsible for paying the interest on this loan while they're enrolled in college. The loan amount limits for Stafford loans are based on the classification of the student (e.g., freshman or sophomore).

Be responsible with your student loans and only take the loan out in the amount that you need! (You don't have to take the full amount.)

Keep in mind that federal and state regulations require that if you are receiving financial aid, you must maintain "satisfactory academic progress." In most cases this means that you must do the following:

1. **Maintain a satisfactory GPA of 2.0.** Your entire academic record will be reviewed, even if you have paid for any of the classes with your own resources.
2. **Make satisfactory academic progress.** Your academic progress will be evaluated at the end of each semester. You will need to successfully pass a certain percentage of the courses you take (67%).
3. **Complete a degree or certificate program within an established period of time.** Check with the Financial Aid Office for details.

Snapshot Summary

4.3 Federal Loan versus Private Loan: A Critical Difference

Private loans and federal loans are totally different and unrelated types of loans. Here are the key differences:

Federal loans have fixed interest rates that are comparatively low.

Private loans have variable interest rates that are very high and can go higher at any time.

Source: Kristof (2008).

Note: Despite the high cost of private loans, they are the fastest-growing type of loans taken out by college students, largely because of aggressive, misleading, and sometimes irresponsible or unethical advertising on loan-shopping Web sites. Students sometimes think they're getting a federal loan only to find out later they have taken on a more expensive private loan.

Remember

Private lenders are like credit card companies: they charge extremely high interest rates, and they can go even higher at any time. They should not be used as a primary loan to help pay for college; they should only be used as a last resort when no other options are available for covering your college expenses.

Student Loans and Credit Scores

Be aware that student loans are a type of loan and can have an effect on your credit score. For many community college students, credit is now a reality and will be for the rest of you when you graduate from college. College loans can hurt or enhance your credit score depending on how you treat the loan.

Your credit score is a number that tells lenders and creditors how financially responsible you are. It assists them in judging the level of risk you present to them as a borrower. This score will dictate how easily you can obtain credit cards, loans, houses, rent an apartment, etc.

Thus, having loans (including student loans) can be good or bad and sometimes both, depending on how you use them and how you repay them. Making your student loan payments in full and on time each month will assist your credit score and helps you to establish a good credit history. However, missing payments or not paying at all can be devastating to your credit and credit score.

Salary Earnings

If you find yourself relying on your salary to pay for college tuition, check with your employer to see whether the company offers tuition reimbursement. You should also check with your campus to determine whether payment plans are available for tuition costs. These plans may differ in terms of how much is due, deadlines for payments, and how any remaining debt owed to the institution is dealt with at the end of the term. You may find that the institution you are attending will not allow you to register for the following term until the previous term is completely paid for.

Research shows that when students work on campus (versus off campus) they are more likely to succeed in college (Astin, 1993; Pascarella & Terenzini, 1991, 2005). This is probably because students become more connected to the college when they work on campus (Tinto, 1993) and because on-campus employers are more flexible than off-campus employers in allowing students to meet their academic commitments while they are employed. For instance, campus employers are more willing to schedule students' work hours around their class schedules and allow students to modify their work schedules when their academic workload increases (e.g., midterm and finals). Thus, we strongly encourage you to seek on-campus employment and capitalize on its capacity to promote your academic success.

Think About It — Journal Entry 4.5

Do you need to work part-time to meet your college expenses?

If yes, do you have to work more than 15 hours per week to make ends meet?

If yes, is there anything you can do to change that?

Monetary Gifts from Family or Friends

Money received as a gift from family or friends who are supporting your education should be used wisely. Although necessities such as food and transportation support your academic goals, money given to you by friends or family members should be used to pay for tuition and textbooks first. Remaining funds can be used for other expenses.

Financial Tools for Saving Money

If you're taking in more money than you're spending, you are saving money, and you can invest the money you've saved in an account that will allow you to earn interest on your savings. This account can help you build up a cash reserve that can be used for future needs or used immediately for emergencies.

"A penny saved is a penny earned."

—Benjamin Franklin, 18th-century inventor, newspaper writer, and signer of the *Declaration of Independence*

Savings Account

A savings account can be opened at virtually any bank and will earn you interest on the money placed in your account. Usually, no minimum amount of money needs to be deposited to open a savings account, and you don't need to maintain a minimum amount of money in the account.

Money-Saving Strategies and Habits

The ultimate goal of money management is to save money and avoid debt. Here are some specific strategies for accomplishing this goal:

1. **Prepare a personal budget.** A budget is simply a plan for coordinating income and expenses to ensure that your cash flow leaves you with sufficient money to cover your expenses. A budget helps you maintain awareness of your financial state or condition; it enables you to be your own accountant by keeping an accurate account of your money.

Student Perspective

"I shouldn't buy random stuff (like hair dye) and other stuff when I don't need it."

—First-year student

Just like managing and budgeting your time, the first step in managing and budgeting your money involves prioritizing. In the case of money management, prioritizing first involves identifying your most important expenses—necessities that are indispensable and that you must have to survive, as opposed to incidentals that are dispensable because you can live without them.

Some people can easily confuse essentials (needs) and incidentals (wants). For instance, if a piece of merchandise happens to be on sale, what this means is that it may be a great bargain for consumers who may want to purchase it; however, it doesn't mean that you need to consume (purchase) it before somebody else does.

Remember

Remaining consciously aware of the distinction between life's essentials *that must be purchased and* incidentals *that may or may not be purchased is an important first step toward preparing an effective budget that enables you to save money and escape debt.*

Author's Experience

Since I was a student who had to manage my own college expenses, I became an expert in managing small budgets. The first thing I always took care of was my tuition. I was going to go to school even if I starved. The next thing I budgeted for was my housing, then food (since I worked in a grocery store, someone would feed me), and then transportation and clothing needs. If I ran out of money, I would then work additional hours if it did not interfere with my academics. I clearly understood that I was working to make a better life for myself and not to just have money to spend at that time. To be successful, I had to be a great money manager because there was so little of it to manage. This took a lot of focus and strong will, but did it ever pay off? Absolutely.

Aaron Thompson

Student Perspective

"I need to save money and not shop so much and impulse buy."

—First-year student

You need to be aware of whether you're spending money on *impulse* and out of *habit* or out of need and after thoughtful reflection. The truth is that humans spend money for a host of psychological reasons (conscious or subconscious), many of which are unrelated to actual need. For example, they spend to build their self-esteem or self-image, to combat personal boredom, or to seek stimulation and an emotional "high" (Furnham & Argyle, 1998). Furthermore, people can become obsessed with spending money, shop compulsively, and become addicted to purchasing products. Just as Alcoholics Anonymous (AA) exists as a support group for alcoholics, Debtors Anonymous exists as a support group for shopaholics and includes a 12-step recovery program similar to AA.

2. **Make all your bills visible and pay them off as soon as possible.** When your bills are visible, they become memorable and you're less likely to forget to pay them or forget to pay them on time. To increase the visibility of your bill payments, keep a financial calendar on which you record key fiscal deadlines for the academic year (e.g., due dates for tuition payments, residential bills, and financial aid applications). Also, try to get in the habit of paying a bill as soon as you open it and have it in your hands, rather than setting it aside and running the risk of forgetting to pay it or losing it. Most companies will charge a late fee if you don't pay your bill on time.
3. **Live within your means.** This strategy is simple: don't purchase what you can't afford. If you are spending more money than you're taking in, it means you're living *beyond* your means. To begin living *within* your means, you have two options:
   a. Decrease your expenses (e.g., reduce your spending); or
   b. Increase your income.

Since most college students are already working while attending college (Orszag, Orszag, & Whitmore, 2001) and working so many hours that it's interfering with their academic performance or progress (King, 2005), the best option for most college students who find themselves in debt is to reduce their spending and begin living within their means.

Author's Experience

When I was young, my mom was always cutting out coupons and looking for what was on sale. If it was not on sale or she did not have a coupon, she usually did not buy it. As a child, it drove me nuts and I thought she was crazy! Now that I am older, I find I am a lot like her when it comes to money. I am always looking for coupons and I rarely buy anything if it is not on sale. Even when I do buy something, I stop and think, "Do I really need this?" or "How much use will I get out of this?" It is because of this that I am able to save up some of my money and do things I really enjoy (season tickets for football games, traveling, etc.), and I am thankful my mom taught me how to save.

Julie McLaughlin

"We choose to spend more money than we have today. Choose debt, or choose freedom, it's your choice."

—Bill Pratt, *Extra Credit: The 7 Things Every College Student Needs to Know About Credit, Debt, and Cash* (2008)

Think About It — *Journal Entry* 4.6

Are you working for money while attending college?

____

If you're not working, are you sacrificing anything that you want or need because you lack money?

____

If you are working,

1. How many hours per week do you currently work?

   ____

2. Do you think that working is interfering with your academic performance or progress? Explain.

   ____

   ____

   ____

"It is preoccupation with possessions, more than anything else, that prevents us from living freely and nobly."

—Bertrand Russell, British philosopher and mathematician

3. Would it be possible for you to reduce the number of weekly hours you now work and still be able to make ends meet?

   ____

   ____

   ____

4. **Economize.** By being intelligent consumers who use critical thinking skills when purchasing products, you can be frugal or thrifty without compromising the quality of your purchases. For example, you can pay less to see the same movie in the late afternoon than you would pay at night. Also, why pay more for brand-name products that are the same as products with a different name? Why pay 33 percent more for Advil® or Tylenol® when the same amount of pain-relieving ingredient (ibuprofen or acetaminophen) is contained in generic brands? Often, what you're paying for when you buy brand-name products is all the advertising these companies pay to the media and to celebrities to publicly promote their products. (That's why people instantly recognize them as familiar brand-name products.)

Remember

Advertising creates product familiarity, not product quality. The more money manufacturers pay for advertising and creating a well-known brand, the more money you pay for the product—not necessarily because you're acquiring a product of higher quality, but most often because you're covering its high cost of advertising.

5. **Downsize. Cut down or cut out spending for products that you don't need.** Don't engage in conspicuous consumption just to "keep up with the Joneses" (your neighbors or friends), and don't allow peer pressure to determine your spending habits. Let your spending habits reflect your ability to think critically rather than your tendency to conform socially.
6. **Live with others rather than living alone.** Although you lose privacy when you share living quarters with others, you save money; if you enjoy the company of those you live with, it also has social benefits.
7. **Give gifts of time rather than money.** Spending money on gifts for family, friends, and romantic partners is not the only way to show that you care. The point of gift giving is not to show others you aren't cheap or to show off your lavish spending skills. Instead, show off your social sensitivity by doing something special or making something meaningful for them. Gifts of time and kindness can often be more personal and more special than store-bought gifts.

Author's Experience

When my wife (Mary) and I were first dating, she was aware that I was trying to gain weight because I was on the thin side. (All right, I was skinny.) One day when I came home from school, I found this hand-delivered package in front of my apartment door. I opened it up and there was a homemade loaf of whole wheat bread made from scratch by Mary. That gift didn't cost her much money, but she took the time to do it and remembered to do something that was important to me (gaining weight), which really touched me; it's a gift I've never forgotten. Since I eventually married Mary and we're still happily married, I guess you could say that inexpensive loaf of bread was the "gift that kept on giving."

Joe Cuseo

8. **Develop your own set of money-saving strategies and habits.** You can save money by starting to do little things that eventually turn into regular money-saving habits, which can add up to big savings over time. Consider the following list of habit-forming tips for saving money that were suggested by students in a first-year seminar class:
   - Don't carry a lot of extra money in your wallet. (It's just like food: if it's easy to get to, you'll be more likely to eat it up.)
   - Shop with a list—get in, get what you need, and get out.
   - Put all your extra change in a jar.

- Put extra cash in a piggy bank that requires you to smash the piggy to get at it.
- Seal your savings in an envelope.
- Immediately get extra money into the bank (and out of your hands).
- Bring (don't buy) your lunch.
- Hide your credit card or put it in the freezer so that you don't use it on impulse.
- Use cash (instead of credit cards) because you can give yourself a set amount of cash and can clearly see how much of it you have at the start of a week and how much is left at any point during the week.
- If your employer has a direct deposit option, use it! This way your money goes directly into your account and you'll be less tempted to spend it.
- Identify wants vs. needs.
- Use Groupon, coupons, etc., whenever possible.

"The safest way to double your money is to fold it over and put it in your pocket."

—Kin Hubbard, American humorist, cartoonist, and journalist

Think About It — Journal Entry 4.7

Do you use any of the strategies on the preceding list? Which ones?

____

____

Have you developed any effective strategies that do not appear on the list? What are they?

____

____

____

____

Author's Experience

When I was four years old living in the mountains of Kentucky, it was safe for a young lad to walk the railroad tracks and roads alone. My mother knew this and would send me to the general store to buy various small items we needed for our household. Since we had little money, she was aware that we had to be cautious and only spend money on the essential necessities we needed to survive. I could only purchase items from the general store that I could carry back home by myself and the ones my mother strictly ordered me to purchase. Most of these items cost less than a dollar, and in many cases you could buy multiple items for that dollar in the early 1960s. At the store I would hand my mother's handwritten list to the owners. They would pick the items for me, and we would exchange the items for my money. On the checkout counter were jars with different kinds of candy or gum. You could buy two pieces for a penny. As a hardworking boy who was doing a good deed for his parents, I didn't think there would be any harm in rewarding myself with two pieces of candy after doing a good deed. After all, I could devour the evidence of my disobedience on my slow walk home. Upon my return, my mother, being the protector of the vault and the sergeant-of-arms in our household, would count each item I brought home to make sure I had been charged correctly. She always found that I had either been overcharged by a cent or that I had spent a cent. In those days, parents believed in behavior modification. After she gave me a scolding, she would say, "Boy, you better learn how to count your money if you're ever going to be successful in life." I learned the value of saving money and the discomfort of overspending at a young age.

Aaron Thompson

9. **When making purchases, always think in terms of their long-term total cost.** It's convenient and tempting for consumers to think in the short term ("I see it; I like it; I want it; and I want it now"). However, long-term thinking is one of the essential keys to successful money management and financial planning. Those small (monthly) installment plans that businesses offer to get you to buy expensive products may make the cost of those products appear attractive and affordable in the short run. However, when you factor in the interest rates you pay on monthly installment plans, plus the length of time (number of months) you're making installment payments, you get a more accurate picture of the product's total cost over the long run. This longer-range perspective can quickly alert you to the reality that a product's sticker price represents its partial and seemingly affordable short-term cost, but its long-term total cost is much less affordable (and perhaps out of your league).

"Ask yourself how much of your income is being eaten up by car payments. It may be time to admit you made a mistake . . . sell it [and] replace it with an older or less sporty model."

—Bill Pratt, *Extra Credit: The 7 Things Every College Student Needs to Know about Credit, Debt, and Cash* (2008)

Furthermore, the long-term price for purchases sometimes involves additional "hidden costs" that don't relate directly to the product's initial price but that must be paid for the product's long-term use. For example, the sticker price you pay for clothes does not include the hidden, long-term costs that may be involved if those clothes require dry cleaning. By just taking a moment to check the inside label, you can save yourself this hidden, long-term cost by purchasing clothes that are machine washable. Or, to use an example of a big-ticket purchase, the extra money spent to purchase a new car (instead of a used car) includes not only paying a higher sticker price but also paying the higher hidden costs of licensing and insuring the new car, as well as any interest fees if the new car was purchased on an installment plan. When you count these hidden, long-term costs in a new car's total cost, buying a good used car is a more effective money-saving strategy than buying a new one.*

Remember

Avoid buying costly items impulsively. Instead, take time to reflect on the purchase you intend to make, do a cost analysis of its hidden or long-term costs, and then integrate these invisible costs with the product's sticker price to generate an accurate synthesis and clearer picture of the product's total cost.

Long-Range Financial Planning: Financing Your College Education

**Thus far, our discussion has focused primarily on short-range and mid-range financial planning strategies that will keep you out of debt on a monthly or yearly basis. We turn now to issues involving long-term financial planning for your entire college experience. While there's no one "correct" strategy for financing a college education, certain strategies are more effective than others. Studies show that financing a college education by obtaining a student loan and working no more than 15 hours per week is an effective long-range strategy for students at all income levels. Students who use this strategy are more likely to graduate from college, graduate in less time, and graduate with higher grades than full-time college students who work part-time for more than 15 hours per week or students who work full-time and attend college part-time (King, 2002; Perna & DuBois, 2010).

Unfortunately, less than 6% of all first-year students use the college-financing strategy of borrowing money in the form of a student loan, attending college fulltime and working part time for 15 or fewer hours per week. Instead, almost 50% of first-year students choose a strategy that research indicates is the least likely to be associated with college success: borrowing nothing and trying to work more than 15 hours per week. Students who use this strategy increase their risk of lowering their grades significantly and withdrawing from college altogether (King, 2005), probably because they can't handle the academic work load required of a full-time student on top of all the hours they're working each week. Working longer hours also increases the likelihood that students switch from full-time to part-time enrollment, which delays their time to graduation and increases their risk of not graduating at all (Tinto, 2012). Thus, a good strategy for balancing learning and earning is to try to limit work for pay to 15 or fewer hours per week.

Some students decide to finance their college education by working full-time and attending college part-time. They believe it will be less expensive in the long run to attend college part-time because it will allow them to avoid any debt from student loans. However, studies show that when students use this strategy, it lengthens their time to degree completion and increases the risk that they will never complete a degree (Orszag, Orszag, & Whitmore, 2001).

Students who work more than 15 hours per week not only take longer to graduate from college, they end up losing money in the long run. The hourly pay most part-time jobs students earn while they're in college is less than half than what they'll earn from working in full-time positions as college graduates (King, 2005). Thus, the longer they take to graduate, the longer they must wait to enter higher-paying, full-time positions that a college diploma qualifies them for; this delays their opportunity to "cash in" on the monetary benefits of a college degree.

Furthermore, studies show that two out of three college students have at least one credit card and nearly one-half of students with credit cards carries an average balance of more than $2,000 per month (Nellie Mae, 2005; Sallie Mae 2009). A debt level this high is likely to force many students into working more than 15 hours a week to pay it off. ("I owe, I owe, so off to work I go.") These students often end up taking fewer courses per term so they can work more hours to pay off their credit card debt, which results in their taking longer to graduate and to start earning a college graduate's salary.

Instead of paying almost 20% interest to credit card companies for their monthly debt, these students would be better off obtaining a student loan at a much lower interest rate, which they will start paying back six months after graduation— when they'll be making more money in full-time positions as college graduates. Despite this clear advantage of student loans compared to credit-card loans, only about 25% of college students with credit cards take out student loans (King, 2002).**

Remember

Student loans are provided by the American government with the intent of helping its citizens become better educated. In contrast, for-profit businesses such as credit card companies lend students money with no intent or interest in helping them become better educated, but with the intent of helping themselves make money—from the high rates of interest they collect from students who do not pay their debt in full at the end of each month.

"Unlike a car that depreciates in value each year that you drive it, an investment in education yields monetary, social, and intellectual profit. A car is more tangible in the short term, but an investment in education (even if it means borrowing money) gives you more bang for the buck in the long run."

—Eric Tyson, financial counselor and national bestselling author of *Personal Finance for Dummies* (2003)

**Keep in mind that not all debt is bad. Debt can be good if it represents an investment in something that will appreciate with time—that is, something that will gain in value and eventually turn into profit for the investor. Purchasing a college education on credit is a good investment because you're investing in yourself and your future, which, over time, will *appreciate*—that is, increase its monetary return in the form of higher salaries and benefits accumulated over the remainder of your life.

In contrast, purchasing a new car is a bad long-term investment because it begins to *depreciate* or lose monetary value immediately after it's purchased. The instant you drive that new car off the dealer's lot, you become the proud owner of a used car that's worth much less than what you just paid for it.**

Think About It — Journal Entry 4.8

In addition to college, what might be other good long-term investments for you to make now or in the near future?

____

____

____

____

____

____

You may have heard the expression: "Time is money." One way to interpret this expression is that the more money you spend, the more time you must spend making money. College students who spend more time earning money to cover the costs of material things they want, but don't need, typically spend less time studying, complete fewer classes, and earn lower grades. You can avoid this negative cycle by viewing academic work as work that "pays" you back in terms of completed courses and higher grades. If you put in more academic time to earn more course credits in less time, you're paid back sooner by graduating sooner and beginning to earn the full-time salary of a college graduate—which will pay you about twice as much per hour than you'll earn doing part-time work without a college degree (plus additional "fringe benefits" like health insurance and paid vacation time). Furthermore, the time you put into earning higher grades in college will earn you more pay in your first full-time position after college because research shows that for students graduating in the same field, those with higher grades earn higher starting salaries (Pascarella & Terenzini, 2005).

Remember

Work for better grades now; work for better pay later.

"I invested in myself—in study, in mastering my tools, in preparation. Many a man who is putting a few dollars a week into the bank would do much better to put it into himself."

—Henry Ford, founder of Ford Motor Co. and one of the richest people of his generation

*You may need to delay your immediate material desires and consumer gratification by not purchasing high-priced products until later in life. Ultimately, financing a college education may require that you give serious thought to your current lifestyle choices and make firm decisions about what you can live without at the moment. For example, a new set of wheels or a more spacious apartment may have to wait until you graduate.

Finally, be sure you take full advantage of your Financial Aid Office during your time in college. This is the campus resource that has been designed specifically to help you finance your college education. If you are concerned about whether you are using the most effective strategy for financing your education, make an appointment of see a professional in your Financial Aid Office. Also, periodically check with this office to see whether you qualify for additional sources of income, such as:

- Part-time employment on campus;
- Low-interest loans;
- Grants; or
- Scholarships.

Keep a watchful eye out for notices posted near your Financial Aid Office about financial aid reminders, application deadlines and updates, money-management workshops, and on-campus employment.

Minimize Your Risk of Identity Theft

Identity thieves steal your personal information to make transactions or purchases in your name. This can damage your credit status and cost you time and money to restore your financial credibility. Listed below are key strategies for reducing your risk of identity theft.

- Don't share personal identity information over the phone with anyone you don't know and trust, especially your social security or credit card number.
- Don't share identity information over the phone with anyone who claims to be an Internal Revenue Service (IRS) agent and threatens you with arrest or deportation, or who requests personal information the purpose of sending you a refund. The IRS will contact you in writing if it needs anything.
- Don't respond to e-mails from anyone claiming to be from the IRS. This is always a scam because the IRS doesn't initiate contact with taxpayers by e-mail or social media to request personal or financial information. (The only legitimate communication you will receive from the IRS is through postal mail.)
- Don't click on links or open e-mail attachments from anyone unfamiliar to you. Scam artists create fake websites and send "phishing" e-mails—which are attempts to acquire personal information such as usernames, passwords, and credit card details, often using the names of trustworthy electronic sources (e.g., an Internet service provider).
- Don't enter your credit card or bank account information on any websites.
- Install firewalls and virus detection software on your computer, to protect yourself against "cyber crime."
- When using your laptop in public, shield your screen from "shoulder surfers."
- Don't carry your Social Security (SSN) card in your wallet or write it on your checks. Only give out your SSN to people you know and trust.
- Conceal your personal identification number (PIN). Don't supply it to anyone and don't keep it in your wallet.
- Shred documents containing personal information you no longer need. (Some identity thieves are "dumpster divers" who go through the garbage to get your personal information.)
- Compare your receipts with your account statements and credit card statements to be sure there are no transactions you didn't authorize. If you have an online

account, you can check your account at any time. It's a good idea to get in the habit of checking it at least once a week (e.g., every Sunday evening).
- If you believe you've been victimized by identity theft, contact your local police department and any of the following credit reporting companies to place a fraud alert.

Summary and Conclusion

The following key strategies for effectively managing money were recommended in this chapter:

- Develop financial self-awareness. Become aware of the amount of money you have flowing in and out.
- Develop a money-management plan. Ensure that the money coming in (income) is equal to or greater than the money going out (expenses).
- Use available financial tools and instruments to track your cash flow and manage your money, such as checking accounts, credit cards, charge cards, and debit cards.
- Explore all sources of income for financing your college education, including the FAFSA, scholarships, grants, loans, monetary gifts from family or friends, salary earnings, and personal savings.
- Use available financial tools for saving money, such as savings accounts and money-market accounts.
- Prepare a personal budget. A simple plan lets you coordinate income and expenses to ensure that your cash flow leaves you with sufficient money to cover your expenses. It enables you to be your own accountant by keeping an accurate account of your money.
- Make all your bills visible and pay them off quickly. When your bills are visible, you're less likely to forget to pay them on time.
- Live within your means. Don't purchase what you can't afford.
- Economize by using critical thinking skills when purchasing products. You can be frugal or thrifty without compromising quality.
- Downsize. Cut down or cut out spending for unneeded products. Let your spending habits reflect your ability to think critically rather than a tendency to be influenced by peer pressure.
- Live with others rather than living alone. Sharing translates to saving, and if you enjoy the company of those you live with, shared living quarters have social benefits.
- Give gifts of time rather than money. Gifts of time and kindness can often be more personal and more special than store-bought gifts.
- Work for better grades now; work for better pay later. Taking out a student loan and working part-time for 15 or fewer hours per week is the most effective financial strategy for students at all income levels.
- Take full advantage of your Financial Aid Office during your time in college. Check periodically with this office to see whether you qualify for additional sources of income, such as part-time employment on campus, low-interest loans, grants, or scholarships.

Managing money is a key personal resource that can promote or sabotage your success in college and in life beyond college. As with time management, if you effectively manage your money and gain control of how you spend it, you can gain greater control over the quality of your life. On the other hand, if you ignore it or abuse it, you raise your level of debt and stress and lower your level of performance. Research shows that accumulating high levels of debt while in college is associated with higher levels of stress, lower academic performance, and greater risk of withdrawing from college. However, the good news is that students who learn to use effective money-management strategies are able to reduce unnecessary spending, accumulation of debt, and stress while improving the quality of their academic performance.*

Chapter 4 Reflection

Name: ______________________

**How are you financing your college education? Do you feel this is the best way for you to pay for college? Why or why not?

Do you feel you have good or poor money management skills? Explain.

List and describe at least five principles discussed in this chapter that you can use to better manage your money.

1.

2.

3.

4.

5.

Now explain HOW you can put these principles into practice.**

1.

2.

3.

4.

5.

Exercise 1. Financial Literacy and Money Management

***Name: ____________________

Materials Required: None

Objective: To identify and define financial literacy terms and to learn tools and strategies to manage your money.

Financial literacy refers to your knowledge of financial terms, concepts and ideas. **Money management** refers to the tools and strategies you use to get or keep your financial life in order.

Part 1: The following is a list of financial terms/concepts, some of which are detailed in the chapter. Circle any that you **couldn't** explain to a friend.

APR	401K	Net/Gross Worth
Stock/Bond	Scholarships	Higher One DMACC OneCard
CD	Pell Grant	Unsubsidized Student Loan
Subsidized Student Loan	Mortgage/Loans	FICO Score
Credit Report	Credit Union	Grace period
Budget	Roth IRA	Checking Account
Savings Account	Interest Rate	Bankruptcy
Compound interest	Simple interest	Credit cards
Debt	Taxes	Income-Based Loan Forgiveness Program

Part 2: The 50/30/20 Plan

One easy way to think about managing your money is to use the 50/30/20 plan: 50% of your money should go to your needs (which includes things like housing and child care as well as anything you are required to make payments on, like car loans or cell phones, if you have a contract); 30% should go to your wants; and 20% should go to savings and/or debt repayment.

Determine for yourself (and family, if applicable) how the 50/30/20 plan would work for you:

Monthly net income: ________ ; 50% of net: ________ ; 30% of net: ________ ; 20% of net: ________

Monthly bills/expenses that should go into the 50% for needs category:

Bill/Expense Amount

Total: ________ Are you over the 50%?***

SQ4R Worksheet

Your Name:

Selection Title/Chapter:

Author(s):

1. ******Survey***: Look at the title, visuals, questions, excerpts, headings and sub-headings. Afterward, answer the questions below.

What do I already know about the topics?	What do I expect to learn?

2. **Question**: Create questions based on your survey of the text. If there are headings, turn them into questions. Include *at least three* below to help focus your attention as you read.

A.
B.
C.
D.
E.

3. **Read** and **Record** (Annotate): Read the selection thoroughly, highlight, and make note of important points, associations, and unfamiliar terms. Complete the chart using **your own words**. Provide a sketch and/or explanation of the visuals. Use and attach a separate sheet if needed.

Page and Paragraph #	Vocabulary Terms	Notes and Definitions	Visuals

(*Continued*)

(*Continued*)

4. **Recite**: Answer your questions from step two.

a.
b.
c.
d.
e.

5. **Review and Reflect**: Check your memory by verbalizing the above information. Below, write a summary **in your own words** of what you have read, connecting the content ideas. Additionally, write a brief reflection including your personal response to the reading (use "I" and make connections to your own experiences, ask more questions, respond to the text, and consider anything you were reminded of or visualized while reading).***

Summary:

Reflection:

Adapted from Florida Online Reading Professional Development. (n.d.). *SQ4R*. Retrieved from the Marco Island Charter Middle School website at http://micms.org/SQ4R.pdf

Strategic Learning and Studying

5

Learning Deeply and Remembering Longer

THOUGHT STARTER | *Journal Entry* 5.1

*What do you think is the key difference between learning and memorizing?

LEARNING GOAL

To develop a set of effective strategies for studying smarter, learning deeply, and retaining what you learn longer.

Stages in the Learning and Memory Process

Learning deeply, and remembering what you've learned, is a process that involves three key stages:

1. **Sensory input (perception).** Taking information into your brain;
2. **Memory formation (storage).** Saving that information in your brain; and
3. **Memory recall (retrieval).** Bringing information back to mind when you need it.

These three stages in the learning-memory process are summarized visually in Figure 5.1.

You can consider these stages of the learning and memory process to be similar to the way information is processed by a computer: (1) information is typed onto the screen (input), (2) the information is saved in a file (storage), and (3) the saved information is recalled and used when it's needed (retrieval). This three-stage process can be used to create a systematic set of strategies for effectively using the two major routes through which you acquire information and knowledge in college: taking notes as you listen to lectures, and reading textbooks.

FIGURE 5.1

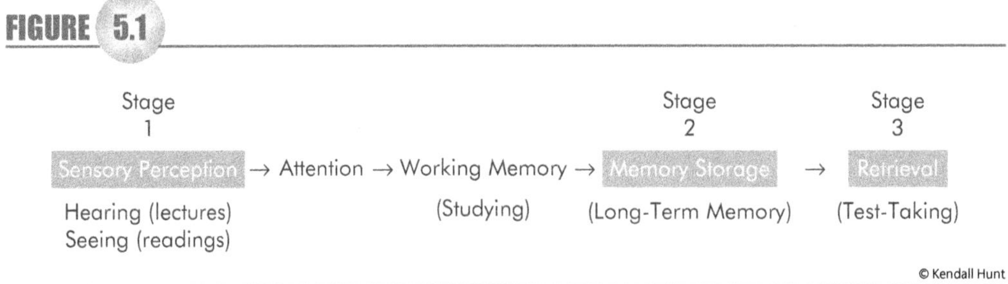

Key Stages in the Learning and Memory Process

Effective Lecture-Listening and Note-Taking Strategies

The importance of effective listening skills in the college classroom is highlighted by a study of more than 400 first-year students who were given a listening test at the start of their first term in college. At the end of their first year in college, 49 percent of those students who scored low on the listening test were on academic probation, compared to only 4.4 percent of students who scored high on the listening test. On the other hand, 68.5 percent of students who scored high on the listening test were eligible for the honors program at the end of their first year—compared to only 4.17 percent of those students who had low listening test scores (Conaway, 1982).

Think About It — Journal Entry 5.2

Do you think writing notes in class helps or hinders your ability to pay attention and learn from your instructors' lectures?

Why?

____

____

____

____

____

____

Studies show that information delivered during lectures is the number one source of test questions (and answers) on college exams (Brown, 1988; Kuhn, 1988). **When lecture information appears on a test that hasn't been recorded in the student's notes, it has only a 5 percent chance of being recalled** (Kiewra et al., 2000). Students who write notes during lectures achieve higher course grades than students who just listen to lectures (Kiewra, 1985, 2005), and students with a more complete set of notes are more likely to demonstrate higher levels of overall academic achievement (Johnstone & Su, 1994; Kiewra & DuBois, 1998; Kiewra & Fletcher, 1984).

Contrary to popular belief that writing while listening interferes with the ability to listen, students report that taking notes actually increases their attention and concentration in class (Hartley, 1998; Hartley & Marshall, 1974). Studies also show that when students write down information that's presented to them, rather than just sitting and listening to it, they're more likely to remember the most important aspects of that information when tested later (Bligh, 2000; Kiewra et al., 1991). One study discovered that students with grade point averages (GPAs) of 2.53 or higher record more information in their notes and retain a larger percentage of the most important information than do students with GPAs of less than 2.53 (Einstein, Morris, & Smith, 1985). These findings are not surprising when you consider that *hearing* information, *writing* it, and then *seeing* it after you've written it produces three different memory traces (tracks) in the brain, which combine to multiply your chances of remembering it. Furthermore, students with a good set of notes have a written record of that information that can be reread and studied later.

These research findings suggest that you should view each lecture as if it were a test-review session during which your instructor is giving out test answers and you're given the opportunity to write all those answers in your notes. Come to class with the attitude that your instructors are dispensing answers to test questions as they speak, and your job is to pick out and pick up these answers.

Remember

If important points your professor makes in class make it into your notes, they can become points learned; these learned points, in turn, will turn into earned points on your exams (and higher grades in the course).

The next sections give strategies for getting the most out of lectures at three stages in the learning process: *before*, *during*, and *after* lectures.

Pre-Lecture Strategies: What to Do before Lectures

1. **Check your syllabus to see where you are in the course and determine how the upcoming class fits into the total course picture.** Checking your syllabus before individual class sessions strengthens learning because you will see how each part (individual class session) relates to the whole (the entire course). This strategy also capitalizes on the brain's natural tendency to seek larger patterns and see the "big picture." Rather than seeing things in separate parts, the brain is naturally inclined to connect parts into a meaningful whole (Caine & Caine, 2011). In other words, the brain looks for meaningful patterns and connections rather than isolated bits and pieces of information (Jensen, 2008). In Figure 5.2, notice how your brain naturally ties together and fills in the missing information to perceive a meaningful whole pattern.
2. **Get to class early so that you can look over your notes from the previous class session and from any reading assignment that relates to the day's lecture topic.** Research indicates that when students preview information related to an upcoming lecture topic, it improves their ability to take more accurate and complete lecture notes (Jairam & Kiewra, 2009; Kiewra, 2005). Thus, a good strategy to help you learn from lectures is to review your notes from the previous class session and read textbook information related to an upcoming lecture topic *before* hearing the lecture. This strategy will help you better understand and take more detailed notes on the lecture. Reviewing previously learned information also activates your previous knowledge, enabling you to build a mental bridge

FIGURE 5.2

You perceive a white triangle in the middle of this figure. However, if you use three fingers to cover up the three corners of the white triangle that fall outside the other (background) triangle, the white triangle suddenly disappears. What your brain does is take these corners as starting points and fill in the rest of the information on its own to create a complete or whole pattern that has meaning to you. (Also, notice how you perceive the background triangle as a complete triangle, even though parts of its left and right sides are missing.)

Triangle Illusion

from one class session to the next, connecting new information to what you already know—a key to deep learning (Bruner, 1990; Piaget, 1978; Vygotsky, 1978). Acquiring knowledge isn't a matter of simply pouring information into the brain as if it were an empty jar. It's a matter of attaching or connecting new ideas to ideas that are already stored in the brain. When you learn deeply, a physical connection is actually made between nerve cells in your brain (Alkon, 1992), as illustrated in Figure 5.3.

Listening and Note-Taking Strategies: What to Do during Lectures

1. **Take your own notes in class.** Don't rely on someone else to take notes for you. Taking your own notes in your own words focuses your attention and ensures that you're taking notes that make sense to you. Research shows that students who record and review their own notes earn higher scores on memory tests for that information than do students who review the notes of others (Jairam & Kiewra, 2009; Kiewra, 2005). These findings point to the importance of taking

FIGURE 5.3

When something is learned, it's stored in the brain as a link in an interconnected network of brain cells. Thus, deep learning involves making connections between what you're trying to learn and what you already know.

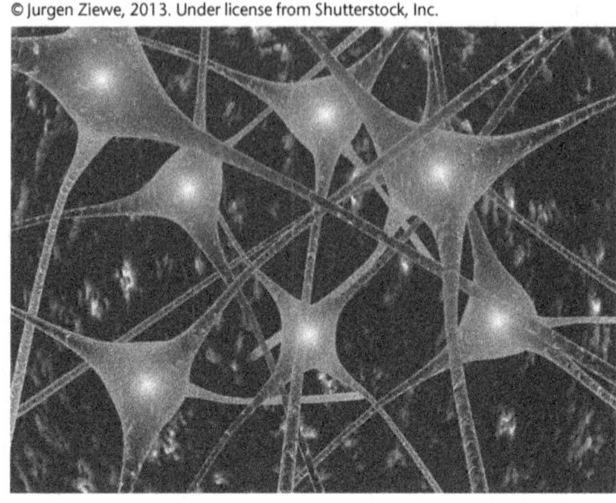

Network of Brain Cells

and studying your own notes because they will be most meaningful to you. You can collaborate with classmates to compare notes for completeness and accuracy or to pick up points you may have missed. However, don't routinely rely on someone else to take notes for you.

2. **Focus full attention on the most important information.** Attention is the critical first step to successful learning and memory. Since the human attention span is limited, it's impossible to attend to and make note of (or take notes on) everything. Thus, you need to use your attention *selectively* to focus on, detect, and select information that matters most. Here are some strategies for attending to and recording the most important information delivered by professors in the college classroom:
   - Pay attention to information your instructors put *in print*—on the board, on a slide, or in a handout. If your instructor takes the time and energy to write it out or type it out, that's usually a good clue that the information is important and you're likely to see it again—on an exam.
   - Pay attention to information presented during the first and last few minutes of class. Instructors are more likely to provide valuable reminders, reviews, and previews at these two points in time.
   - Use your instructor's *verbal and nonverbal cues* to detect important information. Don't just tune in when the instructor is writing something down and tune out at other times. It's been found that students record almost 90 percent of information written on the board, but less than 50 percent of important ideas that professors state but don't write on the board (Johnstone & Su, 1994; Locke, 1977; Titsworth & Kiewra, 2004). Don't fall into the reflexive routine of just writing something in your notes when you see your instructor writing on the board. Listen actively to receive and record important ideas in your notes that you *hear* your instructor saying. In Do It Now! 5.1, you'll find strategies for detecting clues to important information that professors deliver during lectures.

Students who take notes during lectures have been found to achieve higher class grades than those who just listen.

3. **Take organized notes.** Keep taking notes in the same paragraph if the instructor is continuing on the same point or idea. When the instructor shifts to a new idea, skip a few lines and shift to a new paragraph. Be alert to phrases that your instructor may use to signal a shift to a new or different idea (e.g., "Let's turn to . . ." or "In addition to . . ."). Use these phrases as cues for taking notes in paragraph form. By recording different ideas in different paragraphs, you improve the organizational quality of your notes, which will improve your comprehension and retention of them. Also, be sure to leave extra space between paragraphs (ideas) to give yourself room to add information later that you may have initially missed, or to translate the professor's words into your own words that are more meaningful to you. If your instructor provides notes (in handout form, PowerPoints, etc.), it is helpful to take your notes directly on the material provided.

5.1 DO IT NOW

Detecting When Instructors Are Delivering Important Information during Class Lectures

1. Verbal cues
   - Phrases signal important information (e.g., "The point here is . . ." or "What's most significant about this is . . .").
   - Information is repeated or rephrased in a different way (e.g., "In other words . . .").
   - Stated information is followed with a question to check understanding (e.g., "Is that clear?" "Do you follow that?" "Does that make sense?" or "Are you with me?").
2. Vocal (tone of voice) cues
   - Information is delivered in a louder tone or at a higher pitch than usual, which may indicate excitement or emphasis.
   - Information is delivered at a slower rate or with more pauses than usual, which may be your instructor's way of giving you more time to write down these important ideas.
3. Nonverbal cues
   - Information is delivered by the instructor with more than the usual:
     a. facial expressiveness (e.g., raised or furrowed eyebrows);
     b. body movement (e.g., more gesturing and animation); or
     c. eye contact (e.g., looking more directly and intently at the faces of students to see whether they are following or understanding what's being said).
   - The instructor moves closer to the students (e.g., moving away from the podium or blackboard).
   - The instructor's body is oriented directly toward the class (i.e., both shoulders directly or squarely face the class).

Another popular strategy for taking organized notes, the Cornell Note-Taking System, is summarized in Do It Now! 5.2.

4. **Keep taking notes even if you don't immediately understand what your instructor is saying.** If you are uncertain or confused about what your instructor is saying, don't stop writing—your notes will at least leave you with a record of the information to review later when you have more time to think about and grasp their meaning. If you still don't understand it after taking time to review it, check it out in your textbook, with your instructor, or with a classmate.

Remember

Your primary goal during lectures is to get important information into your brain long enough to note it mentally and then physically in your notes. Making sense of that information often has to come later, when you have time to reflect on the notes you took in class.

Post-Lecture Strategies: What to Do after Lectures

1. **As soon as class ends, quickly check your notes for missing information or incomplete thoughts.** Since the information is likely to be fresh in your mind immediately after class, a quick check of your notes at this time will allow you to take advantage of your short-term memory. By reviewing and reflecting on it, you can help move the information into long-term memory before forgetting takes place. This quick review can be done alone or, better yet, with a motivated classmate. If you both have gaps in your notes, check them out with your instructor before he or she leaves the classroom. Even though it may be weeks be-

fore you will be tested on the material, the quicker you address missed points and clear up sources of confusion, the better, because you'll be able to use your knowledge to help you understand and learn upcoming material. Catching confusion early in the game also enables you to avoid the mad last-minute rush of students seeking help from the instructor just before test time. You want to reserve the critical time just before exams for studying a set of notes that you know are complete and accurate, rather than rushing around trying to find missing information and getting cheap fast-food help on concepts that were presented weeks ago.

Think About It — *Journal Entry* 5.2

1. What do you tend to do immediately after a class session ends?

___

___

___

2. Why? What could you do immediately after class to be a more successful student?

___

___

___

___

___

___

2. **Before the next class session meets, reflect on and review your notes to make sense of them.** Your professors will often lecture on information that you may have little prior knowledge about, so it is unrealistic to expect that you will understand everything that's being said the first time you hear it. Instead, you'll need to set aside time for making notes or taking notes on your own notes (i.e., rewriting them in your own words so that they make sense to you).

During this reflect-and-rewrite process, we recommend that you take notes on your notes by:

- Translating technical information into your own words to make it more meaningful to you; and
- Reorganizing your notes to get ideas related to the same point in the same place.

5.2 DO IT NOW

The Cornell Note-Taking System

1. On the page on which you're taking notes, draw a horizontal line about 2 inches from the bottom edge of the paper.
2. If there's no vertical line on the left side of the page, draw one line about 2½ inches from the left edge of the paper (as shown in the scaled-down illustration here).
3. When your instructor is lecturing, use the large space to the right of the vertical line (area A) to record your notes.
4. After a lecture, use the space at the bottom of the page (area B) to summarize the main points you recorded on that page.
5. Use the column of space on the left side of the page (area C) to write questions that are answered in the notes on the right.
6. Quiz yourself by looking at the questions listed in the left margin while covering the answers to them that are found in your class notes on the right.

Note: You can use this note-taking and note-review method on your own, or you could team up with two or more students and do it collaboratively.

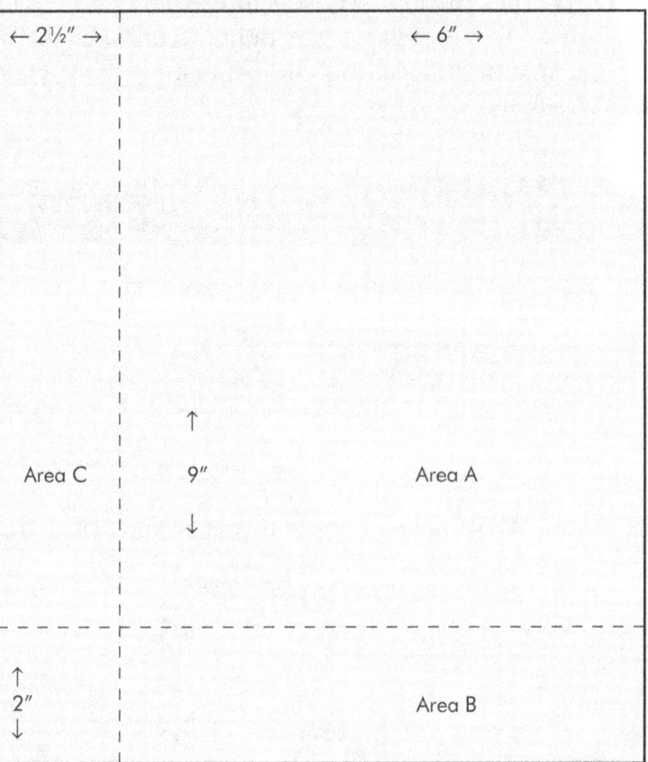

Studies show that when students organize lecture information into meaningful categories, they demonstrate greater recall for that information on a delayed memory test than do students who simply review their notes without organizing them into categories (Howe, 1970; Kiewra, 2005).

Remember

Look at note taking as a two-stage process: Stage 1 involves actively taking notes in class, and Stage 2 takes place later, when you have time to reflect on your notes and process them more deeply.

Author's Experience

My first year in college was mainly spent trying to manipulate my schedule to find some free time. I took all of my classes in a row without a break to save some time at the end of the day for relaxation and hanging out with friends before I went to work. Seldom did I look over my notes and read the material that I was assigned on the day I took the lecture notes and received the assignment. Thus, on the day before the test I was in a panic trying to cram the lecture notes into my head for the upcoming test. Needless to say, I did not perform well on many of these tests. Finally, I had a professor who told me that if I spent time each day after a couple of my classes catching up on reading and rewriting my notes, I would retain the material longer, increase my grades, and decrease my stress at test time. I employed this system, and it worked wonderfully.

Aaron Thompson

Reading Strategically to Comprehend and Retain Textbook Information

Second only to lecture notes as a source of test questions on college exams is information found in assigned readings (Brown, 1988; Cuseo, et al., 2013). You're likely to find exam questions on information contained in your assigned reading that your professors didn't talk about specifically in class (or even mention in class). College professors often expect you to relate or connect what they lecture about in class with material that you've been assigned to read. Furthermore, they often deliver class lectures with the assumption that you have done the assigned reading, so if you haven't done it, you're likely to have more difficulty following what your instructor is talking about in class.

Remember

Do the assigned reading and do it according to the schedule your instructor has established. It will help you better understand class lectures, improve the quality of your participation in class, and raise your overall course grade.

Think About It — *Journal Entry* 5.3

Rate yourself in terms of how frequently you use these note-taking strategies according to the following scale:

4 = always, 3 = sometimes, 2 = rarely, 1 = never

1. I take notes consistently in class.	4	3	2	1
2. I sit near the front of the room during class.	4	3	2	1
3. I sit upright and lean forward while in class.	4	3	2	1
4. I take notes on what my instructors say, not just what they write on the board.	4	3	2	1
5. I pay special attention to information presented at the start and end of class.	4	3	2	1
6. I take notes in paragraph form.	4	3	2	1
7. I review my notes immediately after class to check that they are complete and accurate.	4	3	2	1

What areas do you need to improve in? How can you improve in theses areas?

____

____

____

____

____

____

When completing your reading assignments, use effective reading strategies that are based on sound principles of human learning and memory, such as those listed here.

What follows is a series of research-based strategies for effective reading at three key stages in the learning process: before, during, and after reading.

Pre-Reading Strategies: What to Do before Reading

1. **Before jumping into your assigned reading, look at how it fits into the overall organizational structure of the book and course.** You can do this efficiently by taking a quick look at the book's table of contents to see where the chapter you're about to read is placed in the overall sequence of chapters, especially its relation to chapters that immediately precede and follow it. Using this strategy will give you a sense of how the particular part you're focusing on connects with the bigger picture. Research shows that if learners gain access to advanced knowledge of how information they're about to learn is organized—if they see how its parts relate to the whole—*before* they attempt to start learning the specific parts, they're better able to comprehend and retain the material (Ausubel, Novak, & Hanesian 1978; Chen & Hirumi, 2009). Thus, the first step toward improving reading comprehension and retention of a book chapter is to see how it relates to the whole book before you begin to examine the chapter part by part.

Think About It — Journal Entry 5.4

When you open a textbook to read a chapter, how do you start the reading process? That is, what's the first thing you do? Why do you do this?

____

____

____

____

____

____

2. **Preview the chapter you're about to read by reading its boldface headings and any chapter outline, objectives, summary, or end-of-chapter questions that may be included.** Before jumping right into the content, get in the habit of previewing what's in a chapter to gain an overall sense of its organization and what it's about. If you dive into the specific details first, you lose sight of how the smaller details relate to the larger picture. The brain's natural tendency is to perceive and comprehend whole patterns rather than isolated bits of information. Start by seeing how the parts of the chapter are integrated into the whole. This will enable you to better connect the separate pieces of information you encounter while you read, similar to seeing the whole picture of a completed jigsaw puzzle before you start assembling its pieces.

3. **Take a moment to think about how what you already know relates to the material in the chapter you're about to read.** By thinking about knowledge you possess about the topic you're about to read, you activate the areas of your brain where that knowledge is stored, thereby preparing it to make meaningful connections with the material you're about to read.

Strategies to Use while Reading

1. **Read selectively to locate the most important information.** Rather than jumping into reading and randomly highlighting, effective reading begins with a plan or goal for identifying what should be noted and remembered. Here are three strategies to use while reading to help you determine what information should be noted and retained.
   - **Use boldface or dark-print headings and subheadings as cues for identifying important information.** These headings organize the chapter's major points; thus, you can use them as "traffic" signs to direct you to the most important information in the chapter. Better yet, turn the headings into questions and then read to find answers to these questions. This question-and-answer strategy will ensure that you read actively and with a purpose. (You can set up this strategy when you preview the chapter by placing a question mark after each heading contained in the chapter.) Creating and answering questions while you read also keeps you motivated; the questions help stimulate your curiosity and finding answers to them serves to reward or reinforce your reading (Walter, Knudsbig, & Smith, 2003). Lastly, answering questions about what you're reading is an effective way to prepare for tests because you're practicing exactly what you'll be expected to do on exams—answering questions. You can quickly write the heading questions on separate index cards and use them as flash cards to review for exams. Use the question on the flash card as a way to flash back and trigger your recall of information from the text that answers the question.
   - **Pay special attention to words that are *italicized, underlined, or in boldface print.*** These are usually signs for building-block terms that must be understood and built on before you can proceed to understand higher-level concepts covered later in the reading. Don't simply highlight these words because their special appearance suggests they are important. Read these terms carefully and be sure you understand their meaning before you continue reading.
   - **Pay special attention to the first and last sentences in each paragraph.** These sentences contain an important introduction and conclusion to the ideas covered in the paragraph. It's a good idea to reread the first and last sentences of each paragraph before you move on to the next paragraph, particularly when reading sequential or cumulative material (e.g., science or math) that requires full comprehension of what was previously covered to understand what will be covered next.

Reread your chapter notes and highlights after you've listened to your instructor lecture on the material contained in the chapter. You can use your lecture notes as a guide to help you focus on what information in the chapter your instructor feels is most important. If you adopt this strategy, your reading before lectures will help you understand the lecture and take better class notes, and your reading after lectures will help you locate and learn information in the textbook that your instructor is emphasizing in class—which is likely to be the information your instructor thinks is most important and is most likely to show up on your exams. Thus, it's a good idea to have your class notes nearby when you're completing your reading assignments to help you identify what you should pay special attention to while reading.

Remember

Your goal when reading is not merely to cover the assigned pages, but to uncover the most important information and ideas contained on those pages.

"I would advise you to read with a pen in your hand, and enter in a little book of short hints of what you find that is curious, or that might be useful; for this will be the best method of imprinting such particulars in your memory, where they will be ready."

—Benjamin Franklin, 18th-century inventor, newspaper writer, and signer of the *Declaration of Independence*

2. **Take written notes on what you're reading.** Just as you should take notes in class, you should take notes in response to the author's words in the text. Writing requires more active thinking than highlighting because you're creating your own words rather than passively highlighting words written by somebody else. Don't get into the habit of using your textbook as a coloring book in which the artistic process of highlighting what you're reading with spectacular kaleidoscopic colors distracts you from the more important process of learning actively and thinking deeply.

Highlighting textbooks in spectacular colors is a very popular reading strategy among college students, but it's a less effective strategy for producing deep learning than taking written notes on what you read.

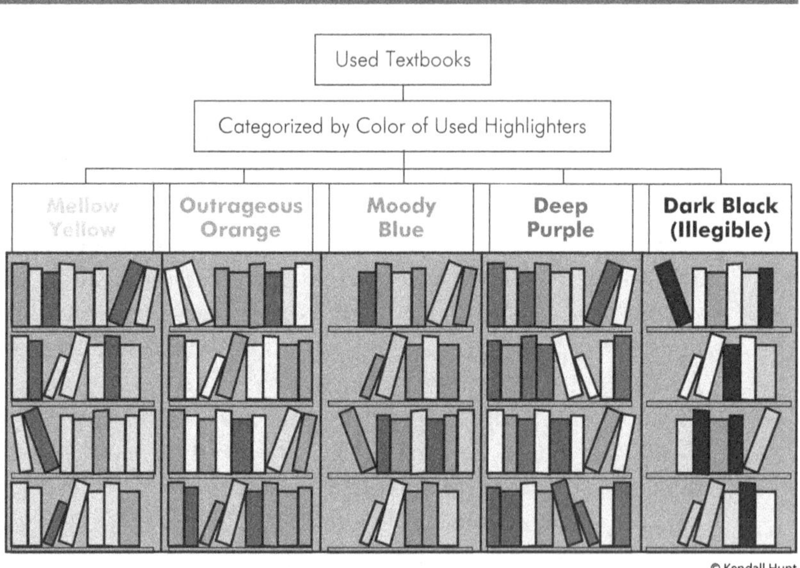

"I had the worst study habits and the lowest grades. Then I found out what I was doing wrong. I had been highlighting with a black magic marker."

—Jeff Altman, American comedian

If you can express what someone else has written in words that make sense to you, this means that you're relating it to what you already know—a sign of deep learning (Demmert & Towner, 2003). A good time to pause and summarize what you've read in your own words is when you encounter a boldface heading, because this indicates you've just completed reading about a major concept and are about to begin a new one.

Remember

Effective reading isn't a passive process of covering pages: it's an active process in which you uncover meaning in the pages you read.

3. **Use the visual aids included in your textbook.** Don't fall into the trap of thinking that visual aids can or should be skipped because they're merely secondary supplements to the written words in the body of the text. Visual aids, such as

charts, graphs, diagrams, and concept maps, are powerful learning and memory tools for a couple of reasons: (1) they enable you to "see" the information in addition to reading (hearing) it, and (2) they organize and connect separate pieces of information into an integrated whole.

Think About It — Journal Entry 5.5

When reading a textbook, do you usually have the following tools on hand?

Highlighter:	yes	no
Pen or pencil:	yes	no
Notebook:	yes	no
Class notes:	yes	no
Dictionary:	yes	no
Glossary:	yes	no

Why or why not?

Furthermore, visual aids allow you to experience a different form of information input than repeatedly processing written words. This occasional change of sensory input brings variety to the reading process, which can recapture your attention and recharge your motivation.

Post-Reading Strategies: What to Do after Reading

1. **End a reading session with a short review of the information you've noted or highlighted.** Most forgetting that takes place after you receive and process information occurs immediately after you stop focusing on the information and turn your attention to another task (Averell & Heathcote, 2011; Baddeley, 1999). (See Figure 5.4.) Taking a few minutes at the end of your reading time to review the most important information works to lock that information into your memory before you turn your attention to something else and forget it.

The graph in Figure 5.4 represents the results of a classic experiment on how well information is recalled at various times after it was originally learned. As you can see on the far left of the graph, most forgetting occurs soon after information has been taken in (e.g., after 20 minutes, the participants in the study forgot more than 60 per-

FIGURE 5.4

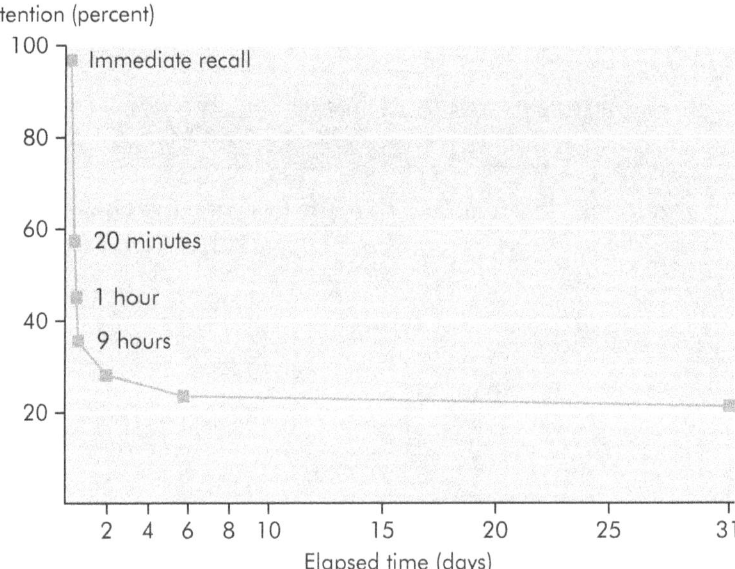

Source: Hermann Ebbinghaus, *Memory: A Contribution to Experimental Psychology*, 1885/1913.

The Forgetting Curve

cent of it). The results of this classic study, which have been confirmed multiple times (Schacter, 2001), point to the importance of reviewing information you've acquired through reading immediately after you've read it. When you do so, your memory for that information will improve dramatically because you're intercepting the forgetting curve at its steepest point of memory loss—immediately after information has been read.

2. **For difficult-to-understand concepts, seek out other information sources.** If you find you can't understand a concept explained in your text, even after rereading and repeatedly reflecting on it, try the following strategy:
   - **Look at how another textbook explains it.** Not all textbooks are created equally: some do a better job of explaining certain concepts than others. Check to see whether your library has other texts in the same subject as your course, or check your campus bookstore for textbooks in the same subject area as the course you're taking. A different text may be able to explain a hard-to-understand concept much better than the textbook you purchased for the course.
   - **Seek help from your instructor.** Your instructor will be available during office hours to review questions. You may also seek help from peer tutoring and the Academic Achievement Center.

Snapshot Summary

5.1 SQ3R: A Method for Improving Reading Comprehension and Retention

A popular reading strategy for organizing and remembering information is the SQ3R method. SQ3R is an acronym for five steps you can take to increase textbook reading comprehension and retention, particularly when reading highly technical or complex material. The following sequences of steps comprise this method:

1. Survey
2. Question
3. Read
4. Recite
5. Review

S = Survey: Get a preview and overview of what you're about to read.

1. Read the title to activate your thoughts about the subject and prepare your mind to receive information related to it.
2. Read the introduction, chapter objectives, and chapter summary to become familiar with the author's purpose, goals, and most important points.
3. Note the boldface headings and subheadings to get a sense of the chapter's organization before you begin to read. This creates a mental structure or framework for making sense of the information you're about to read.
4. Take note of any graphics, such as charts, maps, and diagrams; they provide valuable visual support and reinforcement for the material you're reading.
5. Pay special attention to reading aids (e.g., italics and boldface font) that you can use to identify, understand, and remember key concepts.

Q = Question: Stay active and curious.

As you read, use the boldface headings to formulate questions you think will be answered in that particular section. When your mind is actively searching for answers to questions, it becomes more engaged in the learning process. As you read, add any questions that you have about the reading.

R = Read: Find the answer to the questions you've created.

Read one section at a time, with your questions in mind, and search for answers to these questions. Also, keep an eye out for new questions that need to be asked.

R = Recite: Rehearse your answers.

After you complete reading each section, recall the questions you asked and see whether you can answer them from memory. If not, look at the questions again and practice your answers to them until you can recall them without looking. Don't move on to the next section until you're able to answer all questions in the section you've just completed.

R = Review: Look back and get a second view of the whole picture.

Once you've finished the chapter, review all the questions you've created for different parts or sections. See whether you can still answer them without looking. If not, go back and refresh your memory.

There are variations of the SQ3R strategy. You will find worksheets after each chapter in this text that work you through the SQ4R strategy. SQ5R is also a strategy discussed. The number noted (SQ3R) reflects the number of strategies used after surveying and questioning, which either increases or decreases one's study efforts.

Study Strategies for Learning Deeply and Remembering Longer

The final step in the learning process is to save that information you have in your brain and bring it back to mind at the time you need it—e.g., test time. Described here is a series of effective study strategies for acquiring knowledge, keeping that knowledge in your brain (memory storage), and accessing that information when you need it (memory retrieval).

The Importance of Undivided Attention

The human attention span has limited capacity; we have only so much of it available to us at any point in time, and we can give all or part of it to whatever task we're working on. If study time is spent engaging in other activities besides studying (e.g., listening to music, watching TV, or text messaging friends), the total amount of attention available for studying is subtracted and divided among the other activities. In other words, studying doesn't receive your undivided attention.

Studies show that when people multitask, they don't pay equal attention to all tasks at the same time. Instead, they divide their attention by shifting it back and forth between tasks (Howard, 2014), and their performance on the task that demands the most concentration or deepest thinking is the one that suffers the most (Crawford & Strapp, 1994). Furthermore, research shows that multitasking can increase boredom for the task that requires the most intense concentration. One study found that with even a low level of stimulation from another source of sensory input, such as a TV turned to a low volume in the next room, students were more likely to describe the mental task they were concentrating on as "boring" (Damrad-Frye & Laird, 1989).

Think About It — *Journal Entry* 5.6

Rate yourself in terms of how frequently you use these reading strategies according to the following scale:

4 = always, 3 = sometimes, 2 = rarely, 1 = never

1. I read the chapter outlines and summaries before I start reading the chapter content.	4	3	2	1
2. I preview a chapter's boldface headings and subheadings before I begin to read the chapter.	4	3	2	1
3. I adjust my reading speed to the type of subject I am reading about.	4	3	2	1
4. I look up the meaning of unfamiliar words and unknown terms that I come across before I continue reading.	4	3	2	1
5. I take written notes on information I read.	4	3	2	1
6. I use the visual aids included in my textbooks.	4	3	2	1
7. I finish my reading sessions with a review of important information that I noted or highlighted.	4	3	2	1

What areas need the most improvement? How can you improve in these areas?

When performing complex mental tasks that cannot be done automatically, other tasks and sources of external stimulation interfere with the quiet, internal reflection time needed for permanent connections to form between brain cells—which is what must happen if deep, long-lasting learning is to take place (Jensen, 2008).

Studies show that doing challenging academic work while multitasking divides up attention and drives down comprehension and retention.

Remember

Attention must happen first in order for retention to happen later.

Making Meaningful Associations

Connecting what you're trying to learn to something you already know is a powerful memory-improvement strategy because knowledge is stored in the form of a connected network of brain cells (Coward, 1990; Chaney, 2007). (See Figure 5.3 on p. 130.)

The brain's natural tendency to seek meaningful, connected patterns applies to words as well as images. This is illustrated in the following passage that once appeared anonymously on the Internet. See whether you can read it and grasp its meaning.

> *Aoccdrnig to rscheearch at Cmabridge Uinverstisy, it deos't mattaer in what order the ltteers in a word are, the only iprmoetnt thing is that the frist and lsat ltteer be at the rghit pclae. The rset can be a total mses and you can still raed it wouthit a porbelm. This is bcusae the human mind deos not raed ervey lteter by istlef, but the word as a wlohe. Amzanig huh?*

Notice how easily you found the meaning of the misspelled words by naturally transforming them into correctly spelled words—which you knew because the correctly spelled words were already stored in your brain. Thus, whenever you learn meaningfully, you do so by connecting what you're trying to understand to what you already know.

Learning by making meaningful connections is referred to as *deep learning* (Biggs & Tang, 2007; Entwistle & Ramsden, 1983). It involves moving beyond shallow memorization to deeper levels of understanding. This is a major shift from the old view that learning occurs by passively absorbing information like a sponge—for example, by receiving it from the teacher or text and studying it in the same prepackaged form as you received it. Instead, you want to adopt an approach to learning that involves actively transforming the information you receive into a form that's meaningful to you (Biggs & Tang, 2007; Mayer, 2002). This transforms short-term surface-level learning (memorization of information) into deep and meaningful long-term learning (acquisition of knowledge).

"The extent to which we remember a new experience has more to do with how it relates to existing memories than with how many times or how recently we have experienced it."

—Morton Hunt, *The Universe Within: A New Science Explores the Human Mind*

Student *Perspective*

"When you have to do work, and you're getting it. It's linking what I already know to what I didn't know."

—Student's description of a "good class"

So, instead of immediately trying to learn something by repetition, your first strategy should be to try hooking or hanging it onto something that's already stored in your brain—something you already know and is meaningful to you. It may take a little while and a little work to find the right hook, but once you've found it, you'll learn the information faster and retain it longer. For instance, a meaningful way to learn and remember how to correctly spell one of the most frequently misspelled words in the English language: *separate* (not *seperate*). By remembering that "to par" means "to divide," as in the words par*ts* or par*tition*, it makes sense that the word *separate* should be spelled sep*arate* because its meaning is "to divide into parts."

Each of the academic subjects that comprise the college curriculum has a specialized vocabulary that can sound like a foreign language to someone who has no experience with the subject area. One way you can make a term more meaningful to you is by looking up its word root in the dictionary or by identifying its prefix or suffix, which may give away the term's meaning. For instance, suppose you're taking a biology course and studying the autonomic nervous system—the part of the nervous system that operates without your conscious awareness or voluntary control (e.g., your heart beating and lungs breathing). The meaning of the phrase is given away by the prefix *auto*, which means "self-controlling"—as in the word *automatic* (e.g., automatic transmission).

If looking up the term's root, prefix, or suffix doesn't give away its meaning, see if you can make it meaningful to you in some other way. For instance, suppose you looked up the root of the term *artery* and nothing about the origins of this term suggested its meaning or purpose. You could create your own meaning for this term by taking its first letter (a), and have it stand for "away"—to help you remember that arteries carry blood away from the heart. Thus, you've taken a biological term and made it personally meaningful (and memorable).

Think About It — *Journal Entry* 5.7

Think of a key term or concept you're learning in a course this term that you could form a meaningful association to remember.

1. What is the information you're attempting to learn?

____

____

____

2. What is the meaningful association you could use to help you remember it?

____

____

____

When my son was about three years old, we were riding in the car together and listening to a

Author's Experience

song by the Beatles titled "Sergeant Pepper's Lonely Hearts Club Band." You may be familiar with this tune, but in case you're not, there is a part in it where the following lyrics are sung repeatedly: "Sergeant Pepper's lonely, Sergeant Pepper's lonely, Sergeant Pepper's lonely . . ."

When this part of the song was being played, I noticed that my three-year-old son was singing along. I thought that it was pretty amazing for a boy his age to be able to understand and repeat those lyrics. However, when that part of the song came on again, I noticed that he wasn't singing "Sergeant Pepper's lonely, Sergeant Pepper's lonely." Instead, he was singing "sausage pepperoni, sausage pepperoni" (which were his two favorite pizza toppings).

My son's brain was doing what all brains tend to naturally do. It took unfamiliar information (song lyrics) that didn't make any sense to him and transformed it into a form that was very meaningful to him!

Joe Cuseo

Remember

The more meaningful what you're learning is to you, the deeper you'll learn it and the longer you'll remember it.

Compare and Contrast

When you're studying something new, get in the habit of asking yourself the following questions:

1. Is this idea similar or comparable to something that I've already learned? (Compare)
2. How does this idea differ from what I already know? (Contrast)

Research indicates that this simple strategy is one of the most powerful ways to promote learning of academic information (Marzano, Pickering, & Pollock, 2001). Asking yourself the question "How is this similar to and different from concepts that I already know?" makes learning more personally meaningful because you are relating what you're trying to learn to what you already know.

Integration and Organization

Integrate or connect ideas from your class notes and assigned readings that relate to the same major point by organizing them into the same category. For example, get these related ideas in the same place by recording them on the same index card under the same category heading. Index cards are a good tool for such purposes; you can use each card as a miniature file cabinet for different categories of information. The category heading on each card functions like the hub of a wheel, around which individual pieces of related information are attached like spokes. Integrating information related to the same topic in the same place and studying it at the same time divides the total material you're learning into identifiable and manageable parts. In contrast, when ideas pertaining to the same point or concept are spread all over the place, they're more likely to take that form in your mind—leaving them mentally disconnected and leaving you confused (as well as feeling stressed and overwhelmed).

Remember

Just as important as organizing course materials is organizing course concepts. Ask yourself the following questions: How can this specific concept be categorized or classified? How does this particular idea relate to or "fit into" something bigger?

Spreading out your studying into shorter sessions improves your memory by reducing loss of attention due to fatigue.

Divide and Conquer

Effective learning depends not only on *how* you learn (your method), but also on *when* you learn (your timing). Although cramming just before exams is better than not studying, it's far less effective than studying that's spread out across time. Rather than cramming all your studying into one long session, use the method of *distributed practice*—spread or "distribute" your study time over several shorter sessions. Research consistently shows that short, periodic practice sessions are more effective than a single marathon session.

Distributing study time over several shorter sessions improves your learning and memory by:

- Reducing loss of attention due to fatigue or boredom; and
- Reducing mental interference by giving your brain some downtime to cool down and lock in information it has received before it's interrupted by the need to deal with additional information (Malmberg & Murnane, 2002; Murname & Shiffrin, 1991).

If the brain's downtime is interfered with by the arrival of additional information, it gets overloaded and its capacity for handling information becomes impaired. This is what cramming does—it overloads the brain with lots of information in a limited period of time. In contrast, distributed study does just the opposite—it uses shorter sessions with downtime between sessions, thereby giving the brain the time and opportunity to retain the information that it has received and processed (studied).

Another major advantage of distributed study is that it's less stressful and more motivating than cramming. Shorter sessions provide you with an incentive to start studying because you know that you're not going to be doing it for a long stretch of time or lose any sleep over it. It's easier to maintain your interest and motivation for any task that's done for a shorter rather than a longer period. Furthermore, distributing studying makes exam preparation easier because you know that if you run into difficulty understanding anything, you'll still have plenty of time to get help with it before you're tested and graded on it.

The "Part-to-Whole" Study Method

The part-to-whole method of studying is a natural extension of the distributed practice just discussed. With the part-to-whole method, you break up the material you need to learn into smaller parts and study those parts in separate sessions in advance of the exam; then you use your last study session just before the exam to review (re-study) all the parts you previously studied in separate sessions. Thus, your last session is not a cram session or even a study session: it's a review session.

Research shows that students of all ability levels learn material in college courses more effectively when it's studied in small units and when progression to the next unit takes place only after the previous unit has been mastered or understood (Pascarella & Terenzini, 1991, 2005). This strategy has two advantages: (1) it reinforces your memory for what you previously learned, and (2) it builds on what you already know to help you learn new material. These advantages are particularly important in cumulative subjects that require memory for problem-solving procedures or steps, such as math and science. When you repeatedly practice these procedures, they become more automatic and you're able to retrieve them quicker (e.g., on a timed test). This enables you to use them efficiently without having to expend a lot of mental effort and energy (Samuels & Flor, 1997), freeing your working memory for more important tasks such as critical thinking and creative problem solving (Schneider & Chein, 2003).

Think About It — Journal Entry 5.8

Are you more likely to study in advance of exams or cram just before exams? Why?

Don't buy into the myth that studying in advance is a waste of time because you'll forget it all by test time. As discussed in Chapter 3, this is a myth that procrastinators often use to rationalize their habit of putting off studying until the very last moment, which forces them to cram frantically the night before exams. Do not underestimate the power of breaking material to be learned into smaller parts and studying those parts some time before a major exam. Even if you cannot recall what you previously studied, when you start reviewing it you'll find that you will relearn it much faster than when you studied it the first time. This proves that studying in advance is not a waste of time because it takes less time to relearn the material, indicating that information studied in the earlier sessions was still retained in your brain (Kintsch, 1994).

Build Variety into the Study Process

You can increase your concentration and motivation by using the following strategies to infuse variety and a change of pace into your study routine.

Periodically vary the type of academic work you do while studying. Changing the nature of your work activities or the type of mental tasks you're performing while studying increases your level of alertness and concentration by reducing *habituation*—attention loss that occurs after repeated engagement in the same type of mental task (Thompson, 2009). To combat attention loss due to habituation, occasionally vary the type of study task you're performing. For instance, shift periodically among tasks that involve reading, writing, studying, and problem-solving skills (e.g., math or science problems).

Study different subjects in different places. Studying in different locations provides different environmental contexts for learning, which reduces the amount of interference that normally builds up when all information is studied in the same place (Rankin et al., 2009). In addition to spreading out your studying at different times, it's also a good idea to spread it out in different places. The great public speakers in ancient Greece and Rome used this method of changing places to remember long speeches by walking through different rooms while rehearsing their speeches, learning each major part of a speech in a different room (Higbee, 2001).

Changing the nature of the learning task and place where learning takes place provides a change of pace that infuses variety into the learning process, which, in turn, stimulates your attention, concentration, and motivation. Although it's useful to have a set time and place to study for getting you into a regular work routine, this doesn't mean that learning occurs best by habitually performing all types of academic tasks in the same place. Instead, research suggests that you should periodically change the learning tasks you perform and the environment in which you perform them to maximize attention and minimize interference (Carey, 2014; Druckman & Bjork, 1994).

> **Remember**
>
> *Change of pace and place while studying can stimulate your attention to what you're studying as well as your interest in and motivation for studying.*

Mix long study sessions with short study breaks that involve physical activity (e.g., a short jog or brisk walk). Study breaks that include physical activity not only refresh the mind by giving it a rest from studying, but also stimulate the mind by increasing blood flow to your brain, which will help you retain what you've already studied and regain concentration for what you'll study next.

Learning Styles: Identifying Your Learning Preferences

Student *Perspective*

"I have to *hear* it, *see* it, *write* it, and *talk* about it."

—First-year college student responding to the question "How do you learn best?"

Your learning style is another important personal characteristic you should be aware of when choosing your major. Learning styles refer to individual differences in learning preferences—that is, ways in which individuals prefer to perceive information (receive or take it in) and process information (deal with it after taking it in). Individuals may differ in terms of whether they prefer to take in information by reading about it, listening to it, seeing an image or diagram of it, or physically touching and manipulating it. Individuals may also vary in terms of whether they like to receive information in a structured and orderly format or in an unstructured form that allows them the freedom to explore, play with, and restructure it in their own way. Once information has been received, individuals may also differ in terms of how they prefer to process or deal with it mentally. Some might like to think about it on their own; others may prefer to discuss it with someone else, make an outline of it, or draw a picture of it.

Author's Experience

In my family, whenever there's something that needs to be assembled or set up (e.g., a ping-pong table or new electronic equipment), I've noticed that my wife, my son, and myself have different learning styles in terms of how we go about doing it. I like to read the manual's instructions carefully and completely before I even attempt to touch anything. My son prefers to look at the pictures or diagrams in the manual and uses them as models to find parts; then he begins to assemble those parts. My wife seems to prefer not to look at the manual. Instead, she likes to figure things out as she goes along by grabbing different parts from the box and trying to assemble those parts that look like they should fit together—piecing them together as if she were completing a jigsaw puzzle.

Joe Cuseo

You can take specially designed tests to assess your particular learning style and how it compares with others. There are many of them and most cost money to take. *My Power Learning* is just one example of the many tests you can take. VARK (www.vark-learn.com) is another example.

Probably the most frequently used learning styles test is the Myers-Briggs Type Indicator (MBTI; Myers, 1976; Myers & McCaulley, 1985), which is based on the personality theory of psychologist Carl Jung. The test consists of four pairs of opposing traits and assesses how people vary on a scale (low to high) for each of these four sets of traits.

Learning styles are common ways that people learn. We all have a mix of multiple learning styles, thus we have different and multiple ways of learning. Many students may find that they have a dominant learning style but use other styles that are less dominant. In many cases, you might use different styles for different learning circumstances. No style is set in concrete. They can change and there is no perfect mix for greater learning. You have the ability to increase your lesser used methods to make them more dominant while strengthening your dominant one. Since students have different learning styles and academic fields emphasize different styles of learning, it's important to consider how your learning style meshes with the style of learning emphasized by the field you're considering as a major. If the match seems to be close or compatible, then the marriage between you and that major could be one that leads to a satisfying and successful learning experience.

Although there are many (multiple) learning styles, the three that are considered most common are:

- Visual-Spatial Learning (learning by seeing),
- Auditory-Sequential Learning (learning by hearing),
- Kinesthetic Learning (learning by doing).

In addition to taking formal tests to assess which or how many of these are your learning style(s), you can gain awareness of your learning styles through some simple introspection or self-examination. Take a moment to complete the following sentences that are designed to stimulate personal reflection on your learning style:

I learn best if . . .
I learn most from . . .
I enjoy learning when . . .

Knowing your preferred learning style can make studying easier for you. Once you discover your dominant learning style, research some ways you can incorporate your learning style into your study routine (i.e., if your learning style is visual, read over notes or use flashcards; if you are an auditory learner, read your notes out loud to yourself; if you are a kinesthetic learner, rewrite your notes).

Learn with all of your senses. When studying, try to use as many sensory channels as possible. Research shows that information perceived through multiple sensory modalities is remembered better because it creates multiple interconnections in long-term memory areas of the brain (Bjork, 1994; Shams & Seitz, 2011; Zull, 2002). When a memory is formed in the brain, different sensory aspects of it are stored in different areas. For example, when your brain receives visual, auditory (hearing), and motor (movement) input while learning, each of these forms of sensory input is stored as a memory trace in a different part of the brain. Figure 5.5 shows a map of the outer surface of the human brain; you can see how different parts of the brain are specialized to receive input from different sensory modalities. When you use all of these sensory modalities while learning, multiple memory traces of what you're studying are recorded in different parts of your brain, which leads to deeper learning and stronger memory for what you have learned (Education Commission of the States, 1996).

Learn visually. The human brain consists of two hemispheres (half spheres): the left and the right (see Figure 5.6). Each hemisphere of the brain specializes in a different type of learning. In most people, the left hemisphere specializes in verbal learning, dealing primarily with words. In contrast, the right hemisphere specializes in visual-spatial learning, dealing primarily with perceiving images and objects that occupy physical space. If you use both hemispheres while studying, you lay down two different memory traces in your brain: one in the left hemisphere where words are stored, and one in the right hemisphere where images are stored. This process of laying down a double memory trace (verbal and visual) is referred to as *dual coding* (Paivio, 1990). When this happens, memory for what you're learning is substantially strengthened, primarily because two memory traces are better than one.

FIGURE 5.5

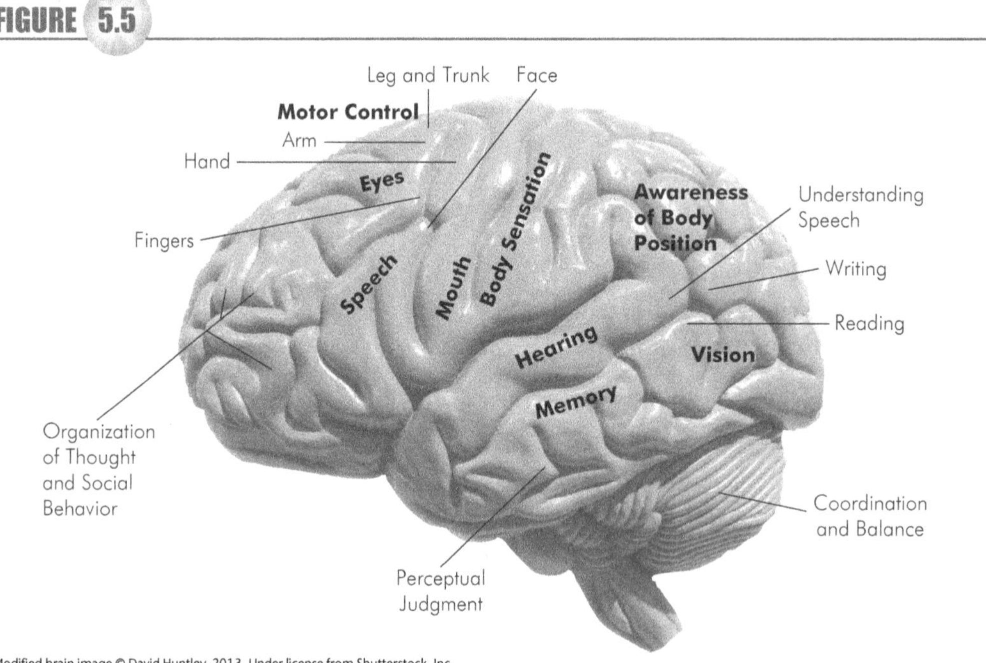

A Map of the Functions Performed by the Outer Surface of the Human Brain

To capitalize on the advantage of dual coding, be sure to use any visual aids that are available to you, including those provided in your textbook and by your instructor in class. You can also create your own visual aids by drawing pictures, symbols, and concept maps, such as flowcharts, Venn diagrams, spiderwebs, wheels with spokes, or branching tree diagrams. (For example, see Figure 5.7 for a tree diagram

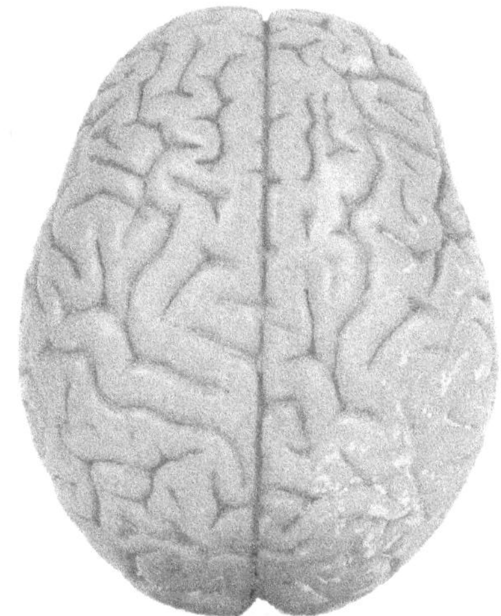

The human brain consists of the left hemisphere, which processes words, and the right hemisphere, which processes images.

that could be used to help you remember the parts and functions of the human nervous system.)

Remember

Drawing and other forms of visual illustration are not just artistic exercises: they can also be powerful learning tools—you can draw to learn! Drawing keeps you actively involved in the process of learning, and by representing what you're learning in visual form, you're able to dual-code the information you're studying, which doubles the number of memory traces recorded in your brain. As the old saying goes, "A picture is worth a thousand words."

FIGURE 5.7

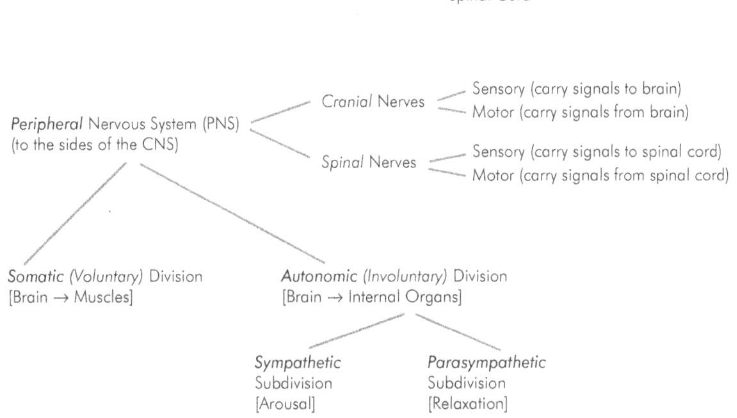

Concept Map for the Human Nervous System

Think About It — Journal Entry 5.9

Think of a course you're taking this term in which you're learning related pieces of information that could be joined together to form a concept map. In the space that follows, make a rough sketch of this map that includes the information you need to remember.

Learn by moving or using motor learning (a.k.a. muscle memory). In addition to hearing and seeing, movement is a sensory channel. When you move, your brain receives kinesthetic stimulation—the sensations generated by your muscles. Research shows that memory traces for movement are commonly stored in an area of your brain that plays a major role in all types of learning (Middleton & Strick, 1994). Thus, associating movement with what you're learning can improve your ability to retain it because you add a muscle memory trace in the motor control area of your brain (see Figure 5.5).

Author's Experience

I was talking about memory in class one day and mentioned that when I temporarily forget how to spell a word, its correct spelling comes back to me once I start to write it. One of my students raised her hand and said the same thing happens to her when she forgets a phone number—it comes back to her when she starts dialing it. Both of these experiences illustrate how motor memory brings information back to mind that was temporarily forgotten, pointing to the power of movement for promoting learning and memory.

Joe Cuseo

You can use movement to help you learn and retain academic information by using your body to act out what you're studying or to symbolize it with your hands (Kagan & Kagan, 1998). For example, if you're trying to remember five points about something (e.g., five consequences of the Civil War), when you're studying these points, count them on your fingers as you try to recall each of them. Also, remember that talking involves muscle movement of your lips and tongue. Thus, if you speak aloud when you're studying, either to a friend or to yourself, your memory of what you're studying may be improved by adding kinesthetic stimulation to the auditory or sound stimulation your brain receives from hearing what you're saying.

Student Perspective

"When I have to remember something, it's better for me to do something with my hands so I could physically see it happening."

—First-year college student

Remember

Try to make the learning process a total body experience—hear it, see it, say it, and move it.

Learn with emotion. Information reaches the brain through your senses and is stored in the brain as a memory trace; the same is true of emotions. Numerous connections occur between brain cells in the emotional and memory centers (Zull, 1998). For instance, when you're experiencing emotional excitement about what you're learning, adrenaline is released and is carried through the bloodstream to the brain. Once adrenaline reaches the brain, it increases blood flow and glucose production, which stimulates learning and strengthens memory (LeDoux, 1998; Rosenfield, 1988). In fact, emotionally intense experiences can release such a substantial amount of adrenaline into the bloodstream that memories of them can be immediately stored in long-term memory and last an entire lifetime. For instance, most people remember exactly what they were doing at the time they experienced such emotionally intense events as the September 11 terrorist attack on the United States, their first kiss, or their favorite team winning a world championship.

What does this emotion-memory link have to do with helping you remember academic information while studying? Research indicates that emotional intensity, excitement, and enthusiasm strengthen memories of academic information just as they do for memories of life events and personal experiences. If you get psyched up about what you're learning, you have a much better chance of learning and remembering it. If you're passionate or intense about what you're learning and convince yourself that it's really important to know, you're more likely to remember it (Howard, 2014; Minninger, 1984). So, keep in mind the importance or significance of what you're learning. For instance, if you're learning about photosynthesis, remind yourself that you're not just learning about a chemical reaction—you're learning about the driving force that underlies all plant life on the planet! If you aren't aware of the importance or significance of a particular concept you're studying, ask your instructor or a student majoring in the field. Enthusiasm can be contagious; you may catch it and become more passionate about learning the concept.

Remember

You learn most effectively when you actively involve all your senses (including bodily movement) and when you learn with passion and enthusiasm. In other words, learning grows deeper and lasts longer when you put your whole self into it—your heart, your mind, and your body.

Learn by collaborating with others. Research indicates that college students who work regularly in small groups of four to six become more actively involved in the learning process and learn more (Light, 2001). To maximize the power of study groups, each member should study individually *before* studying in a group and should come prepared with specific information or answers to share with teammates, as well as questions or points of confusion that the team can attempt to help answer or clarify.

Student Perspective

"I would suggest students get to know [each] other and get together in groups to study or at least review class material. I find it is easier to ask your friends or classmates with whom you are comfortable 'dumb' questions."

—Advice to first-year students from a college sophomore (Walsh, 2005)

Author's Experience

When I was in my senior year of college, I had to take a theory course by independent study because the course would not be offered again until after I planned to graduate. Another senior found himself in the same situation. The instructor allowed both of us to take this course together and agreed to meet with us every two weeks. My fellow classmate and I studied independently for the first two weeks.

I prepared for the biweekly meetings by reading thoroughly, yet I had little understanding of what I had read. After our first meeting, I left with a strong desire to drop the course but decided to stick with it. Over the next two weeks, I spent many sleepless nights trying to prepare for our next meeting and was feeling pretty low about not being the brightest student in my class of two. During the next meeting with the instructor, I found out that the other student was also having difficulty. Not only did I notice, so did the instructor. After that meeting, the instructor gave us study questions and asked us to read separately and then get together to discuss the questions. During the next two weeks, my classmate and I met several times to discuss what we were learning (or attempting to learn). By being able to communicate with each other about the issues we were studying, we both ended up gaining greater understanding. Our instructor was delighted to see that he was able to suggest a collaborative learning strategy that worked for both of us.

Aaron Thompson

Self-Monitor Your Learning

"When you know a thing, to recognize that you know it; and when you do not, to know that you do not know; that is knowledge."

—Confucius, influential Chinese thinker and educator

Successful learners don't just put in study time: they reflect and check on themselves to see if they're putting in quality time and really understanding what they're attempting to learn. They monitor their comprehension as they go along by asking themselves questions such as "Am I following this?" "Do I really understand it?" and "Do I know it for sure?"

How do you know if you really know it? Probably the best answer to this question is "I find *meaning* in it—that is, I can relate to it personally or put it in terms that make sense to me" (Ramsden, 2003).

Discussed below are some strategies for checking whether you truly understand what you're trying to learn. They help you answer the question "How do I know if I really know it?" These strategies can be used as indicators or checkpoints for determining whether you're just memorizing or learning at a deeper level.

Student Perspective

"Most things used to be external to me—out of a lecture or textbook. It makes learning a lot more interesting and memorable when you can bring your experiences into it. It makes you want to learn."

—Returning adult student

- **Can you paraphrase (restate or translate) what you're learning into your own words?** When you can paraphrase what you're learning, you're able to complete the following sentence: "In other words . . ." If you can complete that sentence in your own words, this is a good indication that you've moved beyond memorization to comprehension, because you've transformed what you're learning into words that are meaningful to you. You know you know it if you're not stating it the same way your instructor or textbook stated it, but restating it in words that are your own.
- **Can you explain what you're learning to someone who is unfamiliar with it?** Simply put, if you can't explain it to someone else, you probably don't really understand it yourself. If you can explain to a friend what you've learned, this is a good sign that you've moved beyond memorization to comprehension, because you're able to translate it into language that's understandable to anyone. Studies show that students gain deeper levels of understanding for what they're learning when they're asked to explain it to someone else (Chi, De Leeuw, Chiu, & LaVancher, 1994). Sometimes, we only become aware of how well we know or don't know something when we have to explain it to someone who's never heard it before (just ask any teacher). If you cannot find someone else to explain it to, then explain it aloud as if you were talking to an imaginary friend.

"You do not really understand something unless you can explain it to your grandmother."

—Albert Einstein, considered the "father of modern physics" and named "Person of the (20th) Century" by *Time Magazine*

- **Can you think of an example of what you've learned?** If you can come up with an instance or illustration of what you're learning that's your own—not one given by your instructor or textbook—this is a good sign that you truly understand it. It shows you're able to take a general, abstract concept and apply it to a specific, real-life experience (Bligh, 2000). Furthermore, a personal example is a powerful memory tool. Studies show that when people retrieve a concept from memory, they first recall an example of it. The example then serves as a memory-retrieval cue to trigger their memory of other details about the concept, such as its definition and relationship to other concepts (Norman, 1982; Okimoto & Norman, 2010; Park, 1984).
- **Can you represent or describe what you've learned in terms of an analogy or metaphor that compares it to something with similar meaning, or which works in a similar way?** Analogies and metaphors are basically ways of learning something new by understanding it in terms of its similarity to something you already understand. For instance, the computer can be used as a metaphor for the human brain to get a better understanding of learning and memory as a three-stage process in which information is: (1) inputted—perceived or received (through lectures and readings), (2) stored or saved—by studying, and (3) retrieved—recalled from storage at test time. If you can use an analogy or metaphor to represent what you're learning, you're grasping it at a deep level because you're building a mental bridge that connects it to what you already know (Cameron, 2003).
- **Can you apply what you're learning to solve a new problem that you haven't previously seen?** The ability to use knowledge by applying it in a different situation is a good indicator of deep learning (Erickson & Strommer, 2005). Learning specialists refer to this mental process as *decontextualization*—taking what you learned in one context (situation) and applying it to another (Bransford, Brown, & Cocking, 2000). For instance, you know that you've learned a mathematical concept deeply when you can use that concept to solve math problems that are different from the ones used by your instructor or your textbook. This is why your math instructors rarely include on exams the exact problems they solved in class or were solved in your textbook. They're not trying to "trick" you at test time: they're trying to see whether you've learned the concept or principle deeply.

Student Perspective

"I learn best through teaching. When I learn something and teach it to someone else, I find that it really sticks with me a lot better."

—College sophomore

Think About It — Journal Entry 5.10

Rate yourself in terms of how frequently you use these study strategies according to the following scale:

4 = always, 3 = sometimes, 2 = rarely, 1 = never

1. I block out all distracting sources of outside stimulation when I study.	4	3	2	1
2. I try to find meaning in technical terms by looking at their prefixes or suffixes or by looking up their word roots in the dictionary.	4	3	2	1
3. I compare and contrast what I'm currently studying with what I've already learned.	4	3	2	1
4. I organize the information I'm studying into categories or classes.	4	3	2	1

(continued)

5. I integrate or pull together information from my class notes and readings that relates to the same concept or general category.	4	3	2	1
6. I distribute or spread out my study time over several short sessions in advance of the exam, and I use my last study session before the test to review the information I previously studied.	4	3	2	1
7. I participate in study groups with my classmates.	4	3	2	1

Which of these areas needs improvement? How can you improve in these areas?

____

____

____

____

____

____

Summary and Conclusion

Information delivered during lectures is most likely to form questions and answers on college tests. Students who do not record information presented during lectures in their notes have a slim chance of recalling the information at test time. Thus, effective note taking is critical to successful academic performance in college.

Information from reading assignments is the next most common source of test questions on college exams. Professors often don't discuss information contained in assigned reading during class lectures. Thus, doing the assigned reading, and doing it in a way that's most effective for promoting comprehension and retention, plays an important role in your academic success.

The most effective strategies for promoting effective classroom listening, textbook reading, and studying are those that reflect three college-success principles: (1) active involvement, (2) collaboration, and (3) self-awareness.

Active involvement is critical for learning from lectures (e.g., actively taking notes while listening to lectures) and learning from reading (e.g., actively taking notes while reading). While active involvement is necessary for learning because it engages your attention and enables information to enter the brain, personal reflection is also necessary for deep learning because it keeps that information in the brain by locking it into long-term memory. Reflection also encourages deep learning by promoting self-awareness. Periodically pausing to reflect on whether you're truly understanding what you're studying will make you a more self-aware learner and a more successful student.

Learning is also deepened when it's a multisensory experience—when you engage as many senses as possible in the learning process, particularly the sense of vision. Lastly, learning is strengthened when it's done collaboratively. You can collaborate with peers to take better notes in class, to identify what's most important in your assigned reading, and to study lecture and reading notes in preparation for course exams.*

Case Study

Too Fast, Too Frustrating: A Note-Taking Nightmare

*Susan is a first-year student who is majoring in journalism, and she's enrolled in an introductory course that is required for her major (Introduction to Mass Media). Her instructor for this course lectures at a rapid rate and uses vocabulary words that are new to her. Since she cannot get all her instructor's words down on paper and cannot understand half the words she does manage to write down, she becomes frustrated and stops taking notes. She wants to do well in this course because it's the first course in her major, but she's afraid she will fail it because her class notes are not reflective of the lectures or meaningful.

Discussion Questions

1. Can you relate to this case personally, or do you know any students who are in the same boat as Susan? Explain.

2. What would you recommend that Susan do at this point?

3. Why did you make the preceding recommendation?*

Chapter 5 Reflection

Name: ______________________

**List and describe at least five principles discussed in this chapter that can help you take better notes in class and improve your reading comprehension.

1.

2.

3.

4.

5.

Now explain how you can put these principles into practice.**

For Further Consideration

Test-Taking Tips and Strategies

***Essay Questions**

- Read the directions carefully.
- Budget your exam time; preview the test and look for the questions that are the easiest to answer.
- Plan enough time for each question; allow more time for questions that are worth more points.
- If you have enough time, brainstorm and/or outline your response.
- Rely on facts about the topic, not your feelings and/or opinion.
- Be concise and organized with your answers.
- Know the key task words in essay questions (see "Key Task Words" section).
- Proofread your responses.

Multiple Choice Questions

- Actively review all of the material that will be covered.
- Use flashcards, summary sheets, mind maps, etc. to prepare for the exam.
- Read the questions carefully! Look for words such as *always, never, only, usually.* These terms are absolutes. For example: *Major Depression is **always** accompanied by weight gain.* For this sentence to be true, every single person ever diagnosed with depression would have had to gain weight. Therefore, read questions containing absolutes carefully and consider the true meaning.
- Read carefully for terms such as *not, except,* and *but* that are introduced before the choices.
- If you are stuck or confused by a question, leave it and come back to it later.
- Always double-check to make sure that you are filling in the answer for the right question.
- Complete the entire test and make sure you did not skip any parts of the test.
- Check the back page of the test to ensure you have completed all questions.

True/False Questions

- Remember that for the question to be true, ***every*** detail of the question must be true.
- Questions containing the words such as *always, never,* and *only,* are usually false, whereas, less definite terms such as *often* and *frequently* suggest the statement may be true.
- Do not begin to second-guess what you know or doubt your answers because a sequence of questions appears to be all true or all false.

Matching Questions

- Review all of the terms and descriptions.
- Match the terms you are sure of first.
- As you match terms, cross out both the term and its description.
- Use the process of elimination to assist you in answering the remaining items.

Lab Tests

- Science courses with a lab will typically have lab tests during which you rotate from one lab station to the next.
- Always attend lab.
- Take good notes, including diagrams and other visuals.
- Study your lab notebook carefully.
- Practice labeling your own diagrams and models without looking at your book and/or notes.

Open Book/Open Notes Tests

- It is wrong to assume that you need to study less because you have access to all of the information you need; open-book and open-note exams are typically *harder* than other exams, not easier!
- The best way to prepare is to begin in the same way you would for any other test.
- As you study, create a list of topics and the page numbers where they are covered in the textbook.
- Number the pages of your lecture notes and create an index.
- Create a grid on EXCEL with the topics in alphabetical order; in the other columns place the page numbers in books, notes, etc.
- Use colored tabs in your book to separate topics.
- Monitor your time carefully during the exam.
- Do not waste time looking up information in the book or your notes to "double-check" your answers if you are confident in your choices.
- If you have time at the end of the test, then go back and look up answers and make changes if necessary.

Take-Home Tests

- Are usually more difficult than in-class tests and are often essay tests.
- Require more time, so allow extra time to complete.
- Read the directions and questions as soon as you receive the test to determine how much time you will need.
- Your instructor will expect essay answers to look more like assigned out-of-class papers.
- Determine your instructor's expectations. Are you to work alone? May you collaborate with others?

Key Task Words

- Know the key task words in essay questions.
- Take the time to learn them so you can answer essay questions more accurately and precisely.

Analyze: To divide a subject into its parts in order to understand it better.

Compare: To look at the characteristics of several things and identify their similarities or differences.

Contrast: To identify the differences between things.

Define: To give the meaning of a word or expression; giving an example sometimes helps to clarify a definition.

Describe: To give a general verbal sketch of something in a narrative form.

Discuss: To examine or analyze something in a broad and detailed way; discussion often includes identifying important questions related to an issue and attempting to answer these questions.

Evaluate: To discuss the strengths and weaknesses of something.

Explain: To clarify something, focus on why or how something comes about.

Interpret: To explain the meaning of something.

Justify: To argue in support of some decision or conclusion by showing sufficient evidence or reasons in its favor.

Outline: To present a series of main points in order.

Prove: To give a convincing logical argument and evidence support of some statement.

Review: To summarize and comment on the main parts of a problem or a series of statements.

Summarize: To give information in brief form, omitting examples and details.

Test Anxiety

- Can become debilitating when students put too much pressure on themselves.
- Can be caused by expectations of parents, a spouse, friends, and other people who are close to you.
- Can also be caused by lack of preparation such as not keeping up with assigned readings, assignments, and homework.
- Can be caused by bad experiences with taking exams.
- Can be caused by worrying about the future and what is going to happen.
- Can be caused by not being prepared due to procrastination, which starts a downward spiral leading to pressure to do well on future exams.
- Can be caused by getting behind in a course that builds on prior units (e.g., Math, Foreign Language), which can cause more stress and anxiety as you are attempting to master new material while trying to learn old material as well.

Types of Test Anxiety

- Students may have anxiety in one situation and not in another. For example, you may do well with a chapter exam but have extreme test anxiety with a comprehensive final exam.
- Some students may only have test anxiety dependent on the type of test (e.g., essay exam vs. multiple choice exams).
- Computer proctored exams may cause a student difficulty if he or she lacks good computer skills.
- Test anxiety can also be subject specific; for example, some students may only have math test anxiety.

Symptoms of Test Anxiety

- Butterflies in the stomach
- Feeling queasy or nauseous
- Headaches
- Increased heartbeat
- Hyperventilating
- Shaking
- Sweating
- Muscle cramps
- Going "blank", unable to remember what they *know* they know
- Anger and/or depression due to a cycle of poor testing
- Low self-esteem

What Can You Do?

- Attend preparation workshops and take practice exams.
- If you fear certain types of tests, try predicting the questions and writing sample tests.
- Create practice math exams and time yourself if you have limited test time.
- If you are anxious about computer exams, take practice tests in a computer lab.
- Seek assistance from a DMACC staff and/or faculty member or a DMACC Counselor.
- Take several long deep breaths to restore breathing back to a normal level.
- Use muscle relaxation and visualization.
- Think positively! Focus on your strengths! Avoid negative self-talk!
- Follow a healthy diet.
- Exercise and get plenty of rest.
- Remember that no matter the result, it is not the end of the world.***

References

Bittner, S., Ranch, M., Coon, H. (2009). *DMACC College Seminar: Orientation* (3rd ed.). Dubuque, IA: Kendall-Hunt.

Gardner, J. N., Jewler, A. J., & Barefoot, B.O. (2010). *Your College Experience: Strategies for Success,* concise (8th ed.). Boston: Bedford/St. Martin's.

Gardner, J. N., Jewler, A. J., & Barefoot, B.O. (2009). *Your College Experience: Strategies for Success* (9th ed.). Boston: Bedford/St. Martin's.

SQ4R Worksheet

Your Name:

Selection Title/Chapter:

Author(s):

***1. **Survey**: Look at the title, visuals, questions, excerpts, headings and sub-headings. Afterward, answer the questions below.

What do I already know about the topics?	What do I expect to learn?

2. **Question**: Create questions based on your survey of the text. If there are headings, turn them into questions. Include *at least three* below to help focus your attention as you read.

A.
B.
C.
D.
E.

3. **Read** and **Record** (Annotate): Read the selection thoroughly, highlight, and make note of important points, associations, and unfamiliar terms. Complete the chart using **your own words**. Provide a sketch and/or explanation of the visuals. Use and attach a separate sheet if needed.

Page and Paragraph #	Vocabulary Terms	Notes and Definitions	Visuals

(*Continued*)

(Continued)

4. **Recite**: Answer your questions from step two.

a.
b.
c.
d.
e.

5. **Review and Reflect**: Check your memory by verbalizing the above information. Below, write a summary **in your own words** of what you have read, connecting the content ideas. Additionally, write a brief reflection including your personal response to the reading (use "I" and make connections to your own experiences, ask more questions, respond to the text, and consider anything you were reminded of or visualized while reading).***

Summary:

Reflection:

Adapted from Florida Online Reading Professional Development. (n.d.). *SQ4R*. Retrieved from the Marco Island Charter Middle School website at http://micms.org/SQ4R.pdf

6 DMACC Campus Opportunities and Resources

Ask yourself, "What opportunities await me at DMACC?" "What do I need to know to take every advantage of my college experience?" Let's take a look.

Opportunity #1. Join Phi Theta Kappa

What is Phi Theta Kappa?

Phi Theta Kappa is an international scholastic society recognized by the American Association of Community and Junior Colleges (AACJC). DMACC students with a GPA of 3.5 or higher after accumulating at least twelve community college credits are eligible to join. Students do not have to include grade transcripts that are older than five years for the determination of their eligibility status.

DMACC has a chapter at each of its six campuses. There are more than 1200 chapters worldwide. Phi Theta Kappa has recognized academic excellence in the two-year college since 1918 and has become the largest and most prestigious honor society serving two-year colleges around the world. The innovative programs and services and array of membership benefits offered by Phi Theta Kappa are unequaled among honor societies. Co-curricular programs focus upon the Society's Hallmarks of Scholarship, Leadership, Service, and Fellowship. It is estimated that 100,000 students are inducted into Phi Theta Kappa programs each year.

To join, fill out a membership and return it along with the application fee to your DMACC Campus Phi Theta Kappa Advisor. If you have received an invitation to join this Honor Society, or have further questions regarding this opportunity, contact your DMACC Campus Phi Theta Kappa Advisor.

Opportunity #2. Participate in Student Life

All these opportunities await you in Student Life:

- Student Activities
- Student Activity Council (SAC)
- Student Organizations and Clubs
- Voter Registration
- Ticket Sales
- Intramurals
- Intercollegiate Athletics
- Music, Drama, and Dance

Opportunity #3. Register to Study Abroad in the Spring

DMACC offers students an opportunity to take selected classes during the Spring semester London Study Abroad Program. Students enjoy eight weeks in London studying with a DMACC professor.

In the past, students have taken classes in composition, speech, history, literature, and the humanities; but specific course offerings are announced once the lead professor is selected. Additionally, British professors and scholars at the University of London offer "British Life and Culture," an essential lecture and field trip series covering such topics as the Monarchy and the Royal Family, World War II and the Blitz, and the History of London.

Classes are held at the University of London in the center of the city. In addition to lectures and class discussions, students tour museums, visit historic places, and attend live theatre performances in London and surrounding areas. For a real sense of living in London, students reside with British families.

Students enroll for twelve DMACC credits, which may include independent study, one online course, and internships. Financial aid is available for study abroad. Program arrangements are made in conjunction with the American Institute for Foreign Study (AIFS), specializing in study abroad programs for colleges and universities. The AIFS has an office in London.

Opportunity #4. Already Knowledgeable about a Class? Consider Taking a Challenge Test

Review DMACC Policy ES 4210 for information about Challenge Tests.

Opportunity #5. Register for Cross Enrollment

Under a special agreement, eligible students who have completed 12 college credits may apply to cross enroll in one class each semester (fall and spring only) with tuition waived for that class. Other fees apply depending on the type of course in which the student enrolls.

The following institutions participate in the Cross Enrollment Program:

- Drake University
- Grand View University
- Iowa State University

Opportunity #6. Check out the DMACC Business and Industry Partnerships

AccuMold-Tool and Die & Robotics: A partnership between AccuMold and DMACC was formed to create the opportunity for AccuMold to help train the company's future workforce and at the same time help raise the general awareness of the DMACC Tool & Die and Robotics program. Each year up to four scholarships will be awarded.

Apprenticeship Program: A partnership between DMACC and the Bureau of Apprenticeship Training (BAT). Earn an AAS Degree at DMACC in Technical Studies.

ASEP: The DMACC General Motors Automotive Service Educational Program (GM ASEP) offers students paid work experience at a General Motors dealership and a two-year Associate of Applied Science Degree. Financial aid and scholarships are available to those who qualify.

ASSET: The partnership between Ford and Lincoln-Mercury dealers, Ford Motor Company, community colleges, and technical schools is a two-year program that allows students to earn while they learn and gain hands-on technical experience while earning an Associate's Degree in Automotive Technology.

CAP: The MOPAR CAP program is a partnership program between DMACC and Fiat Chrysler Automobiles and regional Dodge Jeep Chrysler Ram and Fiat dealers. Upon graduation with an AAS degree from the MOPAR Career Automotive Program, students generally continue on with their careers as employees at their sponsoring dealers.

Caterpillar/Ziegler: DMACC and Ziegler have teamed up to bring you BIG opportunities in the field of diesel technology. Your Associate of Applied Science (AAS) degree from DMACC will open doors to an in-demand career in the diesel technology field and will prepare you to work as a service technician.

Machinist Apprenticeship: DMACC's machinist registered apprenticeship program is looking for companies and individuals within companies that want to participate with a registered program through the Department of Labor. After completion of the program you will be a nationally recognized journeyperson machinist.

Opportunity #7. Visit with a Career Center Advisor about Career Planning and Employment Assistance

Career advisors are available on the Ankeny campus in the Career Center in Building 5. Advisors are also available at each campus by appointment to explore and evaluate career and transfer options. Set up an appointment by contacting the campus of your choice and making an appointment.

Opportunity #8. Planning to transfer to a four-year College?

Check out: http://www.transferiniowa.org/ and also DMACC's Education Partnerships.

If you are planning to transfer from DMACC to a four-year college, it is important to begin preparing for your transfer as early as possible to ensure a smooth transition. The information below provides helpful transfer information within Iowa. Advisors are also available to assist you with your out of state transfer plans.

University of Iowa

The **2 + 2 Guaranteed Graduation Plan** is for students who want to earn an Associate of Arts degree at DMACC before transferring to The University of Iowa to earn a bachelor›s degree. The plan connects you with University of Iowa advisors early on so you take the right courses at the right time to complete both degrees in a total of four years. Because of the 2 + 2 graduation guarantee, only certain majors at Iowa are eligible for the 2 + 2 plan.

The **Bachelor of Applied Studies (BAS) program** is designed for graduates of community college (AA, AS, or AAS degrees) who wish to complete a bachelor's degree but, for a variety of reasons, cannot engage in traditional on-campus study

The **Bachelor of Liberal Studies (BLS) program** is designed to serve adults who, for a variety of reasons, might not otherwise be able to attend college as a full-time, on-campus student.

The **RN-BSN program** is mostly online and is for associate degree and diploma-prepared RNs who are ready to expand their nursing skills and professional potential by earning the BSN.

The **BA in Social Work program** prepares students for beginning generalist social work practice with individuals, families, small groups, organizations, and communities. The program gives students a base for a graduate education in social work. Students completing the 2 + 2 Social Work major through DMACC have the option of pursuing a BA completion program in Social Work in Des Moines.

The online **Bachelor of Business Administration in Management** with a concentration in the Entrepreneurial Management track was created for place-bound students.

Buena Vista University 2 + 2

Des Moines Area Community College has an Articulation Agreement with Buena Vista University (BVU). The degree-completion program allows students to take evening or online classes that lead to a Bachelor of Arts degree in Business Management, Elementary Education, Psychology, Human Services, or Business Administration (online) from Buena Vista University.

Simpson College 2 + 2 AA to BA

Students who have earned an Associate of Arts degree at DMACC will have fulfilled the requirements of the Engaged Citizenship Curriculum (all general academic requirements) before starting at Simpson. Simpson has a course articulation guide for DMACC which shows how each class will transfer to Simpson. Credit evaluations are generated quickly upon request and are automatically completed for prospective students and applicants. For additional information on transfer credits, contact the Director of Transfer Enrollment at Simpson College.

University of Northern Iowa 2 + 2

The University of Northern Iowa (UNI) and DMACC offer an Elementary Education Bachelor's degree opportunity through a 2 + 2 program. Students take two years of classes at DMACC and three years of classes through UNI. UNI faculty teach all UNI classes either at DMACC, face-to-face, or via distance education (ICN, Blackboard).

University of Northern Iowa–Admissions Partnership Program (APP)

Students admitted to DMACC who plan to pursue a bachelor's degree at the University of Northern Iowa (UNI) can sign up for the Admissions Partnership Program to streamline the transfer process. Students accepted into the Admissions Partnership Program while enrolled at DMACC benefit from:

- Guaranteed admission to UNI provided all requirements are met.
- Timely progress toward graduation. With the exception of some UNI programs, participation enables students who stay on track to begin at DMACC and graduate from UNI in a total of eight semesters.

- Option to lock-in Bachelor's degree requirements with the same status as a student who enrolls directly at UNI as an entering freshman.
- Academic advising at both DMACC and UNI from the point of acceptance into the APP.
- Early orientation and scheduling for the first semester at UNI.
- Guaranteed placement in UNI housing provided the student complies with established residence policies and application procedures/deadlines.
- Access to UNI campus and student resources.
- Receipt of updated UNI materials and information about campus events and opportunities.
- Updated DMACC transcripts automatically sent to UNI at the end of each semester.

Students who want to be a part of the DMACC/UNI Admissions Partnership Program must enroll at DMACC as a degree-seeking student in a program appropriate for the transfer and then apply to the program.

Iowa State University–Admissions Partnership Program (APP)

Students participating in the Admissions Partnership Program (APP) experience a smooth and successful transition to Iowa State University. Benefits of the program include personalized mentoring and academic counseling, and guaranteed admission to Iowa State University provided all requirements of the program are met.

Drake University–Transfer Resource Initiative (TRI)

Under the Transfer Resource Initiative (TRI) program, you'll enjoy the benefits of being a student at **both schools** while you complete your first two years of college at DMACC. At the end of two years, you can earn an Associate's Degree and move on to Drake University to complete your Bachelor's Degree in as little as two additional years.

Grand View University–Transfer Resource Initiative (TRI)

Under the Transfer Resource Initiative (TRI) program, you'll enjoy the benefits of being a student at both schools while you complete your first two years of college at DMACC. At the end of two years, you can earn an Associate's Degree and then move on to Grand View University to complete your Bachelor's Degree in as little as two additional years.

Grinnell College

DMACC has a new transfer agreement with Grinnell College, allowing qualified students to consider transferring to the private four-year, liberal-arts, college.

This agreement provides a number of unique benefits including application counseling to maximize the chances of admission to Grinnell, an invitation to an exclusive pre-application orientation program, and an opportunity for admitted students to earn both a DMACC Associates Degree and a Grinnell College Bachelor's Degree. DMACC was the first two-year college to sign a transfer agreement with Grinnell College.

Opportunity #9. Determine if you are eligible to receive alternative credit

DMACC offers credit for prior learning opportunities for students with advanced skills or knowledge in fields related to their programs of study. These advanced skills could be gained through work experience, military experience or training, business and industry training, certifications or credentials earned, or previous learning experiences. To determine if you are eligible to receive credit for prior learning, consider these questions:

- Have you received a certificate or credential from participating in a workshop, industry training, or seminar?
- Are you a member or veteran of the Armed Services?
- Have you received training through DMACC's Business Resources (DBR) or Continuing Education?
- Have you taken courses through DMACC's Workforce Training Academy (WTA)?
- Do you have past experiences or skills applicable to your program of study that you would like to explore to see if you could receive alternative credit?

Students who would like to learn more about the process can review the procedure ES 4544 or speak with their academic advisor or program department chairperson.

Now ask yourself, "What resources are available for academic and personal support on my campus?" Let's take a look.

Opportunity #10 Check out Academic and Personal Resources

- Academic Achievement Center
- Academic Advising
- Campus Security and Emergency Auto Service
- Child Care (Ankeny)
- College Communications
- Computer Lab
- Counseling
- Financial Aid
- Library
- Notary Public
- Recreation and Wellness Programs
- Scholarships and Grants
- Services for Students with Disabilities
- SMARTHINKING®, on-line tutoring
- Student Health Services (Ankeny)
- Transfer Planning
- Tutoring
- Veteran's Services

Take every advantage of the opportunities and resources awaiting you.

Chapter 6 Exercises

Exercise 1. Academic Misconduct

Name: ______________________

Materials Required: DMACC Procedure

Objective: To understand the procedure regarding Academic Misconduct

Read the procedure regarding *Academic Misconduct* and then answer the questions.

John arrived at school ill-prepared for a challenging day. He had worked until 10 pm the night before, and then went home and studied until 2 am for a Biology exam. When he awoke, he felt as if he hadn't slept or studied at all. His Biology exam was at 8 am. While taking the exam, he had a difficult time concentrating on the questions and staying awake.

After the Biology class, he went to his Comp I class. The instructor asked the students to write a one-page, in-class essay on a favorite topic. He couldn't believe he had such a difficult assignment after the grueling Biology exam. He began searching the Internet and found some interesting articles on mountain biking, a favorite activity of his. While reading, he kept dozing off, and then found he had only twenty-five minutes left to write the paper. He hurriedly copied some of the material from the Internet and wrote a few of his own ideas. He turned in the paper, left the class, and hurried to work.

The instructor read the paper and completed a Google search for the topic. What will she find?

Did the student exhibit academic misconduct? If so, what type of academic misconduct? What sanctions are possible against this student?

What could John have done differently in his Comp I class?

What other advice might you have for John?

Exercise 2. Grade Appeals

Name: ______________________

Materials Required: DMACC procedure

Objective: To understand the procedure regarding grade appeals

Read the procedure regarding *Appeal of Final Grade* and then answer the questions

Matthew is a second year student at DMACC. He is taking twenty-one credits to enable him to graduate in the spring. He has a D in his economics class. He finds the concepts difficult to understand and the exams challenging. He studies but doesn't retain the information. As the semester progresses, he becomes more and more frustrated with the class. He thinks the instructor should expect less from the students and shouldn't give such difficult exams. He fails the final exam and receives a D- as his final grade. He feels the grade is unfair. He feels the instructor made the class too difficult. He wants to appeal his final grade.

What should he do first?

Do you think the student has a good basis for an Appeal of Final Grade? Why or why not?

What decision making standards are used to determine the outcome of an appeal by the College Review Board?

Exercise 3. Student Conduct

Name: ______________________

Materials Required: DMACC procedure

Objective: To understand the procedure regarding Student Conduct

Read the procedure regarding Student Conduct and then answer the questions.

Karen began abusing alcohol in high school. Once in college, her habit intensified. Sometimes she would go to class after drinking the night before and would still feel hung over.

Sunday night, she spent the evening drinking with friends. During class on Monday her instructor asked her to leave the classroom because she smelled strongly of alcohol.

Did the instructor have the right to ask Karen to leave class?

Was her conduct subject to sanction?

What might the instructor recommend for this student?

Exercise 4. Student Conduct

Name: ______________________

Materials Required: DMACC procedure

Objective: To understand the procedure regarding Student Conduct

Read the procedure regarding Student Conduct and then answer the questions. This exercise applies to campuses that have on-site security.

Chelsea is caught speeding on campus. She is stopped by a campus security officer, who writes her a ticket. She indicates that she was unaware of the speed limit in that area.

Will the security officer give her a break because Chelsea was unaware of the posted speed limit?

Could she appeal the ticket? If yes, how?

What might be the consequences of speeding on campus?

SQ4R Worksheet

Your Name:

Selection Title/Chapter:

Author(s):

1. **Survey:** Look at the title, visuals, questions, excerpts, headings and sub-headings. Afterward, answer the questions below.

What do I already know about the topics?	What do I expect to learn?

2. **Question:** Create questions based on your survey of the text. If there are headings, turn them into questions. Include *at least three* below to help focus your attention as you read.

A.
B.
C.
D.
E.

3. **Read** and **Record** (Annotate): Read the selection thoroughly, highlight, and make note of important points, associations, and unfamiliar terms. Complete the chart using **your own words**. Provide a sketch and/or explanation of the visuals. Use and attach a separate sheet if needed.

Page and Paragraph #	Vocabulary Terms	Notes and Definitions	Visuals

(*Continued*)

(Continued)

4. **Recite**: Answer your questions from step two.

a.
b.
c.
d.
e.

5. **Review and Reflect**: Check your memory by verbalizing the above information. Below, write a summary **in your own words** of what you have read, connecting the content ideas. Additionally, write a brief reflection including your personal response to the reading (use "I" and make connections to your own experiences, ask more questions, respond to the text, and consider anything you were reminded of or visualized while reading).

Summary:

Reflection:

Adapted from Florida Online Reading Professional Development. (n.d.). *SQ4R*. Retrieved from the Marco Island Charter Middle School website at http://micms.org/SQ4R.pdf

Social and Emotional Intelligence 7

Relating to Others and Regulating Emotions

THOUGHT STARTER | *Journal Entry* 7.1

*When you think about someone who's "intelligent," what personal characteristics come to mind? Why?

LEARNING GOAL

To gain a set of social and emotional skills that enhance the quality of your interpersonal relationships and mental health.

The Importance of Interpersonal Relationships for Success, Health, and Happiness

Interpersonal relationships can be a source of social support that promotes success, or a source of social conflict that distracts you from focusing on and achieving your personal goals. As a new college student, you may find yourself surrounded by multiple social opportunities. One of the adjustments you'll need to make is finding a healthy middle ground between too much and too little socializing, as well as forming solid interpersonal relationships that support rather than sabotage your educational success.

Social intelligence, a.k.a. interpersonal intelligence, is the ability to relate effectively to others and is considered to be a major form of human intelligence (Gardner, 1993; Goleman, 2006). Emotional intelligence is emotional self-awareness or empathy (sensitivity to the emotions of others). Both social and emotional intelligence are better predictors of personal and professional success than is intellectual ability (Goleman, 1995, 2006).

Student *Perspective*

"I have often found conflict in living a balanced academic and social life. I feel that when I am enjoying and succeeding in one spectrum, I am lagging in the other."

—First-year student

"I will pay more for the ability to deal with people than any other ability under the sun."

—John D. Rockefeller, American industrialist and philanthropist and once the richest man in the world

Social Intelligence

Studies show that people who have stronger social support networks have a longer life expectancy (Giles, Glonek, Luszcz, & Andrews, 2005) and are more likely to report being happy (Myers, 1993). The development of a strong social support system

Student *Perspective*

"The Internet supposedly increases communication and brings humanity closer together. Instead, in my generation, I'm noticing quite the opposite. There seems to be less face-to-face communication. Everyone is hooked on social networking websites. We cowardly avoid interaction where there are no facial expressions or tones."

—First-year student

is particularly important in today's high-tech world of virtual reality and online (vs. in-person) communication, both of which make it easier to avoid direct contact, not form human connections with others, and increase the risk of isolation, loneliness, and social avoidance (Putman, 2000).

Think About It — *Journal Entry* 7.2

Who are the people in your life that you tend to turn to for social support when you are experiencing stress or need personal encouragement? Why?

"The most important single ingredient in the formula of success is knowing how to get along with people."

—Theodore (Teddy) Roosevelt, 26th president of the United States and winner of the Nobel Peace Prize

Improving the Quality of Interpersonal Relationships

The quality of your interpersonal relationships rests on two skills: (1) communication skills, or how well you send and receive information when interacting with others (verbally and nonverbally), and (2) human relations skills, or how well you relate to and treat people, i.e., "people skills."

Listed here are our top recommendations for strengthening your interpersonal communication skills. Some strategies may appear to be basic and obvious, but they're also powerful. It may be that because they are so basic, people overlook them and forget to use them consistently. Don't be fooled by the seeming simplicity of the following suggestions, and don't underestimate their social impact.

Strategies for Improving the Quality of Interpersonal Communication

"We have been given two ears and but a single mouth in order that we may hear more and talk less."

—Zeno of Citium, ancient Greek philosopher and founder of Stoic philosophy

1. **Work hard at being a good listener.** Studies show that listening is the most frequent human communication activity, followed, in order, by reading, speaking, and writing (Newton, 1990; Purdy & Borisoff, 1996). One study found that college students spend an average of 52.5 percent of each day listening (Barker & Watson, 2000). Being a good listener is one of the top characteristics mentioned by people when they cite the positive features of their best friends (Berndt, 1992). Listening is also one of the top skills employers look for when hiring and promoting employees (Maes, Weldy, & Icenogle, 1997; Winsor, Curtis, & Stephens, 1997; Wolvin, 2010).

   Human relations experts often recommend that people talk less, listen more, and listen more effectively (Nichols, 1995; Nichols & Stevens, 1957). Being a good listener is easier said than done because the ability to listen closely and sensitively is a challenging mental task. Studies show that listening comprehension for spoken messages is less than 50 percent (Nichols & Stevens, 1957; Wolvin & Coakley, 1993), which is not surprising considering that listeners have only one chance to understand words spoken to them. People cannot replay a message delivered in person like they can reread words in print. Studies also show that a person can understand spoken language at a rate almost four times faster than the average person speaks (Adler & Towne, 2001), which leaves our minds plenty of spare time to drift off to something else (e.g., think about what to say next). Since you're not actively doing something while listening, you can easily fall prey to passive listening, whereby you can give others the impression that you're focused on their words but your mind is partially somewhere else. When listening, you need to remain aware of this tendency to drift off and to actively fight it by devoting your full attention to others when they're speaking. Two key strategies for doing so are: (1) focus your attention on what the speaker is saying rather than on what you're going to say next, and (2) actively engage with the speaker's message by occasionally asking questions or seeking clarification about what is being said.

Remember

When you listen closely to those who speak to you, you send them the message that you respect their ideas and that they're worthy of your undivided attention.

2. **Be conscious of the nonverbal messages you send while listening.** Whether or not you're truly listening is often communicated silently through nonverbal body language. It's estimated that 90 percent of communication is nonverbal, because human body language often communicates stronger and truer messages than spoken language (Mehrabian, 1972). Researchers who study lying have identified one of the best ways to detect whether people are telling the truth: see whether their body language matches their spoken language. For example, if people say they're excited or enthusiastic about an idea you're communicating to them but their nonverbal communication indicates otherwise (e.g., their eyebrows don't rise and they sit motionless), you have good reason to doubt their sincerity (Eckman & Friesen, 1969).

"The most important thing in communication is to hear what isn't being said."

—Peter F. Drucker, Austrian author and founder of the study of management

When it comes to listening, body language may be the best way to communicate interest in the speaker's words, as well as interest in the person who's doing the speaking. Similarly, if you are speaking, awareness of your listeners' body language can provide important clues about whether you're holding or losing their interest.

A good mnemonic device (memory-improvement method) for remembering the nonverbal signals you should send others while listening is the acronym SOFTEN, in which each letter stands for an effective nonverbal message:

S = **Smile.** Smiling suggests interest and acceptance, but do it periodically, not continually. (A permanent smile can come across as an artificial pose.)
Sit still. Fidgeting and squirming send the message that the speaker is making you feel anxious or bored.

O = **Open posture.** Avoid closed-posture positions, such as crossing your arms or folding your hands; they can send a message that you're not open to what the speaker is saying or passing judgment on what's being said.

F = **Forward lean.** Leaning back can send a signal that you're not "into" what the person is saying or evaluating (psychoanalyzing) the person saying it.
Face the speaker directly. Line up both shoulders with the speaker rather than turning one shoulder away, as if to give the speaker the cold shoulder.

T = **Touch.** A light touch on the arm or hand can be a good way to communicate warmth, but no rubbing, stroking, or touching in ways that could be interpreted as inappropriate intimacy (or sexual harassment).

E = **Eye contact.** Lack of eye contact sends the message that you're looking around for something more interesting or stimulating than the speaker. However, don't make continual or relentless eye contact because that borders on staring or glaring. Instead, strike a happy medium by making *periodic* eye contact.

N = **Nod your head.** Slowly and periodically, not rapidly and repeatedly—this sends the message that you want the speaker to hurry up and finish up so you can start talking.

Sending positive nonverbal signals when listening encourages others to become more self-confident and enthusiastic speakers, which not only benefits them but also benefits the listener. Listening to speakers who are more self-confident and animated makes listening less challenging and more stimulating.

3. **Be open to different topics of conversation.** Don't be a closed-minded or selective listener who listens to people like you're listening to the radio—selecting or tuning into only those conversational topics that reflect your favorite interests or personal points of view but tuning out everything else.

Remember

People learn most from others whose interests and viewpoints don't necessarily match their own. Ignoring or blocking out information and ideas about topics that don't immediately interest you or support your particular perspective is not only a poor social skill but also a poor learning strategy.

4. **Communicate your ideas precisely and concisely.** When we speak, our goal should be to get to our point, make it, get "off stage," and give someone else a chance to talk. Nobody appreciates "stage hogs" who dominate the conversation and gobble up more than their fair share of conversation time.

   You can make your spoken messages less time-consuming and more to the point by avoiding tangents, unnecessary details, and empty fillers (e.g., "like," "kinda like," "I mean," "I'm all," and "you know"). Fillers such as these just "fill up" time and waste conversation time while adding nothing substantial or meaningful to the conversation. Excessive use of fillers can also result in listeners losing patience, interest, and respect for the speaker (Daniels & Horowitz, 1997).
5. **Take time to gather your thoughts before expressing them.** It's better to think silently *before* speaking aloud than to think aloud *while* talking. Giving forethought to what you're going to say will enable you to speak economically and open up more time for others to speak.
6. **Be comfortable with silent spells that may take place during conversations.** Silence can sometimes make us feel uncomfortable (like being in an elevator with a stranger). To relieve the discomfort of silence, it's tempting to rush in and say anything to get the conversation going again. Although this may be well intended, it can result in speaking before (and without) thinking. Probably more often than not, it's better to hold back our words and think them through before blurting them out.

Silent spots in a conversation shouldn't always be viewed as a "communication breakdown." Instead, they may indicate that the people involved in the conversation are pausing to think deeply about what each other is saying and are comfortable enough with each other to allow these reflective pauses to take place.

Think About It — Journal Entry 7.3

On what topics do you hold strong opinions? Why?

When you express these opinions, how do others usually react to you?

Human Relations Skills (a.k.a. People Skills)

In addition to communicating and conversing well with others, one element of managing interpersonal relationships involves how well you relate to and treat people. You can use several strategies to improve this broader set of human relations or people skills.

"We should be aware of the magic contained in a name. The name sets that individual apart; it makes him or her unique among all others. Remember that a person's name is to that person the sweetest and most important sound in any language."

—Dale Carnegie, author of the bestselling book *How to Win Friends and Influence People* and founder of the Dale Carnegie Course, a worldwide program for business based on his teachings

1. **Remember the names of people you meet.** Remembering people's names communicates to others that you know them as individuals. It makes each person you meet feel less like an anonymous face in a crowd and more like a special and unique individual with a distinctive identity.

   Although people commonly claim they don't have a good memory for names, no evidence shows that the ability to remember names is an inherited trait that people are born with and have no control over; instead, it's a skill that can be developed through personal effort and employment of effective learning and memory strategies.

   You can use the following strategies for remembering names:

   - Consciously pay attention to the name of each person you meet. Make a conscious effort to listen for the person's name rather than focus on the impression you're making on that person, the impression the individual is making on you, or what you're going to say next.

- Reinforce your memory for a new name by saying it or rehearsing it within a minute or two after you first hear it. For instance, if your friend Gertrude has just introduced you to Geraldine, you might say: "Geraldine, how long have you known Gertrude?" By using a person's name soon after you've heard it, you intercept memory loss when forgetting is most likely to occur—immediately after you acquire new information (Underwood, 1983).
- Strengthen your memory of an individual's name by associating it with other information learned about the person. For instance, you can associate the person's name with: (1) your first impression of the individual's personality, (2) a physical characteristic of the person, (3) your topic of conversation, (4) the place where you met, or (5) a familiar word that rhymes with the person's name. By making a mental connection between the person's name and some other piece of information, you help your brain form a physical connection, which is the biological foundation of human memory.

Remember

Developing the habit of remembering names is not only a social skill that can improve your interpersonal interactions and bring you friends, but also a powerful professional tool that can promote your career success in whatever field you may pursue.

In business, remembering people's names can help recruit and retain customers; in politics, it can win votes; and in education, it can promote the teacher's connection and rapport with students.

"If we obey this law, [it] will bring us countless friends. The law is this: Always make the person feel important."

—Dale Carnegie, *How to Win Friends and Influence People*

2. **Refer to people by name when you greet and interact with them.** When you greet a person, be sure to use the person's name in your greeting. Saying, "Hi, Mark," will mean a lot more to Mark than simply saying "Hi" or, worse yet, "Hi, there"—which sounds like you're just acknowledging something "out there" that could be either a human or an inanimate object. By continuing to use people's names after you've learned them, you continue to send them the message that you haven't forgotten their unique identities and you continue to strengthen your memory of their names.
3. **Show interest in others by remembering information about them.** Ask people questions about their personal interests, plans, and experiences. Listen closely to their answers, especially to what seems most important to them, what they care about, or what intrigues them, and introduce these topics when you have conversations with them. For one person that topic may be books, for another it may be sports, and for another it may be relationships. When you see people again, ask them about something they brought up in your last conversation. Try to get beyond the standard, generic questions that people routinely ask after they say "Hello" (e.g., "What's going on?"). Instead, ask about something specific you discussed with them last time you spoke (e.g., "How did that math test go that you were worried about last week?"). This sends a clear message to others that you remember them and care about them. Your memory often reflects your priorities—you're most likely to remember what's most important to you. When you remember people's names and something about them, it lets them know that they're a high priority to you. Furthermore, you're likely to find that others start showing more interest in you after you show interest in them. Another surprising thing may happen when you ask questions that show interest in others: people are likely to say you're a great conversationalist and a good friend.

"You can make more friends in 2 months by becoming interested in other people than you can in 2 years by trying to get other people interested in you."

—Dale Carnegie, *How to Win Friends and Influence People*

Author's Experience

One of my most successful teaching strategies is something I do on the first day of class. I ask my students to complete a student information sheet that includes their name and some information relating to their past experiences, future plans, and personal interests. I answer the same questions I ask my students, writing my information on the board while they write theirs on a sheet of paper. (This allows them to get to know me while I get to know them.) After I've collected all their information sheets, I call out the names of individual students, asking each student to raise a hand when his or her name is called so that I can associate the name and the student's face. To help me remember the names, as I call each name I rapidly jot down a quick word or abbreviated phrase next to the student's name for later review (e.g., a distinctive physical feature or where the student's seated).

I save the student information sheets and refer to them throughout the term. For example, I record the student's name and strongest interest on a sticky note and attach the note to my class notes near topics I'll be covering during the term that relate to the student's interest. When I get to that topic in class (which could be months later), I immediately see the student's name posted by it. When I begin to discuss the topic, I mention the name of the student who had expressed interest in it on the first day of class (e.g., "Gina, we're about to study your favorite topic"). Students often perk up when I mention their names in association with their preferred topics; plus, they're often amazed by my apparent ability to remember so much later in the term the personal interests that they shared on the first day of class. Students never ask how I remember their personal interests, so they're not aware of my sticky note strategy. Instead, they just think I have an extraordinary social memory and social sensitivity (which is just fine with me).

Joe Cuseo

Strategies for Meeting People and Forming Friendships

An important aspect of the college experience is meeting new people, learning from them, and forming lifelong friendships. Here are some practical strategies for increasing the quantity and variety of the people you meet and the quality of friendships you form.

"Be who you are; say what you feel; because those who mind, don't matter, and those who matter, don't mind."

—Theodore Seuss Giesel, a.k.a. Dr. Seuss, famous author of children's books such as *The Cat in the Hat*

1. **Place yourself in situations and locations where you will come in regular contact with others.** Social psychologists have found that the origin of friendships is physical proximity—people are more likely to become friends if they continually find themselves in the same place at the same time (Latané et al., 1995). You can apply this principle by spending as much time on campus as possible and spending time in places where others are likely to be present (e.g., by eating your meals in the student cafeteria and studying in the college library). If you are a commuter student, try to make your college experience as similar as possible to that of a residential student: for example, try to spend study time and social time on campus (e.g., attending campus social or cultural events).

Student Perspective

"I value authenticity in people's actions. I believe in genuine motives [and] none of that ulterior or deceitful stuff."

—First-year student

2. **Put yourself in social situations where you're likely to meet people who have similar interests, goals, and values.** Research supports the proverb, "Birds of a feather flock together." People tend to form friendships with others who share similar interests, values, or goals (AhYun, 2002). When two people have something in common, they're more likely to become friends because they're more likely to enjoy spending time together doing things that relate to their common interests. They're also more likely to get along with each other because they reinforce or validate each other's personal interests and values (Festinger, 1954; Suls, Martin, & Wheeler, 2002).

"Happiness is when what you think, what you say and what you do are in harmony."

—Mahatma Gandhi, nonviolent civil rights leader who led the struggle to free India from colonial rule

An important aspect of the college experience is meeting new people and forming lasting friendships.

One straightforward way to find others with whom you have something in common is by participating in clubs and organizations on campus that reflect your interests and values. If you cannot find one, start one of your own. Also, regularly check your college newspaper, posted flyers on campus, and the Student Information Desk in your Student Activities Center to keep track of social events that are more likely to attract others who share your interests, values, or goals.

3. **Meeting others through social media.** Social media represents another type of venue through which you can network with other college students. You can use social media to meet new people, join groups on campus, and check for announcements of parties or other social events. However, be careful about the people you respond to, and be careful about what you post. Reports indicate that both schools and employers are checking students' social media and using that information to help them decide whether to accept or reject applicants (Palank, 2006; Sinsky, 2011).

Interpersonal Conflict

Disagreement and conflict among people are inevitable aspects of social life. Research shows that even the most happily married couples don't experience continual marital bliss, but have occasional disagreements and conflicts (Gottman, 1994). Thus, conflict is something you cannot expect to escape or eliminate; you can only hope to contain it, defuse it, and prevent it from reaching unmanageable levels. The effective interpersonal communication and human relations skills discussed in this chapter can help minimize conflicts. In addition to these general skills, the following set of strategies may be used to handle interpersonal conflict constructively and humanely.

Minimizing and Resolving Interpersonal Conflicts

1. **Pick the right place and time to resolve conflicts.** Don't discuss sensitive issues when you're fatigued, in a fit of anger, or in a hurry (Daniels & Horowitz, 1997), and don't discuss them in a public arena; deal with them only with the person involved. As the expression goes, "Don't air your dirty laundry in public." Addressing a conflict in public is akin to a public trial; it's likely to embarrass or humiliate the person with whom you are in conflict and cause him/her to resist or resent you.
2. **Check yourself before you express yourself.** When you have a conflict with someone, your ultimate objective should be to solve the problem, not to unload your anger and have an emotionally cathartic experience. Impulsively "dumping" on the other person may give you an immediate sense of relief, but it's not likely to produce permanent improvement in the other person's attitude or behavior toward you. Instead of unloading, take the load off—cool down and give yourself a little down time to reflect rationally before you react emotionally. For example, count to 10 and give your emotions time to settle down before you begin to say anything. Pausing for reflection also communicates to the other person that you're giving careful thought and attention to the matter rather than lashing out randomly.

   If the conflict is so intense that you're feeling incensed or enraged, it may be a good idea to slow things down by writing out your thoughts ahead of time. This strategy will give you time to organize and clarify your ideas by first talking silently to yourself (on paper) before talking out loud to the other person (in person).
3. **Give the person a chance to respond.** Just because you're angry doesn't mean that the person you're angry with must forfeit the right to free speech and self-defense. Giving the other person a chance to speak and be heard will increase the likelihood that you'll receive a cooperative response to your request. It will also prevent you from storming in too quickly before being sure you've got all the facts straight.

   After listening to the other person's response, check your understanding by summarizing it in your own words (e.g., "What I hear you saying is . . ."). This is an important first step in the conflict-resolution process because conflicts often revolve around a simple misunderstanding, failure to communicate, or communication breakdown. Sometimes just taking the time to hear where the other person is coming from before launching into a full-scale complaint or criticism can reduce or resolve the conflict.
4. **Acknowledge the person's perspectives and feelings.** After listening to the person's response, if you disagree with it, don't dismiss or discount the person's feelings. For instance, don't say, "That's ridiculous," or "You're not making any sense." Instead, say, "I see how you might feel that way, but . . ." or "I feel bad that you are under pressure, but . . . ."
5. **If things begin to get heated, call for a time-out and postpone the discussion to allow both of you time to cool off.** When emotion and adrenaline run high, logic and reason often run low. This can result in someone saying something during a fit of anger that, in turn, stimulates an angry response from the other person; then the anger of both individuals continues to escalate and turns into an

intense volley of negativity. For example, the conversation may end up something like this:

Person A: "You're out of control."
Person B: "No, I'm not out of control, you're just overreacting."
Person A: "*I'm* overreacting, you're the one who's yelling!"
Person B: "I'm not yelling, *you're* the one who's raising your voice!"

Exchanges such as these are likely to turn up the emotional heat so high that resolving the conflict is out of the question until both back off, cool down, and try again later.

6. **Make your point assertively (not passively, aggressively, or passive-aggressively).** When you're passive, you don't stand up for your personal rights: you allow others to take advantage of you and push you around. You say nothing when you should say something. You say "yes" when you want to say "no." When you handle conflict passively, you become angry, anxious, or resentful about doing nothing and keeping it all inside. People refer to others who are passive as being a "doormat" or letting others walk all over them.

   When you're aggressive, you stand up for your rights but you also violate the rights of the other person by threatening, dominating, humiliating, or bullying that person. You manage to get what you want but at the other person's expense. Later, you tend to feel guilty about overreacting or coming on too strong (e.g., "I knew I shouldn't have said that").

How Do I Make My Point?

"Seek first to understand, then to be understood."

—Stephen Covey, international bestselling author of *The Seven Habits of Highly Effective People* (1990)

If you tend to be passive, then you will make your point tentatively and nervously while being uncertain and apologetic about that point. You will be intimidated by others in the group and may not make your point at all.

If you tend to be aggressive, you will use a loud, intimidating voice. You will not take people disagreeing with your point lightly. You will use your body language to intimidate people into agreeing with your point and may lose your temper easily if they don't.

If you tend to be passive-aggressive, you will be upset or angry but will not let others see it. Instead, you will try to destroy the person or point that makes you angry behind the scenes. You will say openly that you agree with a point while looking for secret ways to be hostile toward that point.

If you tend to be assertive, you will listen to other points being made. You will be sure of the validity of your point and argue it reasonably and with respect. You will have a strong and sure voice and your tone will not be intimidating. You will not let others in the group be bullied because of their points of view. You will not lose control or lose your temper if people disagree.

Remember

Your goal is reconciliation, not retaliation.

When you're passive-aggressive, you get back or get even with the other person in an indirect and ineffective way by withholding or taking away something (e.g., not speaking to the other person or withdrawing all attention or affection).

In contrast, when you're assertive, you strike the middle ground between aggression and passivity. You handle conflict in a way that protects or restores your rights without taking away or stepping on the rights of the other person. You approach conflict in an even-tempered way rather than in an angry or agitated manner; you speak in a normal volume rather than yelling or screaming; and you communicate at a normal distance rather than getting up close and "into the face" of the other person involved in the conflict. You can resolve conflicts assertively by using the following six strategies:

1. **Focus on the specific behavior causing the conflict, not the person's general character.** Avoid labeling the person as "selfish," "mean," "inconsiderate," and so on. For instance, if you're upset because your roommate doesn't share in cleaning, stay away from aggressive labels such as "You slacker" or "You lazy bum." Attacking others with negative labels such as these does to the other person just what it sounds like: It gives the feeling of being attacked or verbally assaulted. This is likely to put the other person on the defensive and provoke a counterattack on one of your personal characteristics. Before you know it, you're likely to find yourself in a full-out war of words and mutual character assassinations that has escalated well beyond a small-scale skirmish about the specific behavior of one individual.

   Rather than focusing on the person's general character, focus on the behaviors that are causing the problem (e.g., failing to do the dishes or leaving dirty laundry around the room). This will enable the other person to know exactly what actions need to be taken to take care of the problem. Furthermore, it's easier for others to change a specific behavior than it is to change their entire character, which would require a radical change in personality.
2. **Use "I" messages to focus on how the other person's behavior or action affects you.** By using "I" messages, which focus on your perceptions and feelings, you send a message that's less accusatory and threatening (Narciso & Burkett, 1975). In contrast, "you" messages are more likely to make the other person defensive and put them on the offensive—ready to retaliate rather than cooperate (Gibb, 1991).

   For instance, suppose you've received a course grade that's lower than what you think you earned or deserved and you decide to question your instructor about it. You should not begin by saying to the instructor, "*You* gave me the wrong grade," or "*You* made a mistake." These messages are likely to make your professor immediately ready to defend the grade you received. Your professor will be less threatened and more likely to listen to and consider your complaint if you initiate the conversation with an "I" statement, such as "I don't believe I received the correct grade" or "I think an error may have been made in my final grade."

   "I" messages are less aggressive because you're targeting an issue, not a person (McKay, Davis, & Fanning, 2009). By saying, "I feel angry when . . ." rather than "You make me angry when . . ." you send the message that you're taking responsibility for the way you feel rather than guilt-tripping the individual for making you feel that way (perhaps without the person even being aware of how you feel).

   Lastly, when using "I" messages, try to describe what you're feeling as precisely as possible. "I feel neglected when you don't write or call" identifies what you're feeling more precisely than "I wish you'd be more considerate." Describing what you feel in specific terms increases the persuasive power of your message and reduces the risk that the other person will misunderstand or discount it.

Think About It — *Journal Entry* 7.4

Your classmates aren't carrying their weight on a group project that you're all supposed to be working on as a team; you're getting frustrated and angry because you're doing most of the work. What might be an "I" message that you could use to communicate your concern in a nonthreatening way that's likely to resolve this conflict successfully?

"Don't find fault. Find a remedy."

—Henry Ford, founder of Ford Motor Co. and one of the richest people of his generation

3. **Don't make absolute judgments or blanket statements.**
   - "You're no help at all."
   - "You never try to understand how I feel."
   - "I always have to clean up."

   The statements are absolute statements that cover all times, situations, and circumstances, without any room for possible exceptions. Such extreme, blanket criticisms are likely to put the criticized person on the defensive because they state that the person is lacking or deficient with respect to the behavior in question.

"To keep your marriage brimming with love . . . when you're wrong, admit it; when you're right, shut up."

—Ogden Nash, American poet

4. **Focus on solving the problem, not winning the argument.** Try not to approach conflict with the attitude that you're going to "get even" or "prove that you're right." Winning the argument but not persuading the person to change the behavior that's causing the conflict is like winning a battle but losing the war. Instead, approach the conflict with the attitude that it's a problem to be solved and that both parties can win—that is, both of you can end up with a better relationship in the long run if the issue is resolved.
5. **Conclude your discussion of the conflict on a warm, constructive note.** By ending on a positive note, you assure that the other person knows there are no hard feelings and that you're optimistic the conflict can be resolved and your relationship can be improved.
6. **If the conflict is resolved because of some change made by the other person, express your appreciation for the individual's effort.** Even if your complaint was legitimate and your request was justified, the person's effort to accommodate your request shouldn't be taken for granted. At the least, you shouldn't react to a positive change in behavior by rubbing it in with comments such as "That's more like it" or "It's about time!"

   Expressing appreciation to the other person for making a change in response to your request is not only a socially sensitive thing to do, but also a self-serving thing to do. By recognizing or reinforcing the other person's changed behavior, you increase the likelihood that the positive change in behavior will continue.

The Importance of Emotional Intelligence for Educational and Personal Success

The term *intrapersonal intelligence* refers to the ability to be aware of your feelings or emotions (Gardner, 1983). More recently, the term *emotional intelligence* has been coined to describe the ability to identify and monitor your emotions and to be aware of how your emotions are influencing your thoughts and actions (Goleman, 1995; Salovey & Mayer, 1990). Emotional intelligence has been found to be a better predictor of personal and occupational success than is performance on intellectual intelligence tests (Goleman, 1995). Research on college students indicates that those with higher emotional intelligence, such as the ability to identify their emotions and moods, are: (1) less likely to experience boredom (Harris, 2006), and (2) more able to focus their attention and get absorbed (in the zone) when completing challenging tasks (Wiederman, 2007). The connection between emotional intelligence and successful personal performance is further supported by research indicating that people who are able to control their emotions and use them to their advantage are more likely to persist longer at challenging tasks (Simunek, Schutte, Hollander, & McKenley, 2000) and to experience professional success (Goleman, 1995; Saarni, 1999). Success in college is a challenging task that will test your emotional strength and your ability to persist to task completion (graduation).

Research also indicates that experiencing positive emotions, such as optimism and excitement, promotes learning by increasing the brain's ability to take in, store, and retrieve information (Rosenfield, 1988). In one study involving nearly 4,000 first-year college students, it was found that students' level of optimism or hope for success during their first term on campus was a more accurate predictor of their first-year grades than was their SAT score or high school grade point average (Snyder et al., 1991). In contrast, negative emotions such as anxiety and fear can interfere with the brain's ability to store memories (Jacobs & Nadel, 1985), retrieve stored memories (O'Keefe & Nadel, 1985), and engage in higher-level thinking (Caine & Caine, 1991).

College students who score higher on tests of emotional intelligence and emotional management have been found to achieve higher GPAs at the end of their first year (Schutte et al., 1998). Additional research shows that new college students who take seminars or college success courses that include information on emotional control and emotional skill development are more likely to be successful during their first year of college (Schutte & Malouff, 2002).

Stress and Anxiety

Among the most common emotions that humans have to monitor, manage, and regulate are stress and anxiety. College students report higher levels of stress while in college than they did before college (Bartlett, 2002; Sax, 2003).

The "fight-or-flight" reaction occurs when we're under stress because it's a throwback to the time when ancient humans needed to fight with or flee from potential predators. Unlike that of other animals, our hair doesn't rise up and appear more intimidating to foes (but we still get "goosebumps" when we're nervous, and we still refer to scary events as "hair-raising" experiences).

What exactly is stress? The biology of stress originates from the fight-or-flight reaction that's been wired into your body for survival purposes. This automatic reaction prepares you to handle danger or threat by flooding your body with chemicals (e.g., adrenaline and cortisol) in the same way that ancient humans had to handle threats by engaging in fight or flight (escape) when confronted by life-threatening predators.

The word *stress* derives from a Latin root that means "to draw tight." Thus, stress isn't necessarily bad. For example, a tightened guitar string provides better sound than a string that's too lax or loose, a tightened bow delivers a more powerful arrow shot, and a tightened muscle provides more strength or speed. Such productive stress is sometimes referred to as *eustress*—deriving from the root *eu*, meaning "good" (as in the words *euphoria*, meaning "good mood," and *eulogy*, meaning "good words").

If you keep college stress at a moderate level, it can be a productive emotion that promotes your learning and personal development. Stress in moderate amounts can benefit your:

1. Physical performance (e.g., strength and speed);
2. Mental performance (e.g., attention and memory); and
3. Mood (e.g., hope and optimism).

Think About It — Journal Entry 7.5

Can you think of a situation in which you performed at a higher level because you were somewhat nervous or experienced a moderate amount of stress? Describe the situation.

However, if stress is extreme and continues for a prolonged period, it moves from being a productive to a destructive feeling. Using the guitar string as an analogy, if a guitar is strung too tight, the string is likely to snap or break—which isn't productive. Unproductive stress is often referred to as *distress*—from the root *dis* meaning "bad" (as in the words *discomfort* and *disease*). Extreme stress can create feelings of intense anxiety or anxiety disorders (e.g., panic attacks), and if a high level of stress persists for a prolonged period, it can trigger psychosomatic illness—tension-induced bodily disorders (from *psyche,* meaning "mind," and *soma,* meaning "body"). For instance, prolonged distress can trigger indigestion by increasing secretion of stomach acids or contribute to high blood pressure, a.k.a. hypertension. Prolonged stress can also suppress the immune system, leaving you more vulnerable to flu, colds, and other infectious diseases.

Excess stress can interfere with mental performance because the feelings and thoughts that accompany anxiety begin to preoccupy your mind and take up space in your working memory, leaving it with less capacity to process information you're trying to learn and retain. Studies also show that students experiencing higher levels of academic stress or performance anxiety are more likely to use ineffective surface approaches to learning that rely merely on memorization (Ramsden & Entwistle, 1981) rather than effective deep-learning strategies that involve seeking meaning and understanding. Furthermore, high levels of test anxiety are more likely to result in careless concentration errors on exams (e.g., overlooking key words in test questions) and can interfere with memory for information that's been studied (Jacobs & Nadel, 1985; O'Keefe & Nadel, 1985; Tobias, 1985).

Although considerable research points to the negative effects of excess stress, you still need to keep in mind that stress can work either for or against you: you can be either energized or sabotaged by stress depending on its level of intensity and the length of time it continues. You can't expect to stop or eliminate stress, nor should you want to; you can only hope to contain it and maintain it at a level where it's more

Research indicates that college students' stress levels tend to rise when they are experiencing a wave of exams, such as finals.

productive than destructive. Many years of research indicate that personal performance is best when it takes place under conditions of moderate stress because this creates a sense of challenge. On the other hand, too much stress creates performance anxiety, and too little stress results in loss of intensity or indifference (Sapolsky, 2004; Yerkes & Dodson, 1908). (See Figure 7.1.)

Snapshot Summary 7.1 provides a short summary of the signs or symptoms of extreme stress, which indicate that stress has climbed to a level where it's creating distress or anxiety. If these are experienced, particularly for an extended period during which symptoms continue to occur for 2 or more weeks, action should be taken to reduce them.

FIGURE 7.1

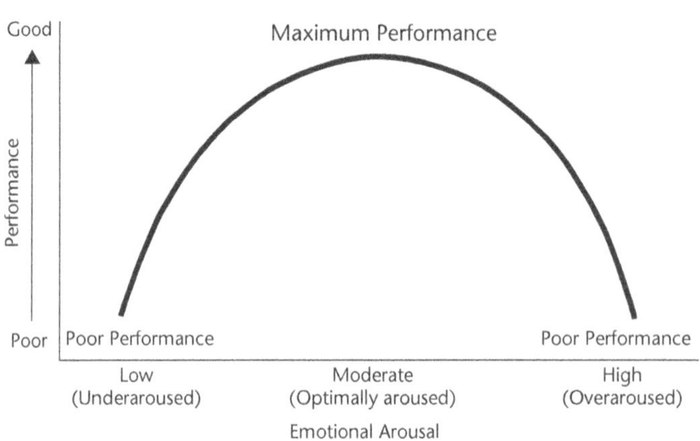

Moderate challenge that produces moderate stress often results in maximum (peak) performance.

Source: Williams, Landers, and Boutcher (1993).

Relationship between Arousal and Performance

Think About It — *Journal Entry* 7.6

How would you rate your level of anxiety in the following situations?

1. Taking tests or exams	high	moderate	low
2. Interacting in social situations	high	moderate	low
3. Making decisions about the future	high	moderate	low

Why did you rate them this way?

____

____

____

____

____

Snapshot Summary

7.1 High Anxiety: Recognizing the Symptoms (Signs) of Distress

- **Jitteriness or shaking**, especially the hands
- **Accelerated heart rate or heart palpitations:** irregular heartbeat
- **Muscle tension:** tightness in the chest or upper shoulders or a tight feeling (lump) in the throat (the expressions "uptight" and "choking" stem from these symptoms of upper-body tension)
- **Body aches:** heightened muscle tension leading to tension headaches, backaches, or chest pain (in extreme cases, it can feel as if a heart attack is taking place)
- **Sweating**, especially sweaty (clammy) palms
- **Cold, pale hands or feet**, symptoms that have led to the expressions "white knuckles" and "cold feet" to describe someone who is very anxious
- **Dry mouth:** decreased production of less saliva (leading to the expression "cotton mouth" and the need for very nervous speakers to have water nearby)
- **Stomach discomfort or indigestion** due to increased secretion of stomach acid (the expression "feeling butterflies in my stomach" relates to this symptom)
- **Gastrointestinal discomfort**, e.g., stomach cramps, constipation, or diarrhea
- **Feeling faint or dizzy** due to constriction of blood vessels that decreases oxygen flow to the brain
- **Weakness and fatigue:** a sustained (chronic) state of arousal and prolonged muscle tension that becomes tiring
- **Menstrual changes:** missing or irregular menstrual periods
- **Difficulty sleeping:** insomnia or interrupted (fitful) sleep
- **Increased susceptibility to colds, flu, and other infections** due to suppression of the body's immune system that leads to more infections*

WHO'S IN CHARGE?

Stress

You have not done well on your first few assignments and tests in college, and it's really starting to get to you. You feel as though there is no hope—you have no future—and soon you stop eating and sleeping. Your life seems to be spinning out of control. You continue to tell yourself that you will amount to nothing and it doesn't matter what you do, the situation is not going to change—you just can't do this school thing! You are ready to give up! Are you in control of this situation, or is someone else? What could you have done to stop yourself from getting to the point where you want to give up? What are some resources you could use to help yourself through this situation?

Research-Based Techniques for Stress Management

*If you perceive your level of stress to be reaching a point where it's beginning to interfere with the quality of your performance or life, you need to take steps to reduce it. Listed here are three stress-management methods whose positive effects have been well documented by research in psychology and biology (Benson & Proctor, 2011; Lehrer, et al., 2007).

Student Perspective

"My stress has caused me to lose a lot of weight; my appetite is cut in half. My sleep pattern is off; I have trouble falling/staying asleep. No matter how stressed I was in high school, this never happened [before]. What can I do to de-stress?"

—First-term college student

Deep (Diaphragmatic) Breathing

The type of breathing associated with excessive stress is hyperventilation—fast, shallow, and irregular breathing through the mouth rather than the chest. Breathing associated with relaxation is just the opposite—slow, deep, and regular breathing that originates from the stomach.

Breathing is something you usually do automatically or involuntarily; however, with some concentration and effort, you can control your breathing by controlling your diaphragm—the body's muscle that enables you to expand and contract your lungs. By voluntarily controlling your diaphragm muscle, you can slow your breathing rate, which, in turn, can bring down your stress level.

Your breathing rate is the pacesetter for the rate at which all other bodily systems operate. For example, when your breathing slows, your heart rate slows, your blood pressure goes down, and your muscle tension is reduced. Thus, if you slow your breathing, you produce a relaxation "wave" or "ripple effect" throughout your body. Deep breathing's ability to trigger relaxation across all systems of the body makes it one of the most powerful stress-management techniques available to you.

You can practice diaphragmatic breathing by inhaling through your nose and exhaling through your mouth, keeping your chest still, and allowing your stomach to rise and fall at a slow, steady pace. To be sure you're breathing through your stomach deeply and consistently, put one hand on your chest and make sure your chest remains still while you breathe; place your other hand on your stomach and make sure that it rises and falls as you breathe in and out, respectively.

If you practice diaphragmatic breathing consistently, it will soon become natural to you, and you'll be able to quickly shift into deep breathing any time you feel yourself becoming anxious or tense (e.g., before a big exam or speech).

Progressive Muscle Relaxation

This stress-management method is similar to stretching exercises used to relax and loosen muscles before and after physical exercise. To achieve total-body (head-to-toe) muscle relaxation, progressively tense and release the five sets of muscles listed here. Hold the tension in each muscle area for about five seconds, and then release it slowly.

1. Wrinkle your forehead muscles, and then release them.
2. Shrug your shoulders up as if to touch your ears, and then drop them.
3. Make a fist with each hand, and then open both.
4. Tighten your stomach muscles, and then release them.
5. Tighten your toes by curling them under your feet, and then raise them as high as you can.

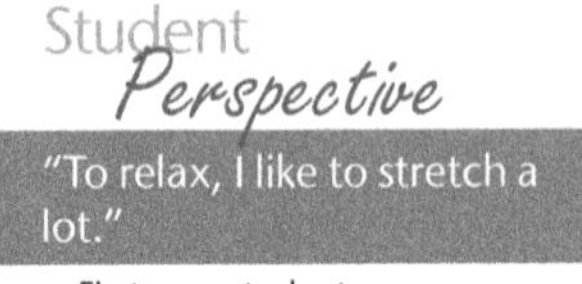

—First-year student

To help tense your muscles, imagine you're using them to push or lift a heavy object. When relaxing your muscles, take a deep breath and think or say, "Relax." By breathing deeply and thinking or hearing "Relax" each time you release your muscles, you associate the word with your muscles becoming relaxed. Then, if you find yourself in a stressful situation, you can take a deep breath, think or say, "Relax," and immediately release tension because that's what your muscles have been trained or conditioned to do.

Mental Imagery

You can use your visual imagination to create sensory experiences that promote relaxation. You can create your own relaxing "mental movie" or "imaginary DVD" by visually placing yourself in a calm, comfortable, and soothing setting. You can visualize ocean waves, floating clouds, floating in a warm sauna, or any sensory experience that tends to relax you. The more senses you use, the more real the scene will seem and the more powerful its relaxing effects will be. Try to use all of your senses—try to see it, hear it, smell it, and feel it. You can also use musical imagination to create calming background music that accompanies your visual image.

Author's Experience

My wife, Mary, is a kindergarten teacher. Whenever her young students start misbehaving and the situation becomes stressful (e.g., during lunchtime when the kids are running wildly, arguing vociferously, and screaming at maximum volume), Mary "plays" relaxing songs in her head. She reports that her musical imagination always works to soothe her nerves, enabling her to remain calm and even-tempered when she must confront children who need to be scolded or disciplined.

Joe Cuseo

Think About It — *Journal Entry* 7.7

What are the most common sources of stress for you?

____

____

____

Would you say that you deal with stress well? Why or why not?

____

____

____

What strategies do you use to cope with stress?

____

____

____

Stress-Reduction Strategies and Practices

In addition to formal stress management techniques, such as diaphragmatic breathing, progressive muscle relaxation, and mental imagery, you can use other habits and simple strategies to reduce stress.

1. **Exercise.** Exercise reduces stress by increasing the release of serotonin, a mellowing brain chemical that reduces feelings of tension (anxiety) and depression. Studies also show that people who exercise regularly tend to report feeling happier (Myers, 1993). Exercise also elevates mood by improving people's sense of self-esteem because it gives them a sense of accomplishment by improving their physical self-image. It is for these reasons that counselors and psychotherapists recommend exercise for patients experiencing milder forms of anxiety or depression (Johnsgard, 2004).
2. **Keep a journal of feelings and emotions.** Writing about our feelings in a personal journal can serve as an effective way to identify our emotions (one form of emotional intelligence) and provide a safe outlet for releasing steam and coping with stress. Writing about our emotions also enables us to become more aware of them, reducing the risk that we'll deny them and push them out of consciousness.
3. **Take time for humor and laughter.** Research on the power of humor for reducing tension is clear and convincing. In one study, college students were suddenly told they had to deliver an impromptu (off the top of their head) speech. This unexpected assignment caused students' heart rates to elevate to an average of 110 beats per minute during delivery of the speech. However, students who watched humorous episodes of sitcoms before delivering their impromptu speeches had an average heart rate during the speech that was significantly lower (80–85 beats per minute), suggesting that humor reduces anxiety (O'Brien, cited in Howard, 2014). Research also shows that if the immune system is suppressed or weakened by stress, humor strengthens it by blocking the body's production of the stress hormone cortisol—a biochemical responsible for suppressing the immune system when we're stressed (Berk, as cited in Liebertz, 2005b).

"There are thousands of causes for stress, and one antidote to stress is self-expression. That's what happens to me every day. My thoughts get off my chest, down my sleeves, and onto my pad."

—Garson Kanin, American writer, actor, and film director

Depression

Along with anxiety, depression is is another mental health issue that commonly afflicts humans and must be managed. Excess stress can turn into anxiety (a heightened state of tension, arousal, and nervous energy), or it can lead to depression (a mental health issue characterized by a loss of optimism, hope, and energy). As its name implies, when people are depressed, their mood is "lowered" or "pushed down". In contrast to anxiety, which typically involves worrying about something that's currently happening or is about to happen (e.g., experiencing test anxiety before an upcoming exam), depression more often relates to something that's already happened. Depression may be related to a loss, such as a lost relationship (e.g., departed friend, broken romance, or death of a family member) or a lost opportunity (e.g., losing a job, failing a course, or failing to be accepted into a major; Bowlby, 1980; Price, Choi, & Vinokur, 2002). It's natural and normal to feel depressed after losses such as these. However, if your depression reaches a point where you can't concentrate and complete your day-to-day tasks, and if this continues for an extended period, you may be experiencing what psychologists call clinical depression (i.e., depression so serious that it requires professional help).

Snapshot Summary 7.2 provides a summary of symptoms or signs that may indicate the presence of depression. If these symptoms continue to occur for two or more weeks, action should be taken to relieve them.

Remember

There is a difference between feeling despondent or "down" and being depressed. When psychologists use the word depression, *they're usually referring to clinical depression—a mood state so low that it's interfering with a person's ability to cope with day-to-day life tasks, such as getting to school or going to work.*

Snapshot Summary

7.2 Recognizing the Symptoms (Signs) of Depression

- Feeling low, down, sad, or blue
- Pessimistic feelings about the future (e.g., expecting failure or feeling helpless or hopeless)
- Decreased sense of humor
- Difficulty finding pleasure, joy, or fun in anything
- Lack of concentration
- Loss of motivation or interest in things previously found to be exciting or stimulating
- Stooped posture (e.g., hung head or drawn face)
- Slower and softer speech rate
- Decreased animation and slower bodily movements
- Loss of energy
- Changes in sleeping patterns (e.g., sleeping more or less than usual)
- Changes in eating patterns (e.g., eating more or less than usual)
- Social withdrawal
- Neglect of physical appearance
- Consistently low self-esteem
- Strong feelings of worthlessness or guilt (e.g., thinking "I'm a failure")
- Suicidal thoughts (e.g., thoughts such as "I can't take it anymore," "People would be better off without me," or "I don't deserve to live")

Think About It — Journal Entry 7.8

Have you, or a member of your family, ever experienced clinical depression?

____

____

What do you think was the primary cause or factor that triggered it?

____

____

____

Strategies for Coping with Depression

Depression can vary widely in intensity. Moderate and severe forms of depression often require professional counseling or psychotherapy.

The following strategies are offered primarily for milder cases of depression that are more amenable to self-help and self-control. These strategies may also be used with professional help or psychiatric medication to reduce the intensity and frequency of depression.

1. **Focus on the present and the future, not the past.** Consciously fight the tendency to dwell on past losses or failures, because you can no longer change or control them. Instead, focus on things you can still control, which are occurring now and will occur in the future.
2. **Deliberately make an effort to engage in positive or emotionally uplifting behavior when you're feeling down.** If your behavior is upbeat, your mind (mood) often follows suit. "Put on a happy face" may be an effective depression-reduction strategy because smiling produces certain changes in your facial muscles, which, in turn, trigger changes in brain chemistry that improve your mood (Liebertz, 2005). In contrast, frowning activates a different set of facial muscles that reduces production of mood-elevating brain chemicals (Myers, 1993).

"Yesterday is gone. Tomorrow has not yet come. We have only today. Let us begin."

—Mother Teresa of Calcutta, Albanian Catholic nun and winner of the Nobel Peace Prize

3. **Continue to engage in activities that are fun and enjoyable for you.** For example, continue to socialize with friends and engage in your usual recreational activities. Falling into the downward spiral of withdrawing from doing the things that bring you joy because you're too down to do them will bring you down even further by taking away the very things that bring you up. Interestingly, the root of the word *recreation* means "to re-create" or "create again," which suggests that recreation can revive, restore, and renew you—physically and emotionally.
4. **Try to continue accomplishing things.** By staying busy and getting things done when you feel down, you help boost your mood by experiencing a sense of accomplishment and boosting your self-esteem. Doing something nice for someone can be a particularly effective way to elevate your mood.

"The best way to cheer yourself up is to try to cheer somebody else up."

—Samuel Clemens, a.k.a. Mark Twain, writer, lecturer, and humorist

5. **Intentionally seek out humor and laughter. In addition to reducing anxiety, laughter can lighten and brighten a dark mood.** Furthermore, humor improves memory (Nielson, as cited in Liebertz, 2005a), which is an important advantage for people experiencing depression, because depression interferes with concentration and memory. Research supporting the benefits of humor for the body and mind is so well established that humor has become a legitimate academic field of study known as gelontology—the study of laughter (from the Greek *gelos* for "laughter" and *ology*, meaning "study of").
6. **Make a conscious effort to focus on your personal strengths and accomplishments.** Another way to drive away the blues is by keeping track of the good developments in your life. You can do this by keeping a positive events journal in which you note the good experiences in your life, including things you're grateful for, as well as your accomplishments and achievements. Positive journal entries will leave you with a visible, uplifting record that you can review anytime you're feeling down. Furthermore, a positive events journal can provide you with a starting point for developing a formal resume, portfolio, and personal strengths sheet, which you can provide to those who serve as your personal references and who write your letters of recommendation.

One strategy for coping with depression is to write down the positive events in your life in a journal.

7. **If you're unable to overcome depression on your own, seek help from others.** College students are more likely than ever to seek professional help if they're feeling depressed (Kadison & DiGeronimo, 2004). This is good news because it suggests that seeking help is no longer viewed in a negative manner or as a sign of personal weakness; instead, today's college students are willing to share their feelings with others and improve the quality of their emotional life.

In some cases, you may be able to help yourself overcome emotional problems through personal effort and effective coping strategies. This is particularly true if you experience depression or anxiety in milder forms and for limited periods. However, overcoming more serious and long-lasting episodes of clinical depression or anxiety isn't as simple as people make it out to be when they glibly say, "Just deal with it," "Get over it," or "Snap out of it."

In mild cases of anxiety and depression, it's true that a person may be able to deal with or get over it, but in more serious cases, depression and anxiety may be strongly related to genetic factors that are beyond the person's control. The genes that trigger anxiety and depression often have a delayed effect; their influence doesn't kick in until the late teens and early 20s. Thus, individuals who may have experienced no issues during childhood may begin to experience them for the first time while they're in college. These cases of depression and anxiety often cannot be solved by willpower alone because they're often related to underlying imbalances in brain chemicals caused by the individual's genetic makeup.

Certainly, you wouldn't tell a person with diabetes, "Come on; snap out of it. Get your insulin up." This sounds ridiculous because you know that this illness is caused by a chemical imbalance (shortage of insulin) in the body. Similarly, mental health issues can be caused by a chemical imbalance (e.g., shortage of serotonin) in the brain. You wouldn't expect people suffering from diabetes to be able to exert self-control over a problem caused by their blood chemistry; similarly, you shouldn't expect people suffering from mental health issues to be able to exert self-control over a problem caused by their brain chemistry.

When professional assistance is needed for depression, anxiety, or any other mental health issue, an effective (and convenient) place to start is the Counseling Center on campus. Counselors in this center are trained to provide professional counseling.

Medications for mental health issues are designed to compensate or correct chemical imbalances in the brain. Thus, taking medication for mental health issues may be viewed as a way of helping the brain to produce chemicals that it should be producing on its own but isn't producing because of its genetic makeup. When humans experience intense physical pain, we understand and accept their need to take painkilling drugs (e.g., over-the-counter or prescription painkillers) to provide relief for their symptoms. Similarly, we should understand that humans experiencing mental health issues (e.g., depression or anxiety) may need to take psychiatric medication to provide relief for their symptoms.

Think About It — *Journal Entry* 7.9

If you thought you were experiencing a serious episode of anxiety or depression, would you feel comfortable seeking help from a professional?

____

If yes, why? If no, why not?

____

____

____

____

____

____

Summary and Conclusion

The quality of our interpersonal relationships is strengthened by our communication skills (verbal and nonverbal) and human relations (people) skills. We can improve our interactions and relationships by working hard at remembering the names and interests of people we meet, being good listeners, and being open to different topics of conversation.

Interpersonal conflict is an inevitable aspect of social life; we can't completely eliminate it, but we can minimize and manage it with effective strategies that enable us to resolve conflicts assertively rather than aggressively, passively, or passive-aggressively.

Today's college students report higher levels of stress than students in years past. Strategies for reducing excess stress include formal stress-management techniques (e.g., diaphragmatic breathing and progressive muscle relaxation), good physical habits (e.g., exercising and reducing intake of caffeine or other stimulants), and positive ways of thinking (e.g., focusing on the present and the future, rather than the past, and making a conscious effort to focus on our personal strengths and accomplishments).

Intellectual ability is only one form of human intelligence. Social and emotional intelligence are at least as important for being successful, healthy, and happy. The strategies discussed in this chapter are not merely "soft skills": they're actually "hard-core" skills essential for success in college and beyond.

Interpersonal relationships are strengthened by communication skills (verbal and nonverbal) and human relations or people skills. You can improve the quality of your interpersonal communication and social relationships by:

- Being a good listener;
- Recognizing nonverbal messages you send while listening;
- Opening your mind to different topics of conversation;

- Recalling people's names;
- Greeting people by name when you interact with them; and
- Remembering information about others, thereby expressing interest in them.

Interpersonal conflict occurs throughout social life. However, you can minimize and manage such conflict by:

- Choosing the best place and time to resolve conflicts;
- Cooling off emotionally before expressing your thoughts verbally;
- Letting the person respond;
- Actively listening to the person's response;
- Making your point assertively rather than aggressively, passively, or both;
- Focusing on solving the problem rather than winning the argument;
- Ending the conversation on a warm, constructive note; and
- Expressing your appreciation for the person's effort to change in response to your request.

Today's college students report higher levels of stress than students in years past. Strategies that have been found effective for reducing excessive stress or anxiety include:

- Deep (diaphragmatic) breathing;
- Progressive muscle relaxation;
- Mental imagery;
- Journaling; and
- Humor and laughter.

Depression is another common mental health issue that people must manage. Self-help strategies for coping with depression include:

- Focusing on the present and the future rather than the past;
- Intentionally improving your mood by engaging in enjoyable or emotionally uplifting activities;
- Continuing to accomplish things;
- Seeking out humor and experiencing laughter;
- Consciously focusing on personal strengths and accomplishments; and
- Seeking help from others, including professional help.

Communicating and relating effectively with others are important life skills and forms of human intelligence. Similarly, emotional intelligence—the ability to identify and manage emotions when dealing with others and remain aware of how emotions influence thoughts and actions—has been found to be an important life skill that influences academic, personal, and professional success. The research and strategies discussed in this chapter point strongly to the conclusion that the quality of relationships and emotional life plays a pivotal role in promoting success, health, and happiness.*

Chapter 7 Exercises

7.1 College Stress: Identifying Potential Sources and Possible Solutions

*Read through the following 29 college stressors and rate them in terms of how stressful each one is for you on a scale from 1 to 5 (1 = lowest, 5 = highest):

Potential Stressors	*Stress Rating*				
Tests and exams	1	2	3	4	5
Assignments	1	2	3	4	5
Class workload	1	2	3	4	5
Pace of courses	1	2	3	4	5
Performing up to expectations	1	2	3	4	5
Handling personal freedom	1	2	3	4	5
Time pressure (e.g., not enough time)	1	2	3	4	5
Organizational pressure (e.g., losing things)	1	2	3	4	5
Living independently	1	2	3	4	5
The future	1	2	3	4	5
Decisions about a major or career	1	2	3	4	5
Moral and ethical decisions	1	2	3	4	5
Finding meaning in life	1	2	3	4	5
Emotional issues	1	2	3	4	5
Physical health	1	2	3	4	5
Social life	1	2	3	4	5
Intimate relationships	1	2	3	4	5
Sexuality	1	2	3	4	5
Family responsibilities	1	2	3	4	5
Family conflicts	1	2	3	4	5
Family pressure	1	2	3	4	5
Peer pressure	1	2	3	4	5
Loneliness or isolation	1	2	3	4	5
Roommate conflicts	1	2	3	4	5
Conflict with professors	1	2	3	4	5
Campus policies or procedures	1	2	3	4	5
Transportation	1	2	3	4	5
Technology	1	2	3	4	5
Safety	1	2	3	4	5

Review your ratings and write down three of your top (highest-rated) stressors. Identify: (1) a coping strategy you may use on your own to deal with that source of stress and (2) a campus resource you could use to obtain help with that source of stress.*

Stressor: ______________________________

Personal coping strategy:

Campus resource:

Stressor: ______________________________

Personal coping strategy:

Campus resource:

Stressor: ______________________________

Personal coping strategy:

Campus resource:

Name: ______________________

For Further Consideration

Staying Healthy in College and Beyond: Taking Care of Yourself While You Study and Learn

***Along with the importance of healthy social relationships, positive mental health, and exercise, most experts agree that the quality and length of sleep and healthy eating habits are important aspects of a healthy lifestyle. As a student, concentrating on good health at this important and busy time in your life will be beneficial now and in the future.

Sleep

What do college students need to know about the importance of sleep? Let's review some interesting information from articles about sleep.

1. Inadequate sleep can make a person more vulnerable to colds, increase blood pressure, and create a higher risk for many health concerns such as heart disease, obesity, depression, and anxiety (President and Fellows of Harvard College, 2010).

2. Sleep helps the immune system work properly. When people do not receive the needed amount of sleep, their immune systems can become weaker, making them more susceptible to illnesses and making it more difficult for their bodies to fight off these illnesses (Blakeslee, 1993, as cited in Cuseo, Thompson, McLaughlin, & Moono, 2013).

3. Receiving the adequate amount of sleep, specifically the needed amount of REM sleep (otherwise known as dream sleep), is helpful when dealing with stress (Cuseo et al., 2013). When people are under a large amount of stress, they tend to have a higher frequency of REM sleep (Greenberg, Pillard, & Pearlman, 1972, as cited in Cuseo et al.). Voelker (2004, as cited in Cuseo et al.) found that when people spend a small amount of time in REM sleep, it negatively impacts their mental health. REM sleep is thought to help balance the chemicals in our brain that are related to anxiety and depression, and therefore is an important piece for maintaining positive mental health and a positive mood (Cuseo et al.).

4. Myers (1993) found that those who receive adequate amounts of sleep are more likely to report being happy with their lives.

5. One theory related to sleep is that it helps in the forming and storing of memories (Cuseo et al., 2013). One study found that the loss of REM sleep at night led to less recall of information that had been learned that day (Peigneux, Laureys, Delbeuck, & Maquet, 2001, as cited in Cuseo et al.). Horne (1988, as cited in Cuseo et al.) found that students who received a small amount of sleep had difficulty remembering new information they had learned in class.

6. Both sleeping too little and sleeping too much are problematic for good health. Strive for eight hours of sleep (Tufts University, 2004).

President and Fellows of Harvard College (2010) state "sleep decisions are a quality-of-life issue. Whatever your interests and goals, getting enough sleep puts you in a better position to enjoy and achieve them" (p. 13).

Tips for Getting the Sleep You Need

Cuseo et al. (2013) make the following suggestions related to sleep:

1. Make sleep a priority.
2. Try to get into a normal pattern of sleep by going to bed and waking at the same basic time.
3. Establish a relaxing bedtime ritual each night.
4. Sleep in a room with a temperature that is comfortable to you and in a bed that is comfortable.
5. Avoid intense mental activity before going to bed.
6. Avoid exercise before going to bed.
7. Avoid caffeine, food, or alcohol before going to bed.

Healthy Eating and Nutrition

Patrick J. Skerrett, Executive Editor, *Harvard Health,* blogged on September 14, 2011, about a revised eating guide as an improvement to the federal authorities' MyPlate. Skerrett and his colleagues at Harvard Health Publications, along with nutrition experts, developed a newer version which they named the "Healthy Eating Plate." "We gave MyPlate a makeover to provide consumers with an easy to use but specific guide to healthy eating based on the best science available," says Dr. Anthony Komaroff, a professor of medicine at Harvard Medical School and Editor in Chief of Harvard Health Publications" (Skerrett, 2011, n.p.).

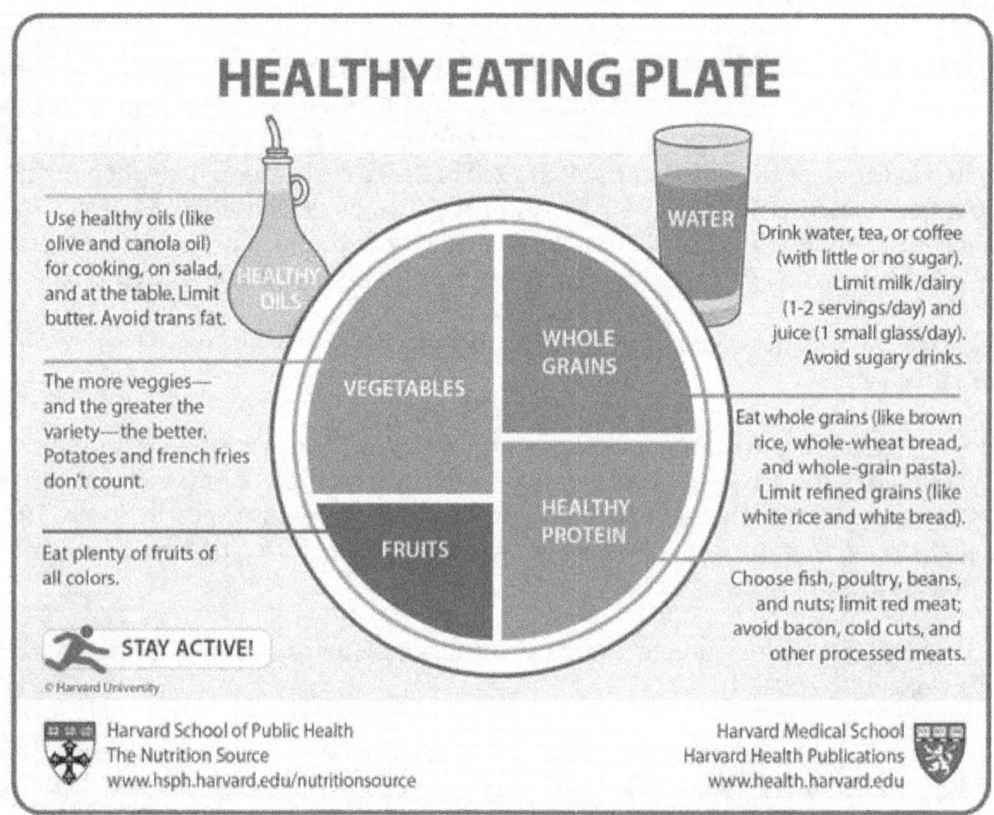

As printed in image and Harvard University. For more information visit: www.health.harvard.edu.NOTE: Harvard Health Publications does not endorse any products or medical peosedures.

Some of the basic recommendations made by the Healthy Eating Plate include: fruits and vegetables constituting half of the meal, restricting refined grains which increase blood sugar, choosing healthy sources of protein, using healthy oils for cooking-related needs, and staying active (Skerrett, 2011).***

References

Cuseo, J. B., Thompson, A., McLaughlin, J. A., & Moono, S. H. (2013). *Thriving in the community college & beyond: Strategies for academic success and personal development* (2nd ed.), Second Edition. Dubuque, IA: Kendall Hunt.

Myers, D. G. (1993). *The pursuit of happiness: Who is happy—and why?* New York, NY: Morrow.

Skerrett, P. J. (2011, September 14). Harvard to USDA: Check out the healthy eating plate [Harvard Health Blog]. Retrieved from http://www.health.harvard.edu/blog/harvard-to-usda-check-out-the-healthy-eating-plate-201109143344

Tufts University, Eds. (2004). And to all a good night: How sleep deprivation may lead to chronic disease. *Tufts University Health & Nutrition Letter*, 22, 8–11.

SQ4R Worksheet

Your Name:

Selection Title/Chapter:

Author(s):

***1. **Survey**: Look at the title, visuals, questions, excerpts, headings and sub-headings. Afterward, answer the questions below.

What do I already know about the topics?	What do I expect to learn?

2. **Question**: Create questions based on your survey of the text. If there are headings, turn them into questions. Include *at least three* below to help focus your attention as you read.

A.
B.
C.
D.
E.

3. **Read** and **Record** (Annotate): Read the selection thoroughly, highlight, and make note of important points, associations, and unfamiliar terms. Complete the chart using **your own words**. Provide a sketch and/or explanation of the visuals. Use and attach a separate sheet if needed.

Page and Paragraph #	Vocabulary Terms	Notes and Definitions	Visuals

(Continued)

(Continued)

4. **Recite**: Answer your questions from step two.

a.
b.
c.
d.
e.

5. **Review and Reflect**: Check your memory by verbalizing the above information. Below, write a summary **in your own words** of what you have read, connecting the content ideas. Additionally, write a brief reflection including your personal response to the reading (use "I" and make connections to your own experiences, ask more questions, respond to the text, and consider anything you were reminded of or visualized while reading).***

Summary:

Reflection:

Adapted from Florida Online Reading Professional Development. (n.d.). *SQ4R*. Retrieved from the Marco Island Charter Middle School website at http://micms.org/SQ4R.pdf

Diversity and the Community College Experience 8

Appreciating the Value of Human Differences for Promoting Learning and Personal Development

THOUGHT STARTER *Journal Entry* 8.1

*Complete the following sentence:

When I hear the word *diversity,* the first thoughts that come to my mind are . . .

____

____

____

____

____

____

LEARNING GOAL

To appreciate the value of human differences and acquire skills for making the most of diversity in college and beyond.

The Spectrum of Diversity

The word *diversity* derives from the Latin root *diversus,* meaning "various." Thus, human diversity refers to the variety of differences that exist among the people that comprise humanity (the human species). In this chapter, we use *diversity* to refer primarily to differences among the major groups of people who, collectively, comprise humankind or humanity. The relationship between diversity and humanity is represented visually in Figure 8.1.

The relationship between humanity and human diversity is similar to the relationship between sunlight and the spectrum of colors. Just as the sunlight passing through a prism is dispersed into all groups of colors that make up the visual spectrum, the human species that's spread across the planet is dispersed into all groups of people that make up the human spectrum (humanity).

As you can see in Figure 8.1, groups of people differ from one another in numerous ways, including physical features, religious beliefs, mental and physical abilities, national origins, social backgrounds, sex, sexual orientation, and other personal dimensions.

"We are all brothers and sisters. Each face in the rainbow of color that populates our world is precious and special. Each adds to the rich treasure of humanity."

—Morris Dees, civil rights leader and cofounder of the Southern Poverty Law Center

FIGURE 8.1

SPECTRUM
of
DIVERSITY

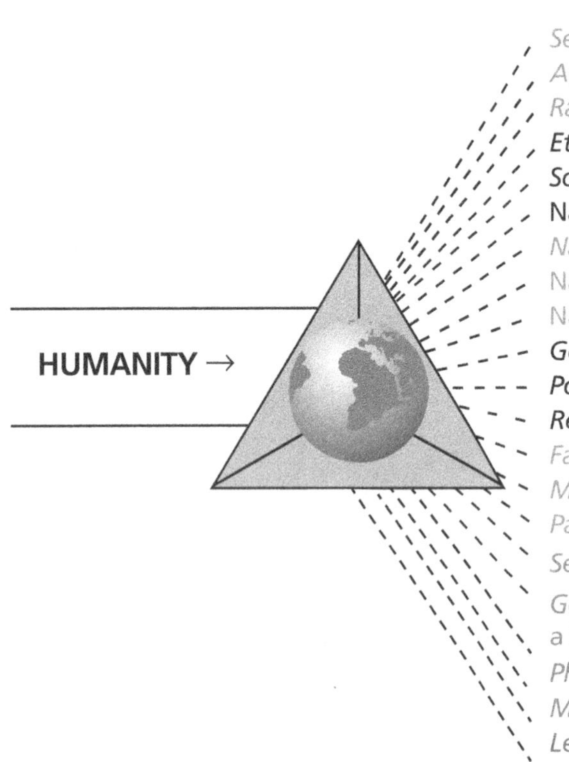

Sex (continuum including male and female)
Age (stage of life)
Race (e.g., White, Black, Asian)
Ethnicity (e.g., Native American, Hispanic, Irish, German)
Socioeconomic status (job status/income)
National *citizenship* (citizen of U.S. or another country)
Native (first-learned) *language*
National *origin* (nation of birth)
National *region* (e.g., raised in north/south)
Generation (historical period when people are born and live)
Political ideology (e.g., liberal/conservative)
Religious/spiritual beliefs (e.g., Christian/Buddhist/Muslim)
Family status (e.g., single-parent/two-parent family)
Marital status (single/married)
Parental status (with/without children)
Sexual orientation (e.g., heterosexual/homosexual/bisexual)
Gender Identity (One's sense of self as male, female, a blend of both, or neither)
Physical ability/disability (e.g., able to hear/hearing impaired)
Mental ability/disability (e.g., mentally able/challenged)
Learning ability/disability (e.g., absence/presence of dyslexia)
Mental health/illness (e.g., absence/presence of depression)

_ _ _ _ _ _ = dimension of diversity

*This list represents some of the major dimensions of human diversity; it does not represent a complete list of all possible forms of human diversity. Also, disagreement exists about certain dimensions of diversity (e.g., whether certain groups should be considered races or ethnic groups).

Humanity and Diversity

Think About It — *Journal Entry* 8.2

Look at the diversity spectrum in Figure 8.1 and look over the list of groups that make up the spectrum. Do you notice any groups that are missing from the list that should be added, either because they have distinctive backgrounds or because they have been targets of prejudice and discrimination?

____

____

____

____

____

Since diversity has been interpreted (and misinterpreted) in different ways by different people, we begin by defining some key terms related to diversity that should lead to a clearer understanding of its true meaning and value.*

What Is Racial Diversity?

A *racial group (race)* is a group of people who share distinctive physical traits, such as skin color or facial characteristics. The variation in skin color we now see among humans is largely due to biological adaptations that have evolved over thousands of years among groups of humans who migrated to different climatic regions of the world. Currently, the most widely accepted explanation of the geographic origin of modern humans is the "Out of Africa" theory. Genetic studies and fossil evidence indicate that all Homo sapiens inhabited Africa 150,000–250,000 years ago; over time, some migrated from Africa to other parts of the world (Mendez, et al., 2013; Meredith, 2011; Reid & Hetherington, 2010). Darker skin tones developed among humans who inhabited and reproduced in hotter geographical regions nearer the equator (e.g., Africans). Their darker skin color helped them adapt and survive by providing them with better protection from the potentially damaging effects of intense sunlight (Bridgeman, 2003). In contrast, lighter skin tones developed over time among humans inhabiting colder climates that were farther from the equator (e.g., Scandinavia). Their lighter skin color enabled them to absorb greater amounts of vitamin D supplied by sunlight, which was in shorter supply in those regions of the world (Jablonksi & Chaplin, 2002).

Author's Experience

My mother was from Alabama and was dark in skin color, with high cheekbones and long curly black hair. My father stood approximately six feet tall and had light brown straight hair. His skin color was that of a Western European with a slight suntan. If you did not know that my father was of African American descent, you would not have thought of him as Black. All of my life I have thought of myself as African American, and all of the people who are familiar with me thought of me as African American. I have lived half of a century with that as my racial description. Several years ago, after carefully looking through records available on births and deaths in my family history, I discovered that fewer than 50 percent of my ancestors were of African lineage. Biologically, I am no longer Black. Socially and emotionally, I still am. Clearly, race is more of a social concept than a biological fact.

Aaron Thompson

**Currently, the U.S. Census Bureau has identified five races (U.S. Census Bureau, 2012):

White: a person whose lineage may be traced to the original people inhabiting Europe, the Middle East, or North Africa.

Black or African American: a person whose lineage may be traced to the original people inhabiting Africa.

American Indian or Alaska Native: a person whose lineage may be traced to the original people inhabiting North and South America (including Central America), and who continue to maintain their tribal affiliation or attachment.

Asian: a person whose lineage may be traced to the original people inhabiting the Far East, Southeast Asia, or the Indian subcontinent, including: Cambodia, China, India, Japan, Korea, Malaysia, Pakistan, the Philippine Islands, Thailand, and Vietnam.

Native Hawaiian or Other Pacific Islander: a person whose lineage may be traced to the original people inhabiting Hawaii, Guam, Samoa, or other Pacific islands.

It's important to keep in mind that racial categories are not based on scientific evidence; they merely represent group classifications constructed by society (Anderson & Fienberg, 2000). No identifiable set of genes distinguishes one race from another; in fact, there continues to be disagreement among scholars about what groups of people constitute a human race or whether distinctive races actually exist (Wheelright, 2005). In other words, you can't do a blood test or some type of internal genetic test to determine a person's race. Humans have simply decided to categorize themselves into races on the basis of certain external differences in their physical appearance, particularly the color of their outer layer of skin. The U.S. Census Bureau could have decided to divide people into "racial" categories based on other physical characteristics, such as eye color (blue, brown, and green), hair color (brown, black, blonde, or red), or body length (tall, short, or mid-sized).

While humans may display diversity in the color or tone of their external layer of skin, the reality is that all members of the human species are remarkably similar at an internal biological level. More than 98% of the genes of all humans are exactly the same, regardless of what their particular race may be (Bronfenbrenner, 2005). This large amount of genetic overlap accounts for our distinctively "human" appearance, which clearly distinguishes us from all other living species. All humans have internal organs that are similar in structure and function, and despite variations in the color of our outer layer of skin, when it's cut, all humans bleed in the same color.**

Author's Experience

*I was proofreading this chapter while sitting in a coffee shop in the Chicago O'Hare airport. I looked up from my work for a second and saw what appeared to be a White girl about 18 years old. As I lowered my head to return to my work, I did a double-take to look at her again because something about her seemed different or unusual. When I looked at her more closely the second time, I noticed that although she had light skin, the features of her face and hair appeared to be those of an African American. After a couple of seconds of puzzlement, I figured it out: she was an *albino* African American. That satisfied me for the moment, but then I began to wonder: Would it still be accurate to say that she was "Black" even though her skin was light? Would her hair and facial features be sufficient for her to be considered or classified as Black? If yes, then what about someone who had a dark skin tone but did not have the typical hair and facial features characteristic of Black people? Is skin color the defining feature of being African American, or are other features equally important? I was unable to answer these questions, but I found it amusing that these thoughts were taking place while I was working on a book dealing with diversity. Later, on the plane ride home, I thought again about that albino African American girl and realized that she was a perfect example of how classifying people into races is based not on objective, scientifically determined evidence but on subjective, socially constructed categories.

Joe Cuseo

Categorizing people into distinct racial or ethnic groups is becoming even more difficult because members of different ethnic and racial groups are ncreasingly forming cross-ethnic and interracial families. By 2050, the number of Americans who identify themselves as being of two or more races is projected to more than triple, growing from 5.2 million to 16.2 million (U.S. Census Bureau, 2008).

Think About It — Journal Entry 8.3

What race do you consider yourself to be? Would you say you identify strongly with your race, or are you rarely conscious of it? Explain.

___

___

___

___

Cultural differences can exist within the same society (multicultural society), within a single nation (domestic diversity), or across different nations (international diversity).

What Is Culture?

Culture may be defined as a distinctive pattern of beliefs and values learned by a group of people who share the same social heritage and traditions. In short, culture is the whole way in which a group of people has learned to live (Peoples & Bailey, 2011); it includes style of speaking (language), fashion, food, art, music, values, and beliefs.

A major advantage of culture is that it helps bind its members together into a supportive, tight-knit community; however, it can also blind them to other cultural perspectives. Since culture shapes the way people think, it can cause groups of people to view the world solely through their own cultural lens or frame of reference (Colombo, Cullen, & Lisle, 1995). Optical illusions are a good illustration of how cultural perspectives can blind people or lead them to inaccurate perceptions. For instance, compare the lengths of the two lines in Figure 8.2.

FIGURE 8.2

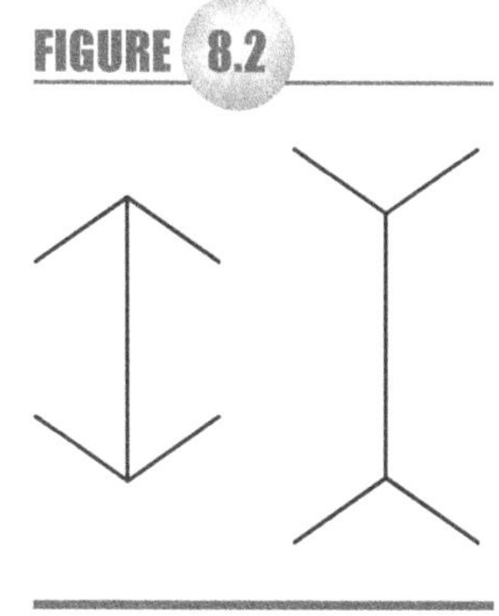

Optical Illusion

If you perceive the line on the right to be longer than the line on the left, welcome to the club. Virtually all Americans and people from Western cultures perceive the line on the right to be longer. Actually, both lines are equal in length. (If you don't believe it, take out a ruler and check it out.) Interestingly, this perceptual error is not made by people from non-Western cultures that live in environments populated with circular structures rather than structures with linear patterns and angled corners, like Westerners use (Segall, Campbell, & Herskovits, 1966).

The key point underlying this optical illusion is that cultural experiences shape and sometimes distort perceptions of reality. We think we are seeing things objectively or "as they really are," but we are often seeing things subjectively from our limited cultural vantage point. Being open to the viewpoints of diverse people who perceive the world from different cultural vantage points widens our range of perception and helps us overcome our "cultural blind spots." As a result, we tend to perceive the world around us with greater clarity and accuracy.

Remember

The reality of our own culture is not the reality of other cultures. Our perceptions of the outside world are shaped (and sometimes distorted) by our prior cultural experiences.

What Is an Ethnic Group?

An ethnic group (ethnicity) is a group of people who share the same culture. Thus, *culture* refers to *what* an ethnic group has in common and *ethnic group* refers to a group of people *who* share the same culture. Unlike a racial group, whose members share physical characteristics that they are born with and that have been passed on biologically, an ethnic group's shared characteristics have been passed on through socialization—that is, their common characteristics have been *learned* or acquired through shared social experiences.

Currently, European Americans are the majority ethnic group in the United States because they account for more than 50 percent of the American population. Native Americans, African Americans, Hispanic Americans, and Asian Americans are considered to be ethnic minority groups because each of these groups represents less than 50 percent of the American population.

Think About It — Journal Entry 8.4

Which ethnic group or groups do you belong to or identify with? What are the most common cultural values shared by your ethnic group or groups?

Student Perspective

"I'm the only person from my 'race' in class."

—Hispanic student commenting on why he felt uncomfortable in his Race, Ethnicity, & Gender class

"As the child of a Black man and a White woman, someone who was born in the racial melting pot of Hawaii, with a sister who's half Indonesian but who's usually mistaken for Mexican or Puerto Rican, and a brother-in-law and niece of Chinese descent, with some blood relatives who resemble Margaret Thatcher and others who could pass for Bernie Mac, family get-togethers over Christmas take on the appearance of a UN General Assembly meeting. I've never had the option of restricting my loyalties on the basis of race, or measuring my worth on the basis of tribe."

—Barack Obama (2006)

As with the concept of race, whether a particular group of people is defined as an ethnic group can be arbitrary, subjective, and interpreted differently by different groups of people. Currently, the only races recognized by the U.S. Census Bureau are White, Black, and Asian; Hispanic is not defined as a race but is classified as an ethnic group. However, among those who checked "some other race" in the 2000 census, 97 percent were Hispanic. This fact has been viewed by Hispanic advocates as a desire for their "ethnic" group to be reclassified as a racial group (Cianciotto, 2005).

This disagreement illustrates how difficult it is to conveniently categorize groups of people into particular racial or ethnic groups. The United States will continue to struggle with this issue because the ethnic and racial diversity of its population is growing and members of different ethnic and racial groups are forming cross-ethnic and interracial families. Thus, it is becoming progressively more difficult to place people into distinct categories based on their race or ethnicity. For example, by 2050, the number of people who will identify themselves as being of two or more races is projected to more than triple, growing from 5.2 million to 16.2 million (U.S. Census Bureau, 2008).

What Is Humanity?

It is important to realize that human *variety* and human *similarity* exist side by side and complement each other. Diversity is a "value that is shown in mutual respect and appreciation of similarities and differences" (Public Service Enterprise Group, 2009). Experiencing diversity not only enhances our appreciation of the unique features of different cultures, but also provides us with a larger perspective on the universal aspects of the human experience that are common to all humans, no matter what their particular cultural background may be. For example, despite our racial and cultural differences, all people express the same emotions with the same facial expressions (see Figure 8.3).

FIGURE 8.3

Humans all over the world display the same facial expressions when experiencing certain emotions. See if you can detect the emotions being expressed in the following faces. (To find the answers, turn your book upside down.)

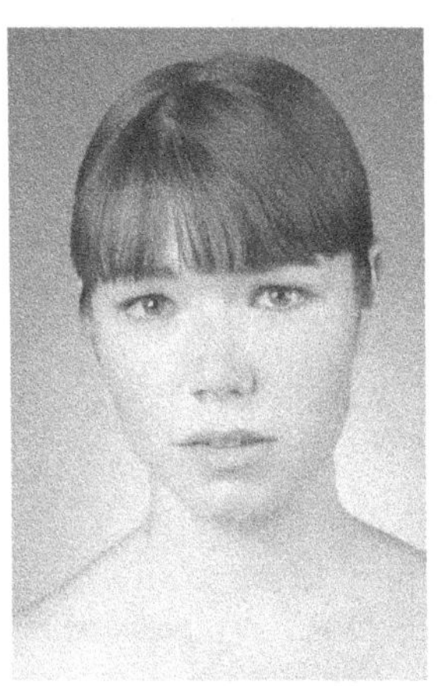

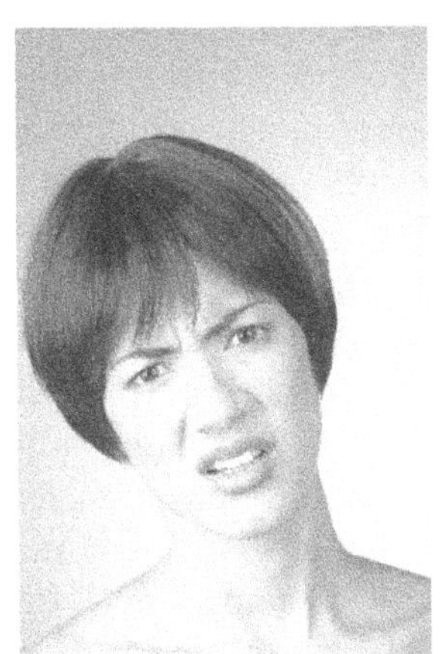

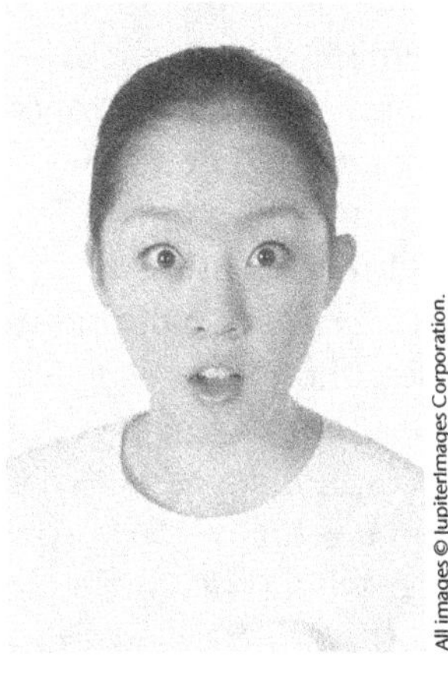

Answers: The emotions shown. Top, left to right: anger, fear, and sadness. Bottom, left to right: disgust, happiness, and surprise.

Think About It — Journal Entry 8.5

List three human experiences that you think are universal—that is, they are experienced by all humans in all cultures:

1. ______________________________

2. ______________________________

3. ______________________________

Other human characteristics that anthropologists have found to be shared across all groups of people in every corner of the world include storytelling, poetry, adornment of the body, dance, music, decoration of artifacts, families, socialization of children by elders, a sense of right and wrong, supernatural beliefs, explanations of diseases and death, and mourning of the dead (Pinker, 2000). Although different ethnic groups may express these shared experiences in different ways, these universal experiences are common to all humans.

Remember

Diversity represents variations on the common theme of humanity. Although people have different cultural backgrounds, they are still cultivated from the same soil—they are all grounded in the common experience of being human.

"We are all the same, and we are all unique."

—Georgia Dunston, African American biologist and research specialist in human genetics

Thus, different cultures associated with different ethnic groups may be viewed simply as variations on the same theme: being human. You may have heard the question "We're all human, aren't we?" The answer to this important question is "yes and no." Yes, we are all the same, but not in the same way.

A good metaphor for understanding this apparent contradiction is to visualize humanity as a quilt in which we are all joined together by the common thread of humanity—by the common bond of being human. Yet the different patches that make up the quilt represent diversity—the distinctive or unique cultures that comprise our common humanity. The quilt metaphor acknowledges the identity and beauty of all cultures. It differs from the old American melting pot metaphor, which viewed differences as something that should be melted down or eliminated, or the salad bowl metaphor, which suggested that America is a hodgepodge or mishmash of different cultures thrown together without any common connection. In contrast, the quilt metaphor suggests that the cultures of different ethnic groups should be recognized and celebrated. Nevertheless, our differences can be woven together to create a unified whole—as in the Latin expression *E pluribus unum* ("Out of many, one"), the motto of the United States, which you will find printed on all U.S. coins.

"We have become not a melting pot but a beautiful mosaic."

—Jimmy Carter, 39th president of the United States and winner of the Nobel Peace Prize

To appreciate diversity and its relationship to humanity is to capitalize on the power of our differences (diversity) while still preserving our collective strength through unity (humanity).

Remember

By learning about diversity (our differences), we simultaneously learn about our commonality (our shared humanity).

Author's Experience When I was 12 years old and living in New York City, I returned from school one Friday afternoon and my mother asked me if anything interesting happened at school that day. I mentioned to her that the teacher went around the room, asking students what we had eaten for dinner the night before. At that moment, my mother began to become a bit agitated and nervously asked me, "What did you tell the teacher?" I said, "I told her and the rest of the class that I had pasta last night because my family always eats pasta on Thursdays and Sundays." My mother exploded and fired back at me, "Why couldn't you tell her that we had steak or roast beef?" For a moment, I was stunned and couldn't figure out what I had done wrong or why I should have lied about eating pasta. Then it suddenly dawned on me: My mother was embarrassed about being an Italian American. She wanted me to hide our family's ethnic background and make it sound like we were very "American." After this became clear to me, a few moments later, it also became clear to me why her maiden name was changed from the Italian-sounding DeVigilio to the more American-sounding Vigilis and why her first name was changed from Carmella to Mildred. Her family wanted to minimize discrimination and maximize their acculturation (absorption) into American culture.

I never forgot this incident because it was such an emotionally intense experience. For the first time in my life, I became aware that my mother was ashamed of being a member of the same group to which every other member of my family belonged, including me. After her outburst, I felt a combined rush of astonishment and embarrassment. However, these feelings eventually faded and my mother's reaction ended up having the opposite effect on me. Instead of making me feel inferior or ashamed about being Italian American, her reaction that day caused me to become more aware of, and take more pride in, my Italian heritage.

As I grew older, I also grew to understand why my mother felt the way she did. She grew up in America's "melting pot" era—a time when different American ethnic groups were expected to melt down and melt away their ethnicity. They were not to celebrate diversity: they were to eliminate it.

Joe Cuseo

What Is Individuality?

It's important to keep in mind that *individual* differences within the same racial or ethnic group are greater than the *average* differences between two different groups. For example, although you live in a world that is conscious of differences among races, differences in physical attributes (e.g., height and weight) and behavior patterns (e.g., personality characteristics) among individuals within the same racial group are greater than the average differences among various racial groups (Caplan & Caplan, 2008).

As you proceed through this book, keep in mind the following distinctions among humanity, diversity, and individuality:

- **Diversity.** We are all members of *different groups* (e.g., different gender and ethnic groups).
- **Humanity.** We are all members of the *same group* (the human species).
- **Cultural competence.** The ability to *appreciate and capitalize* on human differences by interacting effectively with people from diverse cultural backgrounds.
- **Individuality.** We are all *unique individuals* who differ from other members of any group to which we may belong.*

"Every human is, at the same time, like all other humans, like some humans, and like no other human."

—Clyde Kluckholn, American anthropologist

Major Forms or Types of Diversity

International Diversity

**If it were possible to reduce the world's population to a village of precisely 100 people, with all existing human ratios remaining about the same, the demographics of this world village would look something like this:

61 would be Asians; 13 would be Africans; 12 would be Europeans; 9 would be Latin Americans; and 5 would be North Americans (citizens of the United States and Canada)
50 would be male, 50 would be female
75 would be non-white; 25 white
67 would be non-Christian; 33 would be Christian
80 would live in substandard housing
16 would be unable to read or write
50 would be malnourished and 1 would be dying of starvation
33 would be without access to a safe water supply
39 would lack access to modern sanitation
24 would have no electricity (and of the 76 who have electricity, most would only use it for light at night)
8 people would have access to the Internet
1 would have a college education
1 would have HIV
2 would be near birth; 1 near death
5 would control 32% of the entire world's wealth; all 5 would be U.S. citizens
48 would live on less than $2 a day
20 would live on less than $1 a day (Family Care Foundation, 1997–2012).

In this world village, English would not be the most common language spoken— it would be third, following Chinese and Spanish (Lewis, Paul, & Fennig, 2014).

The need for American college students to develop an appreciation of international diversity is highlighted by a study conducted by an anthropologist who went "undercover" to pose as a student in a university residence hall. She found that the biggest complaint international students had about American students was their lack of knowledge of other countries and the misconceptions they held about people from different nations (Nathan, 2005). When you take the time to learn about other countries and the cultures of people who inhabit them, you move beyond being just a citizen of your own nation, you become *cosmopolitan*—a citizen of the world.**

Ethnic and Racial Diversity

*America is rapidly becoming a more racially and ethnically diverse nation. In 2008, the minority population in the United States reached an all-time high of 36.6 percent of the total population. The population of ethnic minorities is now growing at a much faster rate than the White majority. This trend is expected to continue, and by the middle of the 21st century, the minority population will have grown from one-third of the U.S. population to more than one-half (54 percent), with more than 60 percent of the nation's children expected to be members of minority groups (U.S. Census Bureau, 2008).

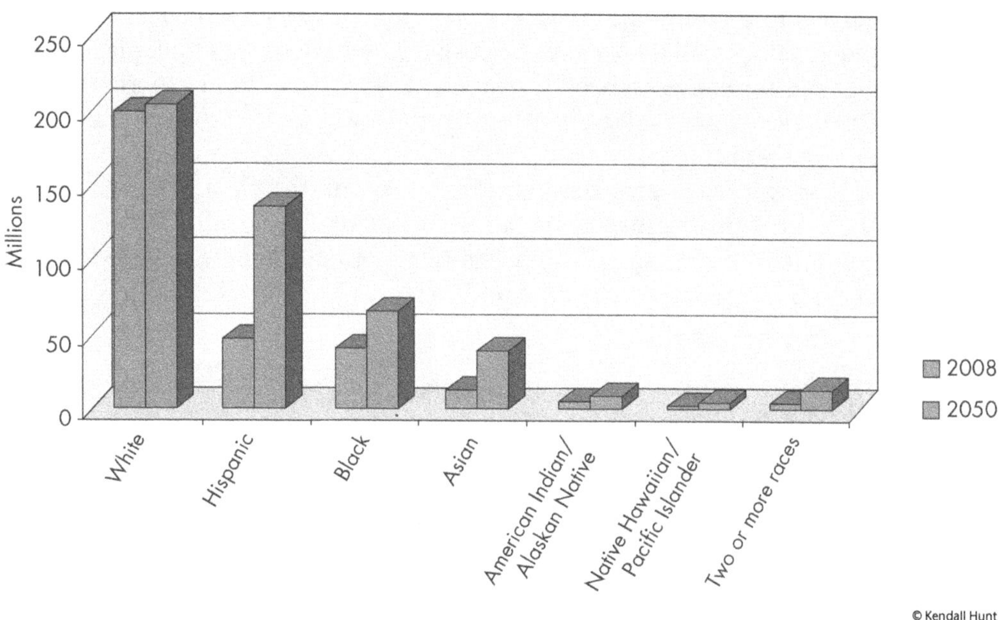

The "New Majority"

By 2050, the U.S. population is projected to be more than 30 percent Hispanic (up from 15 percent in 2008), 15 percent Black (up from 13 percent), 9.6 percent Asian (up from 5.3 percent), and 2 percent Native American (up from 1.6 percent). The native Hawaiian and Pacific Islander population is expected to more than double between 2008 and 2050. In the same time frame, the percentage of Americans who are White will drop from 66 percent (2008) to 46 percent (2050). (See Figure 8.4.)

Socioeconomic Diversity

Diversity also appears in the form of socioeconomic status or social class, which is typically stratified (divided) into lower, middle, and upper classes, depending on level of education and income. Groups occupying lower social strata have significantly fewer social and economic opportunities or privileges (Feagin & Feagin, 2007).*

**Young adults from high-income families are more than seven times likely to have earned a college degree and hold a prestigious job than those from low-income families (Olson, 2007). Sharp discrepancies also exist in income level among different racial, ethnic, and gender groups. In 2012, the median income for non-Hispanic white households was $57,009, compared to $39,005 for Hispanics and $33,321 for African Americans (DeNavas-Walt, Proctor, & Smith, 2013). From 2005 to 2009, household wealth fell by 66% for Hispanics, 53% for Blacks, and 16% for Whites, largely due to the housing and mortgage collapse—which had a more damaging effect on lower-income families (Kochlar, Fry, & Taylor, 2011).

Despite its overall wealth, the United States is one of the most impoverished of all developed countries in the world (Shah, 2008). The poverty rate in the United States is almost twice the rate of other economically developed countries around the world (Gould & Wething, 2013). In 2012, more than 16% of the American population, and almost 20% of American children, lived below the poverty line ($23,050 yearly income for a family of four) (U.S. Census Bureau, 2013).**

Generational Diversity

*Humans are also diverse with respect to the generation in which they grew up. *Generation* refers to a group of individuals born during the same historical period whose attitudes, values, and habits have been shaped by events that took place in the world during their formative years of development. Each generation experiences different historical events, so it's likely that generations will develop different attitudes and behaviors as a result.

Snapshot Summary 8.1 provides a brief summary of the major generations, the key historical events that occurred during the formative periods of the people in each generation, and the personal characteristics that have been associated with a particular generation (Lancaster & Stillman, 2002).

Snapshot Summary

8.1 Generational Diversity

- **The Traditional Generation, a.k.a. the Silent Generation** (born 1922–1945). This generation was influenced by events such as the Great Depression and World Wars I and II. Characteristics associated with this generation include loyalty, patriotism, respect for authority, and conservatism.
- **The Baby Boomer Generation** (born 1946–1964). This generation was influenced by events such as the Vietnam War, Watergate, and the human rights movement. Characteristics associated with this generation include idealism, importance of self-fulfillment, and concern for equal rights.
- **Generation X** (born 1965–1980). This generation was influenced by Sesame Street, the creation of MTV, AIDS, and soaring divorce rates that produced the first "latchkey children"—youngsters who let themselves into their homes after school with their own keys because their mothers were working outside the home. Characteristics associated with this generation include self-reliance, resourcefulness, and being comfortable with change.
- **Generation Y, a.k.a. Millennials** (born 1981–current). This generation was influenced by the September 11, 2001, terrorist attack on the United States, the shooting of students at Columbine High School, and the collapse of the Enron Corporation. Characteristics associated with this generation include a preference for working and playing in groups, being technologically savvy, and a willingness to provide volunteer service in their community (the civic generation). They are also the most ethnically diverse generation, which may explain why they are more open to diver-sity and see it as a positive experience.

Diversity and the College Experience

There are more than 3,000 public and private colleges in the United States. They vary in size (small to large) and location (urban, suburban, and rural), as well as in their purpose or mission (research universities, comprehensive state universities, liberal arts colleges, and community colleges). This variety makes the American higher education system the most diverse and accessible in the world. The diversity of educational opportunities in American colleges and universities reflects the freedom of opportunity in the United States as a democratic nation (American Council on Education, 2008).

The U.S. system of higher education is also becoming more diverse with respect to the people enrolled in the system. (See Snapshot Summary 8.2 for recent statistics related to diversity in U.S. community colleges). The ethnic and racial diversity of students in American colleges and universities is rapidly rising. In 1960, Whites made up almost 95 percent of the total college population; in 2005, that percentage

Snapshot Summary

8.2 Diversity in America's Community Colleges

58% of community college students are women
53% are 22 years of age or older
Among full-time students, 50% are employed part-time and 27% are employed full-time
Among part-time students, 50% are employed full-time and 33% are employed part-time
39% are the first in their family to attend college
36% are members of a minority ethnic or racial group
17% are single parents

Source: American Association of Community Colleges (2009).

had decreased to 69 percent. At the same time, there was an increase in the percentage of Asian, Hispanic, Black, and Native American students attending college (Chronicle of Higher Education, 2003).

The rise in ethnic and racial diversity on American campuses is particularly noteworthy when viewed in light of the historical treatment of minority groups in the United States. In the early 19th century, education was not a right but a privilege available only to those who could afford to attend private schools. Members of certain minority groups were left out of the educational process altogether or were forced to be educated in racially segregated settings. For example, Americans of color were once taught in separate, segregated schools that were typically inferior in terms of educational facilities. This continued until the groundbreaking U.S. Supreme Court ruling in *Brown v. Board of Education* in 1954, which changed the face of education for people of color by ruling that "separate educational facilities are inherently unequal." The decision made it illegal for Kansas and 20 other states to deliver education in segregated classrooms.

"Of all the civil rights for which the world has struggled and fought for 5,000 years, the right to learn is undoubtedly the most fundamental."

—W. E. B. DuBois, African American sociologist, historian, and civil rights activist

Think About It — Journal Entry 8.6

1. Are you the first in your family to attend college?

____

2. Whether yes or no, how does that make you feel?

____

____

____

____

____

Author's Experience

My mother was a direct descendent of slaves and moved with her parents from the Deep South at the age of 17. My father lived in an all-Black coal mining camp, into which my mother and her family moved in 1938. My father remained illiterate because he was not allowed to attend public schools in eastern Kentucky.

In the early 1960s my brother, my sister, and I were integrated into the White public schools. Physical violence and constant verbal harassment caused many other Blacks to forgo their education and opt for jobs in the coal mines at an early age. But my father remained constant in his advice to me: "It doesn't matter if they call you n_____; but don't you ever let them beat you by walking out on your education." He would say to me, "Son, you will have opportunities that I never had. Just remember, when you do get that education, you'll never have to go in those coal mines and have them break your back. You can choose what you want to do, and then you can be a free man."

My parents, who could never provide me with monetary wealth, truly made me proud of them by giving me the gift of insight and an aspiration for achievement.

Aaron Thompson

Think About It — Journal Entry 8.7

1. What diverse groups do you see represented on your campus?

____

____

____

2. Are there groups on your campus that you did not expect to see or to see in such large numbers?

____

____

____

3. Are there groups on your campus that you expected to see but do not see or see in smaller numbers than you expected?

____

____

____

The Benefits of Experiencing Diversity

Diversity Promotes Self-Awareness

Learning from people with diverse backgrounds and experiences sharpens your self-knowledge and self-insight by allowing you to compare and contrast your life experiences with others whose life experiences differ sharply from your own. This comparative perspective gives you a reference point for viewing your own life, which places you in a better position to see more clearly how your unique cultural background has influenced the development of your personal beliefs, values, and lifestyle. By viewing your life in relation to the lives of others, you see more clearly what is distinctive about yourself and how you may be uniquely advantaged or disadvantaged.

When students around the country were interviewed about their diversity experiences in college, they reported that these experiences often helped them learn more about themselves and that their interactions with students from different races and ethnic groups produced "unexpected" or "jarring" self-insights (Light, 2001).

Student Perspective

"I remember that my self-image was being influenced by the media. I got the impression that women had to look a certain way. I dyed my hair, wore different clothes, more makeup . . . all because magazines, TV, [and] music videos 'said' that was beautiful. Luckily, when I was 15, I went to Brazil and saw a different, more natural beauty and came back to America more as myself. I let go of the hold the media image had on me."

—First-year college student

Remember

The more opportunities you create to learn from others who are different from yourself, the more opportunities you create to learn about yourself.

Diversity Stimulates Social Development

Interacting with people from various groups widens your social circle. By widening the pool of people with whom you have contact, you increase your capability and confidence in relating to people with varied life experiences, as well as your ability to converse with people on a wider range of topics. Just as seeking variety in what you eat provides greater stimulation to your taste buds, seeking variety in the people with whom you interact stimulates your social life and social skills. Research indicates that students who have more diversity experiences in college report higher levels of satisfaction with their college experience (Astin, 1993).

"Variety is the spice of life."

—American proverb

Vive la différence! ("Long live difference!")

—French saying

Diversity Enriches a College Education

Diversity magnifies the power of a college education because it helps liberate you from the tunnel vision of ethnocentric (culture-centered) and egocentric (self-centered) thinking, enabling you to get beyond yourself and your own culture to see yourself in relation to the world around you. Just as the various subjects you take in the college curriculum open your mind to multiple perspectives, so does your experience with people from varied backgrounds; it equips you with a wide-focus lens that allows you to take a multicultural perspective. A multicultural perspective helps you become aware of cultural "blind spots" and avoid the dangers of groupthink—the tendency for tight, like-minded groups of people to think so much alike that they overlook flaws in their own thinking that can lead to poor choices and faulty decisions (Janis, 1982).

"Without exception, the observed changes [during college] involve greater breadth, expansion, and appreciation for the new and different."

—Ernest Pascarella and Pat Terenzini, *How College Affects Students* (2005)

Diversity Strengthens Learning and Critical Thinking

Research consistently shows that we learn more from people who are different from us than we do from people who are similar to us (Pascarella, 2001; Pascarella & Terenzini, 2005). When your brain encounters something that is unfamiliar or different than you're accustomed to, you must stretch beyond your mental comfort zone and work harder to understand it because doing so forces you to compare and contrast it to what you already know (Acredolo & O'Connor, 1991; Nagda, Gurin, & Johnson, 2005). This mental "stretch" requires the use of extra psychological effort and energy, which strengthens and deepens learning.

"When all men think alike, no one thinks very much."

—Walter Lippmann, distinguished journalist and originator of the term *stereotype*

Diversity Promotes Creative Thinking

"When the only tool you have is a hammer, you tend to see every problem as a nail."

—Abraham Maslow, humanistic psychologist, best known for his self-actualization theory of achieving human potential

Experiences with diversity supply you with a broader base of knowledge and wider range of thinking styles that better enable you to think outside your own cultural box or boundaries. In contrast, limiting your number of cultural vantage points is akin to limiting the variety of mental tools you can use to solve new problems, thereby limiting your creativity.

Drawing on different ideas from people with diverse backgrounds and bouncing your ideas off them is a great way to generate energy, synergy, and serendipity—unanticipated discoveries and creative solutions. People who approach problems from diverse perspectives are more likely to look for and discover "multiple partial solutions" (Kelly, 1994). Diversity expands students' capacity for viewing issues or problems from multiple vantage points, equipping them with a wider variety of approaches to solving unfamiliar problems they may encounter in different contexts and situations.

Diversity Enhances Career Preparation and Success

Learning about and from diversity has a practical benefit: it better prepares you for the world of work. Whatever career you may choose to pursue, you are likely to find yourself working with employers, employees, co-workers, customers, and clients from diverse cultural backgrounds. America's workforce is now more diverse than at any other time in the nation's history, and it will grow ever more diverse. For example, the percentage of America's working-age population that represents members of minority groups is expected to grow from 34 percent in 2008 to 55 percent in 2050 (U.S. Bureau of Labor Statistics, 2008).

In addition to increasing diversity in America, today's work world is characterized by a global economy. Greater economic interdependence among nations, more international trading (imports and exports), more multinational corporations, and almost-instantaneous worldwide communication increasingly occur—thanks to advances in the World Wide Web (Dryden & Vos, 1999; Smith, 1994). Because of these trends, employers of college graduates now seek job candidates with the following skills and attributes: sensitivity to human differences, the ability to understand and relate to people from different cultural backgrounds, international knowledge, and foreign language skills (Fixman, 1990; National Association of Colleges & Employers, 2003; Office of Research, 1994; Smith, 1997). In one national survey, policymakers, business leaders, and employers all agreed that college graduates should be more than just "aware" or "tolerant" of diversity: they should have *experience* with diversity (Education Commission of the States, 1995).

"Empirical evidence shows that the actual effects on student development of emphasizing diversity and of student participation in diversity activities are overwhelmingly positive."

—Alexander Astin, *What Matters in College* (1993)

The wealth of diversity on college campuses today represents an unprecedented educational opportunity. You may never again be a member of a community that includes so many people from such a rich variety of backgrounds. Seize this opportunity! You're now in the right place at the right time to experience the people and programs that can infuse and enrich the quality of your college education with diversity.

Stumbling Blocks and Barriers to Experiencing Diversity

Stereotypes

The word *stereotype* derives from a combination of two roots: *stereo* (to look at in a fixed way) and *type* (to categorize or group together, as in the word *typical*). Thus, stereotyping is viewing individuals of the same type (group) in the same (fixed) way.

In effect, stereotyping ignores or disregards a person's individuality; all people who share a similar group characteristic (e.g., race or gender) are viewed as having the same personal characteristics, as in the expression, "You know what they are like; they're all the same." Stereotypes involve bias, which literally means "slant." A bias can be either positive or negative. Positive bias results in a favorable stereotype; negative bias produces an unfavorable stereotype.

Think About It — Journal Entry 8.8

1. Have you ever been stereotyped, such as based on your appearance or group membership? If so, how did it make you feel and how did you react?

2. Have you ever unintentionally perceived or treated someone in terms of a group stereotype rather than as an individual? What assumptions did you make about that person? Was that person aware of, or affected by, your stereotyping?

Whether you are male or female, don't let gender stereotypes limit your career options.

Author's Experience

When I was six years old, I was told by another six-year-old from a different racial group that all people of my race could not swim. That six-year-old happened to be of a different racial group. Since I could not swim at that time and she could, I assumed she was correct. I asked a boy, who happened to be of the same racial group as that little girl, if that statement were true; he responded: "Yes, it is true." Since I was from an area where few other African Americans were around to counteract this belief about Blacks, I bought into this stereotype for a long time until I finally took swimming lessons as an adult. I am now a lousy swimmer after many lessons because I did not even attempt to swim until I was an adult. The moral of this story is that group stereotypes can limit the confidence and potential of individuals who are members of the stereotyped group.

Aaron Thompson

"Let us all hope that the dark clouds of racial prejudice will soon pass away and the deep fog of misunderstanding will be lifted from our fear-drenched communities, and in some not too distant tomorrow the radiant stars of love and brotherhood will shine over our great nation."

—Martin Luther King, Jr., civil rights activist and clergyman

Prejudice

If virtually all members of a stereotyped group are judged or evaluated in a negative way, the result is prejudice. (The word *prejudice* literally means to "pre-judge.") Technically, prejudice may be either positive or negative; however, the term is most often associated with a negative prejudgment or stigmatizing—associating inferior or unfavorable traits with people who belong to the same group. Thus, prejudice may be defined as a negative judgment, attitude, or belief about another person or group of people, which is formed before the facts are known. Stereotyping and prejudice often go hand in hand because individuals who are placed in a negatively stereotyped group are commonly prejudged in a negative way.

Someone with a prejudice toward a group typically avoids contact with individuals from that group. This enables the prejudice to continue unchallenged because there is little or no chance for the prejudiced person to have positive experiences with a member of the stigmatized group that could contradict or disprove the prejudice. Thus, a vicious cycle is established in which the prejudiced person continues to avoid contact with individuals from the stigmatized group, which, in turn, continues to maintain and reinforce the prejudice.

"'See that man over there?'
'Yes.'
'Well, I hate him.'
'But you don't know him.'
'That's why I hate him.'"

—Gordon Allport, *The Nature of Prejudice* (1954)

Discrimination

Literally translated, the term *discrimination* means "division" or "separation." Whereas prejudice involves a belief or opinion, discrimination involves an *action* taken toward others. Technically, discrimination can be either negative or positive—for example, a discriminating eater may be careful about eating only healthy foods. However, the term is most often associated with a negative action that results in a prejudiced person treating another person, or group of people, in an unfair way. Thus, it could be said that discrimination is prejudice put into action. Hate crimes are examples of extreme discrimination because they are acts motivated solely by prejudice against members of a stigmatized group. Victims of hate crimes may have their personal property damaged or they may be physically assaulted. Other forms of discrimination are more subtle and may take place without people being fully aware that they are discriminating.

Think About It — Journal Entry 8.9

Prejudice and discrimination can be subtle and only begin to surface when the social or emotional distance among members of different groups grows closer. Rate your level of comfort (high, moderate, or low) with the following situations.

Someone from another racial group:

1.	Going to your school	high	moderate	low
2.	Working in your place of employment	high	moderate	low
3.	Living on your street as a neighbor	high	moderate	low
4.	Living with you as a roommate	high	moderate	low
5.	Socializing with you as a personal friend	high	moderate	low
6.	Being your most intimate friend or romantic partner or	high	moderate	low
7.	Being your partner in marriage	high	moderate	low

For any item you rated "low," what do you think was responsible for the low rating?

Think About It — Journal Entry 8.10

1. Have you ever held a prejudice against a particular group of people?

2. If you have, what was the group, and how do you think your prejudice developed?

The following practices and strategies may be used to accept and appreciate individuals from other groups toward whom you may hold prejudices, stereotypes, or subtle biases that bubble beneath the surface of your conscious awareness:

1. **Consciously avoid preoccupation with physical appearances.** Go deeper and get beneath the superficial surface of appearances to judge people not in terms of how they look, but in terms of who they are and how they act. Remember the old proverb "It's what's inside that counts." Judge others by the quality of their personal character, not by the familiarity of their physical characteristics.
2. **Perceive each person with whom you interact as a unique human being.** Make a conscious effort to see each person with whom you interact not merely as a member of a group, but as a unique individual. Form your impressions of each person case by case rather than by using some rule of thumb.

"The common eye sees only the outside of things, and judges by that. But the seeing eye pierces through and reads the heart and the soul, finding there capacities which the outside didn't indicate or promise."
—Samuel Clemens, a.k.a. Mark Twain; writer, lecturer, and humorist

This may seem like an obvious and easy thing to do, but research shows that humans have a natural tendency to perceive and conceive of individuals who are members of unfamiliar groups as being more alike (or all alike) than members of their own group (Taylor, Peplau, & Sears, 2006). Thus, you may have to consciously resist this tendency to overgeneralize and "lump together" individuals into homogeneous groups and make an intentional attempt to focus on treating each person you interact with as a unique human.

"Stop judging by mere appearances, and make a right judgment."
—Bible, John 7:24

Remember

While it is valuable to learn about different cultures and the common characteristics shared by members of the same culture, differences exist among individuals who share the same culture. Don't assume that all individuals from the same cultural background share the same personal characteristics.

Interacting and Collaborating with Members of Diverse Groups

Once you overcome your biases and begin to perceive members of diverse groups as unique individuals, you are positioned to take the next step of interacting, collaborating, and forming friendships with them. Interpersonal contact between diverse people takes you beyond multicultural awareness and moves you up to a higher level of diversity appreciation that involves intercultural interaction. When you take this step to cross cultural boundaries, you transform diversity appreciation from a value or belief system into an observable action and way of living.

Your initial comfort level with interacting with people from diverse groups is likely to depend on how much experience you have had with diversity before college. If you have had little or no prior experience interacting with members of diverse groups, it may be more challenging for you to initiate interactions with diverse students on campus.

However, if you have had little or no previous experience with diversity, the good news is that you have the most to gain from experiencing diversity. Research consistently shows that when humans experience social interaction that differs radically from their prior experiences, they gain the most in terms of learning and cognitive development (Piaget, 1985; Acredolo & O'Connor, 1991).

Think About It — *Journal Entry* 8.11

Rate the amount or variety of diversity you have experienced in the following settings:

1.	The high school you attended	high	moderate	low
2.	The college or university you now attend	high	moderate	low
3.	The neighborhood in which you grew up	high	moderate	low
4.	Places where you have worked or been employed	high	moderate	low

Which setting had the most and which had the least diversity?

___

___

___

What do you think accounts for this difference?

___

___

___

___

___

___

What follows is a series of strategies for meeting and interacting with people from diverse backgrounds:

1. **Intentionally create opportunities for interaction and conversation with individuals from diverse groups.** Consciously resist the natural tendency to associate only with people who are similar to you. One way to do this is by intentionally placing yourself in situations where individuals from diverse groups are nearby and potential interaction can take place. Research indicates that meaningful interactions and friendships are more likely to form among people who are in physical proximity to one another (Latané, Liu, Nowak, Bonevento, & Zheng, 1993). Studies show that stereotyping and prejudice can be sharply reduced if contact between members of different racial or ethnic groups is frequent enough to allow time for the development of friendships (Pettigrew, 1998). You can create this condition in the college classroom by sitting near students from different ethnic or racial groups or by joining them if you are given the choice to select whom you will work with in class discussion groups and group projects.
2. **Take advantage of the Internet to "chat" with students from diverse groups on your campus or with students in different countries.** Electronic communication can be a more convenient and more comfortable way to initially interact with members of diverse groups with whom you have had little prior experience.

After you've communicated successfully *online,* you may then feel more comfortable about interacting with them *in person.* Online and in-person interaction with students from other cultures and nations can give you a better understanding of your own culture and country, as well as increase awareness of its customs and values that you may have taken for granted (Bok, 2006).

3. **Seek out the views and opinions of classmates from diverse backgrounds.** For example, during or after class discussions, ask students from different backgrounds if there was any point made or position taken in class that they would strongly question or challenge. Seeking out divergent (diverse) viewpoints has been found to be one of the best ways to develop critical thinking skills (Kurfiss, 1988).
4. **Join or form discussion groups with students from diverse backgrounds.** You can gain exposure to diverse perspectives by joining or forming groups of students who differ from you in terms of such characteristics as gender, age, race, or ethnicity. You might begin by forming discussion groups composed of students who differ in one way but are similar in another way. For instance, form a learning group of students who have the same major as you do but who differ with respect to race, ethnicity, or age. This strategy gives the diverse members of your group some common ground for discussion (your major) and can raise your group's awareness that although you may be members of different groups, you can, at the same time, be similar with respect to your educational goals and life plans.

Remember

Including diversity in your discussion groups not only provides social variety, but also promotes the quality of the group's thinking by allowing its members to gain access to the diverse perspectives and life experiences of people from different backgrounds.

5. **Form collaborative learning teams.** A learning team is more than a discussion group or a study group. It moves beyond discussion to collaborative learning—in other words, members of a learning team "colabor" (work together) as part of a joint and mutually supportive effort to reach the same goal. Studies show that when individuals from different ethnic and racial groups work collaboratively toward the attainment of a common goal, it reduces racial prejudice and promotes interracial friendships (Allport, 1954; Amir, 1976). These positive findings may be explained as follows: if individuals from diverse groups work together on the same team, no one is a member of an "out" group: instead, all are members of the same "in" group (Pratto et al., 2000; Sidanius et al., 2000).

Summary and Conclusion

Diversity refers to differences among groups of people who, together, comprise humanity. Experiencing diversity enhances our appreciation of the unique features of different cultures, and it provides us with a larger perspective on those aspects of the human experience that are common to all people, no matter what their particular cultural background happens to be.

Culture is a distinctive pattern of beliefs and values learned by a group of people who share the same social heritage and traditions. A major advantage of culture is that it helps bind groups of people into supportive, tight-knit communities. However, it can also lead its members to view the world solely through their own cultural lens, known as ethnocentrism, which can blind them from seeing the world and from taking on other cultural perspectives. Ethnocentrism can contribute to stereotyping—viewing individual members of the same group in the same way and thinking they all have similar personal characteristics.

If members of a stereotyped group are judged or evaluated in a negative way, the result is prejudice—a negative prejudgment about another person or group of people, which is formed before the facts are known. Stereotyping and prejudice often go hand in hand because if the stereotype is negative, individual members of the stereotyped group are then prejudged in a negative way. Discrimination takes prejudice one step further by converting the negative prejudgment into action that results in unfair treatment of others. Thus, discrimination is prejudice put into action.

If stereotyping and prejudice are overcome, you are then positioned to experience diversity and reap its multiple benefits, which include sharpened self-awareness, social stimulation, broadened personal perspectives, deeper learning and higher-level thinking, and career success.

College campuses today have such diversity that the educational opportunities available are unprecedented. This may be the only time in your life when you are part of an organization or community that includes so many diverse members. Seize this unique opportunity to experience the diversity of people and programs available to you and profit from the power of diversity.*

Chapter 8 Exercises

Name: ______________________

8.1 Multigroup Self-Awareness

*You can be members of multiple groups at the same time, and your membership in these groups can influence your personal development and self-identity. In the figure that follows, consider the shaded center circle to be yourself and the six nonshaded circles to be six groups you belong to that you think have influenced your personal development or personal identity.

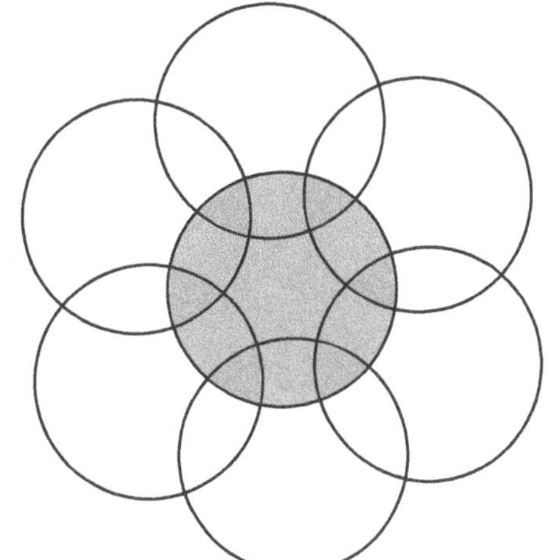

Fill in the nonshaded circles with the names of groups to which you belong that have had the most influence on your personal development. You can use the diversity spectrum that appears on the first page of this chapter to help you identify different groups. Do not feel you have to come up with six groups and fill all six circles. What is more important is to identify those groups that have had a significant influence on your personal development or identity.

Self-Assessment Questions

1. Which one of your groups has had the greatest influence on your personal identity, and why?
2. Have you ever felt limited or disadvantaged by being a member of any group or groups?
3. Have you ever felt that you experienced advantages or privileges because of your membership in any group or groups?

8.2 Switching Group Identity

Imagine you were to be born again as a member of a different racial or ethnic group.

1. What group would you want it to be? Why?

2. With your new group identity, what things would change in your personal life?

3. What things would remain the same in your life even though your group identity has changed?*

Source: Adapted from University of New Hampshire Office of Residential Life (2001).

8.3 Hidden Bias Test

**Go to www.tolerance.org/activity/test-yourself-hidden-bias and take one or more of the hidden bias tests on this website. These tests assess subtle bias with respect to gender, age, ethnic minority groups, religious denominations, sexual orientations, disabilities, and body weight.

After completing the test, answer the following questions:

1. Did the results reveal any biases you weren't unaware of?

2. Did you think the assessment results were accurate or valid?

3. What do you think best accounts for or explains your results?

If your closest family member and best friend took the test, how do you think their results would compare with yours?**

SQ4R Worksheet

Your Name:

Selection Title/Chapter:

Author(s):

***1. **Survey**: Look at the title, visuals, questions, excerpts, headings and sub-headings. Afterward, answer the questions below.

What do I already know about the topics?	What do I expect to learn?

2. **Question**: Create questions based on your survey of the text. If there are headings, turn them into questions. Include *at least three* below to help focus your attention as you read.

A.
B.
C.
D.
E.

3. **Read** and **Record** (Annotate): Read the selection thoroughly, highlight, and make note of important points, associations, and unfamiliar terms. Complete the chart using **your own words**. Provide a sketch and/or explanation of the visuals. Use and attach a separate sheet if needed.

Page and Paragraph #	Vocabulary Terms	Notes and Definitions	Visuals

(*Continued*)

(*Continued*)

4. **Recite**: Answer your questions from step two.

a.
b.
c.
d.
e.

5. **Review and Reflect**: Check your memory by verbalizing the above information. Below, write a summary **in your own words** of what you have read, connecting the content ideas. Additionally, write a brief reflection including your personal response to the reading (use "I" and make connections to your own experiences, ask more questions, respond to the text, and consider anything you were reminded of or visualized while reading).***

Summary:

Reflection:

Adapted from Florida Online Reading Professional Development. (n.d.). *SQ4R*. Retrieved from the Marco Island Charter Middle School website at http://micms.org/SQ4R.pdf

Appendix A

Exercises

Meeting with a DMACC Advisor

Name: ______________________

Materials Required: Student prepared information and your developed *Completion Plan*

Objective: To meet with an academic advisor for course planning and support.

Due Date: _________ (As established by the instructor)

Assignment:

Part 1. Contact the student advising office and schedule an appointment to meet with an advisor. Note the appointment in your planner.

Part 2. Prepare for the appointment by considering the questions noted below.
1.How are you doing in your current classes?

2. Do you want to make a change in your program of study or do you have questions about a particular program?

3. Are you planning to continue at DMACC the next semester and/or transfer?

4. If transferring, what information do you have about the transferring college? What information do you need?

The First Day of Class

Name: ______________________

Materials Required: Access to Catalog Program Descriptions

Objective: To cover important information needed by students the first class day.

1. What is your current Program of Study? ________________________________ Do you need to change your current Program of Study? If yes, you will need a *Program Change Form*. Ask your instructor for the form, complete the form including the program change, and submit the form to the Admissions Office as soon as possible.
2. The *Catalog Program Description* is a road map that will guide you in selecting classes and will help to ensure that you take the classes required for your Program of Study.
3. Starting the *Completion Plan.*
4. Confirming your DMACC username and password.
5. Accessing the DMACC Web Information System.
6. Accessing Blackboard.

How to Read a Catalog Program Description

Name: ______________________

Materials Required: Internet access

Information Needed:

Core Requirements are those courses that constitute the body of a traditional liberal arts curriculum in the first two-years of a baccalaureate degree. Essentially, these courses have universal transfer status among receiving institutions.

A *Degree* is a title conferred by a college or university upon completion of a particular program of academic work. Some typical college degrees are Associate in Arts (AA), Associate in Science (AS), Associate in Applied Science (AAS), Bachelor of Arts (BA), and Bachelor of Science (BS).

Electives are courses students elect to take outside of the core requirements. Depending on the number of elective courses required, electives may cover a variety of subject areas or concentrate on one major area.

Preparatory Education Courses are courses designed to aid students whose educational background requires additional strengthening to achieve success in regular college-level courses. Preparatory education courses below the 100 level do not transfer to other colleges or universities or apply to a student's program of study at DMACC.

A *Program of Study* is the student's major area of concentration within the degree selection.

Semester Credit Hour is a unit of measurement used to determine approximately how many hours students are required to spend in class each week, and how many units will be accumulated towards graduation.

Objective: To review the Catalog Program Description for your program of study and use the information to build your *Completion Plan.*

Due Date: ________________ (As established by the instructor)

1. Your instructor will provide you with a Catalog Program Description.
2. Review your Catalog Program Description and complete the following:
   - Summarize the program entry requirements.
   - Summarize the graduation requirements.
   - Summarize the core requirements.
   - What is the diversity requirement?
   - What are the total number of credits required for your degree?

Emergency! You Need a Back-Up Plan!

Name: ______________________

Materials Required: None

Objective: To build on your college readiness checklist that was developed during your orientation session and to ensure that you have a back-up plan to prevent you from missing classes.

The Top Ten Emergencies that Impact Attendance

1. Car problems
2. If you have children, daycare
3. Personal Illness
4. Family Illness
5. Conflicting work hours
6. Family demands
7. Poor finances (i.e. can't afford gas)
8. Motivation
9. Bad weather
10. Personal or family appointments

Keeping in mind that your goal is to be in class every day, develop two back-up options to address each of the top ten emergencies listed above that are relevant to your life. Be realistic. Take time to thoughtfully consider realistic scenarios that apply to your personal life. Often the biggest difference between attending class and missing class is prior planning for potential emergencies.

As a college student, truly, your most important goal that will impact your success is attending every class. Even if you have legitimate reasons for not attending class and even if your instructor is understanding, poor attendance is directly correlated to poor grades. Therefore, you will be well served by establishing back-up plans in advance of possible emergencies.

Visiting the Academic Achievement Center (AAC) within the first three – weeks of class

Name: ______________________

Materials Required: None

Objective: To find the Academic Achievement Center and determine its benefits for you during the semester.

Due Date: __________________ (Established by the instructor prior to week 4)

1. Find the Academic Achievement Center on your campus. List the Building and room location.

2. List the times when the AAC is open **AND** what subjects are available.

3. List the current classes you're taking and how the AAC could be of help to you in each of your classes. Keep in mind the AAC is your one-stop shop for academic assistance from faculty members. The AAC is a great place to meet with a study group or simply study.

DMACC Learning Opportunity

Name: ____________________

Materials Required: None

Objective: To connect with others and build a sense of community, while learning about something new or providing a service.

Answer the questions below based on your learning activity.

Activity: ____

Date of the activity: ____________________

Vision

- What was your goal for this learning opportunity?

Ethics and Integrity

- How did this opportunity benefit the public good or help you to understand behaviors that lead to public good?
- How did this opportunity help you to develop or define your own personal values?

Service Orientation

- How did this opportunity connect you to others and get you to think outside yourself?

Communication Skills

- How did this opportunity increase your communication skills?

Self-awareness

- How did this opportunity increase your realization of your own personal strengths and weaknesses?

Teamwork in diverse groups

- What did you learn from others by working together to accomplish common goals?

Academics

- What new knowledge did you acquire?

Appendix B

Handouts

Grade Point Average (GPA)

Materials Required: DMACC Handbook

Objective: To learn how to calculate your grade point average (GPA)

Refer to the table at the end of each exercise to determine the grade point averages. A blank grid is also available for determining your midterm or end-of-term GPA.

COURSE	GRADE	NUMERICAL VALUE	NUMBER OF CREDITS	QUALITY POINTS
SDV 108: The College Experience	A		1	
SDV 115: Study Strategies	B		2	
BIO 112: General Biology	B–		4	
SOC 110: Introduction to Sociology	C		3	
SPC 126: Interpersonal & Small Group Communication	C+		3	
Total				
Divide Total Quality Points _______ by Total Number of Credit Hours = _________ GPA				

Letter Grade	GPA	Letter Grade	GPA
A	4.00	**C**	2.00
A–	3.67	**C–**	1.67
B+	3.33	**D+**	1.33
B	3.00	**D**	1.00
B–	2.67	**D–**	0.67
C+	2.33	**F**	0.00

COURSE	GRADE	NUMERICAL VALUE	NUMBER OF CREDITS	QUALITY POINTS
CHM 105: Survey of Chemistry	B+		3	
RDG 038: College Preparatory Reading	A		3	
ENG 060: College Preparatory Writing	C+		3	
MAT 772: Applied Math	C		3	
Total				
Divide Total Quality Points ________ by Total Number of Credit Hours = _________ GPA				

Letter Grade	GPA	Letter Grade	GPA
A	4.00	**C**	2.00
A–	3.67	**C–**	1.67
B+	3.33	**D+**	1.33
B	3.00	**D**	1.00
B–	2.67	**D–**	0.67
C+	2.33	**F**	0.00

COURSE	GRADE	NUMERICAL VALUE	NUMBER OF CREDITS	QUALITY POINTS
Total				
Divide Total Quality Points ________ by Total Number of Credit Hours = _________ GPA				

Graduation Plan
Course Planning Form

Student Name: ____________________ DMACC ID#: ____________

Program of Study: ____________________ Date: ____________

Semester: Fall Year

Course	Credits

Semester: Spring Year

Course	Credits

Semester: Summer Year

Course	Credits

Semester: Fall Year

Course	Credits

Semester: Spring Year

Course	Credits

Semester: Summer Year

Course	Credits

Semester: Fall Year

Course	Credits

Semester: Spring Year

Course	Credits

Semester: Summer Year

Course	Credits

Total Credits ______

DES MOINES COMMUNITY COLLEGE
EDUCATIONAL SERVICES PROCEDURES

Section: STUDENT RECORDS
Procedure: Satisfactory Academic Progress
Effective: August 25, 2011
Number: ES 4560

I. Institutional Regulations

A. To define the requirements for academic progress and establish the procedures necessary to enforce those requirements. No program of study at Des Moines Area Community College may establish academic progress standards lower than those specified in this procedure.
B. A program of study at Des Moines Area Community College may establish academic progress standards higher than those specified above, but such standards must first be recommended by the respective academic dean or campus executive dean, approved by the Academic Standards Commission, and approved by the Senior Vice President, Academic Affairs.

II. Procedures

A. Academic Progress
   1. The following requirements only apply to credit enrollment at Des Moines Area Community College.
   2. Students who have attempted 1 or more credits with any of the grades or marks listed in Procedure ES4552 at Des Moines Area Community College are subject to the following satisfactory academic progress standards:
      a. Earn a cumulative grade point average (G.P.A.) of 2.00 or higher.
      b. Successful completion of 67% of attempted credits. Successful completion is defined as achieving a grade of "D-" or better.
      c. Guidelines for placing a student on "ACADEMIC WARNING":
         1. A student whose cumulative G.P.A. falls below 2.00 at the end of any term will be placed on ACADEMIC WARNING for the next term of enrollment.
         2. A student whose cumulative credit completion rate falls below 67% at the end of any term will be places on ACADEMIC WARNING.
         3. A student on ACADEMIC WARNING will return to a status of "good academic standing" when his/her cumulative G.P.A. is raised to 2.00 or higher and his/her cumulative credit completion rate is above 67% or above.
         4. A student on ACADEMIC WARNING will continue on academic warning status if his/her term G.P.A. for the term following his/her placement on academic warning is 2.00 or higher but the cumulative G.P.A. remains below 2.00 and/or their cumulative credit completion rate is 67% or lower. This rule will also apply for subsequent terms of enrollment.
      d. Guidelines for placing a student on "ACADEMIC CONDITIONAL ENROLLMENT":
         1. A student on academic warning who earns a term G.P.A. of less than 2.00 and/or has not completed 67% of credits attempted for the term will be placed on ACADEMIC CONDITIONAL ENROLLMENT for the following term of enrollment. Students who receive federal financial aid may be subject to financial aid suspension. See ES 4300 Financial Aid Satisfactory Academic Progress policy.
         2. If the student is registered for the following term and is placed on ACADEMIC CONDITIONAL ENROLLMENT for that term, he/she will be required to meet at the campus of their choice with a counselor or advisor no later than the fifth day of the ACADEMIC CONDITIONAL ENROLLMENT term to review his/her course selections and to complete an Academic Improvement Plan (AIP). Failure to comply will result in the student's being administratively dropped from all courses.
         3. If the student placed on ACADEMIC CONDITIONAL ENROLLMENT is not yet registered for the next term, he or she must meet with a counselor/advisor and complete an Academic Improvement Plan (AIP) prior to registering for any credit course work.
         4. A student on ACADEMIC CONDITIONAL ENROLLMENT who earns a term G.P.A. of 2.00 or higher but whose cumulative G.P.A. remains below a 2.00 and/or has not completed 67% of credits attempted for the term will be remain on ACADEMIC CONDITIONAL ENROLLMENT .
         5. A student on ACADEMIC CONDITIONAL ENROLLMENT who earns a term G.P.A. and a cumulative G.P.A. of 2.00 or higher and has completed 67% of cumulative credits attempted will be placed in good standing.
      e. Guidelines for placing a student on "ACADEMIC DISQUALIFICATION": A student on ACADEMIC CONDITIONAL ENROLLMENT who earns a term G.P.A. of less than 2.00 and/or

does not complete 67% of term credits attempted will be placed on ACADEMIC DISQUALIFICATION and will not be allowed to enroll in credit course work for a period of one semester (or one summer semester plus one fall semester in the case of a suspension at the end of the spring semester).

f. Guidelines for re-enrollment of DISQUALIFIED students:
    1. After non-enrollment for a minimum of one semester, as defined above in 'Guidelines for placing a student on "Academic Disqualification", a student on ACADEMIC DISQUALIFICATION may re-enroll after completing an updated AIP.
    2. In all instances, a re-enrolled student will be placed on ACADEMIC CONDITIONAL ENROLLMENT.
    3. Individual programs of study may impose additional re-enrollment requirements.

g. A student placed on ACADEMIC DISQUALIFICATION may appeal that placement before the deadline to the Academic Reinstatement Committee chaired by the Director of Student Development. The appeal must be made in writing and must at a minimum explain the reasons for the past unsatisfactory academic performance and how the student proposes to improve his/her performance. The committee may grant or deny the appeal based on the written statement or the committee chairperson may choose to conduct a personal interview with the student or require the student to undergo counseling or academic assessment before making a decision. If the appeal is granted, the committee chairperson is authorized to impose reasonable restrictions on the student's subsequent enrollment.

h. Students may appeal an ACADEMIC DISQUALIFICATION status only one time. Subsequent appeals will not be accepted.

APPROVED: ______________________ Date: 8-10-11

Executive Dean, Student Services

______________________ Date: 8-10-11

Senior Vice President, Academic Affairs

Check one: ☐ **DMACC - ACADEMIC IMPROVEMENT PLAN (AIP)**
☐ **DMACC - GRADUATION PLAN**

PART 1 Student Information

DMACC ID or SSN ☐☐☐☐☐☐☐☐☐

Date ____________________

Name ____
(Last) (First) (M)

Program: ____

Term ____________________

PART 2 Reasons for AIP/Graduation Plan (Check all that apply)

❑ Conditional Enrollment ❑ Student has been academically disqualified and desires to re-enroll.

❑ Financial aid warning ❑ Financial aid cancelation ❑ Graduation plan – extending aid

PART 3 Reasons for not meeting Academic Progress Standards/Degree Completion Requirements

❑ Attendance ❑ Health issues ❑ Financial issues ❑ Extending aid

❑ Time management/study skills ❑ Other (specify) ____________________

PART 4 Class Schedule

Semester: __________

Course #	Credits

Semester: __________

Course #	Credits

Semester: __________

Course #	Credits

Per ES4560 the number of credits and courses allowed in a semester may be limited for students not achieving satisfactory academic progress.

PART 5 - Plan for Academic Improvement/Degree Completion

What will you do differently this term to achieve academic success/degree completion? (Be specific – "study 20 hours/week'"; "arrange for tutor")

____

____

Counselor/Advisor comments:

____

____

____

Student's Signature____________________ Counselor/Advisor:____________________

Satisfactory Academic Progress

SAP = Completing 67% of attempted credits and earning a 2.00 GPA each term

If either of these conditions are NOT met:

Academic SAP

1. First term – Academic warning; no holds
2. Second term – Conditional enrollment; hold placed on record until AIP is completed
3. Third term – Academic disqualification
   a. Need to sit out one semester (either fall or spring; summer does not count) OR file academic DQ appeal
   b. If the student sits out for a term, needs to complete a new AIP prior to registering for classes.

Financial Aid SAP

1. First term – financial aid warning
2. Second term – financial aid cancellation
   a. Pay for classes out of pocket and meet SAP OR file a financial aid appeal
   b. If the student pays for classes out of pocket, will need to file a new financial aid appeal for the following term.

If a student fails or withdraws from *all* of their classes during their ***first*** semester, they are automatically placed on financial aid suspension.

There are limits to the number of times a student can file either a financial aid or DQ appeal. Maximum number of appeals granted - 2 - UNLESS there are new extenuating circumstances.

*Both types of appeals require documentation & an AIP.

If either appeal is granted, the student must meet SAP that semester.

Student stays on financial aid warning and/or conditional enrollment UNTIL cumulative GPA is 2.00 and student has successfully completed 67% of attempted credits.

Terminology

Academic Advisor—An individual employed by the college to assist students in all aspects of program and course information.

Audit—To attend a class without receiving credit or grade.

Core—Those courses that constitute the body of traditional liberal arts curriculum in the first two years of a baccalaureate degree. Essentially, these courses have universal transfer status among receiving institutions.

Corequisite—A course that must be taken concurrently with another course.

Counselor—An individual employed by the college to assist students with all aspects of program and course information and on life issues, including academic, career, and personal concerns.

Course Competencies—Learning outcomes and concepts that make up the general knowledge or skills of a course.

Course Description—Statements identifying the contents of a course. Course descriptions are found in the online college catalog.

Cross Enrollment—Under a special agreement, DMACC students may cross enroll in one class, per term at Drake, Grand View or Iowa State. No additional tuition is charged for these courses. Students must have earned 12 semester hours with a minimum 2.0 GPA at DMACC and be current, full-time students in good standing. The credits earned while on the cross-enrollment plan will be added to the DMACC transcript. Not available for the summer term.

Degree—A title conferred by a college or university upon completion of a particular program of academic work. Some typical college degrees are Associate in Arts (AA), Associate in Science (AS), Associate in Applied Science (AAS), Bachelor of Arts (BA), and Bachelor of Science (BS).

Drop/Add—After completing registration, students may change their schedules by adding and/or dropping classes. For a full semester length class, students may drop the class up to the end of the tenth week of the term. The drop period is prorated for classes with duration less than the full term.

Electives—Courses students elect to take outside of the core requirements. Depending on the number of elective courses required, electives may cover a variety of subject areas or concentrate on one major area.

Full-time Student—To be classified as full-time, students must take a minimum of 12 credit hours during the fall and spring terms and 8 hours during the summer.

Part-time Student—To be classified as part-time, students carry from 1–11 credit hours during the fall and spring terms and 1–7 credit hours during the summer.

Preparatory Education Courses—Courses designed to aid students whose educational background requires additional strengthening to achieve success in regular college-level courses. Preparatory education courses below the 100 level do not transfer to other colleges or universities or apply to a student's program of study at DMACC.

Prerequisite—Successful completion of a course or other criterion necessary for students to enroll in a higher-level course.

Semester Credit Hour—A unit of measurement used to determine approximately how many hours students are required to spend in class each week, and how many units will be accumulated towards graduation.

Semester or Term—An enrollment period (15 weeks in the fall and spring session and 10 weeks in the summer).

Transfer—The conveyance of students' credits from one college to another.

CPSIA information can be obtained
at www.ICGtesting.com
Printed in the USA
LVHW011021040619
619987LV00001B/1/P